TESTING THE ROOSEVELT COALITION

ꕥ *Twentieth-Century America Series*

Testing the Roosevelt Coalition

CONNECTICUT SOCIETY AND POLITICS

IN THE ERA OF WORLD WAR II

John W. Jeffries

☆

THE UNIVERSITY OF TENNESSEE PRESS

KNOXVILLE

ᔥ Twentieth-Century America Series

DEWEY W. GRANTHAM, GENERAL EDITOR

Publication of this book was assisted by a grant from the University of Maryland Baltimore County.

Library of Congress Cataloging in Publication Data

Jeffries, John W   1942-
    Testing the Roosevelt coalition.

    (Twentieth-century America series)
    Bibliography: p.
    Includes index.
    1. Connecticut—Politics and government—1865–1950. 2. Political participation—Connecticut—History. I. Title.
F100.J43   320.9′746′04   78-14550
ISBN 0-87049-255-1

For Renate

PREFACE

The usual story of the United States during the Second World War centers on fighting, foreign policy, and mobilization for war. Apart from the "miracles of production," domestic events scarcely figure in the tale. Historians have especially neglected the mundane but important experiences, concerns, and attitudes of home-front Americans. Even politics, that customary staple of American historiography, have received scant attention, and wartime elections have been examined cursorily and primarily at the national level.

The World War II American home front deserves closer study. Indeed it requires such study, for knowledge of the home-front experience is important not only in its own right but also for understanding the course of mid-twentieth-century American history. The nation that emerged victorious, powerful, and prosperous from World War II was different from the prewar United States—different in temper, different in important social and economic patterns, different, too, in what the government did at home and abroad, and different largely because of the war. The effects of the war, moreover, continued to ramify well beyond the immediate postwar years. Yet American life was not transformed but rather altered, sometimes marginally and slowly, by the war, and it revealed major continuities in the period of World War II; if the impact of the war should not be underestimated, neither should it be exaggerated. An examination of American society and politics in the era of World War II illuminates at once the contours of the home-front experience, the impact of the war, and the manifold connections between the interwar and postwar years. Basic to the politics of the war years, and a key to understanding the era, was the testing of the Roosevelt Coalition forged in the 1930s. Enduring the new circumstances and the trial of the war years, this coalition would remain central to American politics—and to American life—for decades to come. Its World War II career thus has special importance.

No state is exactly the nation in miniature, nor do the politics of any one state fully typify or explain national political developments. Still, an examination of Connecticut society and politics during the war years has important wider implications and reveals much about the experience of war in kindred states and in the nation generally. In its economic and social structure, and consequently in its politics, Connecticut was not simply a New England state but was rather a representative northern industrial state. Although without a metropolis to compare with New York or Boston, Connecticut was primarily urban. The state's economy, while similar to those of Massachusetts and Rhode Island, also had much in common with the expanding economies of the newer industrial states to the west and south. With its large proportion of "new immigrants," especially Italians, Poles, and Jews, Connecticut resembled such states as New York and New Jersey as much as it did Massachusetts, for example, where the Irish were relatively more important. And while the state's twentieth-century political history and voting patterns have approximated those of Massachusetts and Rhode Island, Connecticut's support of Democratic presidential candidates since 1936 has more closely paralleled levels and trends in other industrial states, New York and Pennsylvania especially. In the presidential and congressional elections from 1936 to 1948, the Democratic percentage of the vote in Connecticut varied (except for 1938) within just a point or two of the Democratic share of the aggregate vote of the major industrial states of the Northeast and Midwest. Connecticut's Roosevelt Coalition, moreover, based on working-class, ethnic, urban voters, fits clearly into the mold of the classic industrial-state Roosevelt Coalition described by historians and political scientists. Connecticut, then, provides a good place to examine the impact of World War II on the people and politics of an urban-industrial-ethnic state with representative voting trends and a characteristic Roosevelt Coalition.

It does so all the more because of the nature of its wartime history. Connecticut's remarkable wartime economic boom makes the state a good case study of the World War II economic mobilization and its consequences. The boom meant prosperity, of course, but prosperity accompanied by various tensions, frustrations, and problems; and the troubles, like the effort (or lack of it) to cope with them, were much the same in Connecticut as in other war-boom areas. In those aspects of its wartime economic and social history, and in other important ones too, Connecticut reveals not only the impact of the war but also the persistence of old attitudes, values, and practices and the powerful influence of the past on the present and future that were fundamental parts of national life in the era. The experiences of Connecticut's major European ethnic groups and blacks also paralleled those in other states. With an eighth and more of its population Italian-Americans, moreover, Connecticut provides a revealing look at the largely ignored but eventful and important wartime story of the nation's millions of Italian-Americans. And so as well do Connecticut's wartime politics tell much about broader developments and patterns. Issues, party strategies, voting patterns, the ebb and flow of political strength, and above all the history of the Roosevelt Coalition—tested by new circumstances and new issues, eroded and somewhat altered, but nonetheless largely intact at the end of the war—all these aspects of Connecticut politics were of a piece with those elsewhere. In the presidential elections of 1940 and 1944, Connecticut was about one percentage point less Democratic than the nation, one percentage point more Democratic than the collective northern industrial states. Parts of Connecticut's wartime history, to be sure, must be understood more or less narrowly in terms of Connecticut itself; but much of that history, and especially the larger social, economic, and political patterns, was consistent with and helps illuminate developments elsewhere on the American home front.

Politics provide the basic focus and organizing theme for my examination of Connecticut. This study is informed, indeed, by a persuasion that American politics stand in close relation to the American culture broadly defined—to the experiences, concerns, and attitudes of the people generally and of identifiable and reasonably coherent groups in the society. In analyzing Connecticut politics I have thus looked at many things. I have explored the social bases of the state's politics and examined important developments and attitudes in the war years, and I have tried to show their political implications. While "politics" is not quite the same as "government," the use of government in America is intrinsically political; consequently I have paid attention to the state and federal governments. I have also tried to show how and why Connecticut political parties decided on policy positions and candidates. I have devoted much space to close scrutiny of campaigns and voting returns. Examined together, and in the context of the social and political culture, what candidates did and said and how people voted reveal much about the impact of events, illuminate dominant concerns, and help toward understanding not just the decisions but also the divisions and directions of the society.

Properly to study wartime Connecticut and its politics requires a focus substantially broader than the period between Pearl Harbor and V-J Day. Although World War II ended in the late summer of 1945, the entire 1945–46 biennium, involving as it did the transition from war to peace and from Franklin D. Roosevelt to Harry S Truman, is important to understanding the wartime experience. So too are the political developments of those years, and the voting patterns of 1946—and of 1948 as well—are essential to analysis of the political impact of the war, especially on the Roosevelt Coalition. The study of Connecticut society and politics in the era of World War II must begin before Pearl Harbor just as it must extend beyond V-J Day. As early as 1940, the war significantly affected Connecticut's people and politics. Nor indeed does the year 1940 provide an adequate starting point, for it is necessary to understand something about the state's social, economic, and political structure and development. To examine the effects of the war years on the Roosevelt Coalition in particular, it is essential to see how and why Connecticut politics had changed in the preceding decade, to understand the bases and contours of Connecticut's Roosevelt Coalition. History is continuous, and if study of the war years is important for understanding the postwar era, so wartime Connecticut is best approached and comprehended from the perspective of its people's past.

ACKNOWLEDGMENTS

Many people gave me generous and important assistance at every stage of my work from prospectus to publication. I am glad here to acknowledge, though I cannot discharge, the many debts I incurred along the way. My research was made far easier by the ready and expert help of numerous library staffs, particularly those of the Connecticut State Library, the Yale University Library, the Franklin D. Roosevelt Library, and the University of Maryland Baltimore County Library. They and the other library and archives staffs upon whom I relied have my gratitude. So also do the numerous people who read and helped improve various versions of my work. I must especially thank John Morton Blum, Dewey W. Grantham, John L. McCarthy, Elting E. Morison, R. Hal Williams, Allan M. Winkler, and C. Vann Woodward for their discerning comments and suggestions. Jack Zaiman of the *Hartford Courant* also read an early draft, and in two interviews he shared with me some of his vast knowledge of Connecticut politics and politicians going back to the 1930s. John L. McCarthy provided indispensable tutoring in the use of statistics and computers, and Colin B. Burke also helped me with statistics; neither should be held accountable for any errors of statistical method or execution. The staff of the University of Tennessee Press provided friendly and efficient assistance in bringing my study to publication. True to his reputation, Dewey W. Grantham proved a kind, astute, and altogether helpful editor, and he has my special thanks. My largest scholarly debt is to John Morton Blum, who encouraged and assisted me from the beginning and who gave unstintingly of his time, expertise, and insights in talking through questions with me and in editing several drafts. I owe him much, both personally and professionally. Joseph F. Mulligan, Director of Graduate Studies and Research at the University of Maryland Baltimore County, helped me procure a grant at a critical time, and the University provided financial and clerical assistance that facilitated publishing this book. I am fortunate to be part of a closeknit and supportive family, whose warm encouragement and backing have in this endeavor, as in so many others, been invaluable. My most important debt is to my wife, Renate, and to our children, Martha and Bill. They have in many essential ways sustained me throughout the long enterprise, and I thank them, Renate especially, for that and for much else besides.

June 1978   JOHN W. JEFFRIES

CONTENTS

TABLES

TESTING THE ROOSEVELT COALITION

I

MAKING THE ROOSEVELT COALITION
Connecticut Society and Politics in the Interwar Years

Connecticut in the 1920s shared the normalcy of the American nation. Corporate business grew in size and prestige; social and economic problems also grew, but went almost unattended; and the public, beguiled by consumerism and apparent prosperity and beset by ethnocultural tensions, was for most of the decade largely apathetic to politics and public policy. Like the nation, too, Connecticut was governed by a business-oriented, "respectable" Republican party. Prosperity, overwhelming small-town and rural voting support, and a reputation for thrifty and efficient government provided virtually invincible political strength to the Yankee Republicans, often businessmen, who ruled the state.

Yet the small town-Yankee-business cast of Connecticut politics reflected the decade better than it did the state. The land primarily of Yankee farms and towns lay far in the past. Industrialization had come early to Connecticut, and with it had come urbanization. As factories and cities had changed the face of the state, so had immigrants altered its population. By the 1920s first- and second-generation Americans comprised nearly two-thirds of Connecticut's people, and ethnicity pervaded most aspects of Connecticut life. The urban labor force, largely foreign stock, more truly represented Connecticut society than did the regnant Yankee businessmen. Nor did business in the 1920s have economic soundness to match its political strength. All that made 1920s-style normalcy transitory, not fundamental, and made Republican dominance less secure than it seemed in the Harding-Coolidge era.

3

The decade beginning in the late 1920s brought shock, upheaval, and profound political change to Connecticut as it did to the nation. By the eve of World War II, the state had undergone a trying period of social turmoil and deep economic depression. As they usually do in America, such experiences found political expression. Benefiting from the developments of the decade and from the longer-range changes in the social bases of Connecticut politics, the Democrats rose from the inept and hopeless minority party of the mid-1920s to the powerful majority party of the mid-1930s. Ethnocultural tensions, the Great Depression, the New Deal, and Franklin D. Roosevelt combined to alter the shape and substance of Connecticut politics and to produce the landslide victory of the Roosevelt Coalition in 1936. Events of the late 1930s, however, proved that Democrats could not presume an easy dominance of the state's politics. Although the changes in Connecticut politics proved lasting and although Democrats retained an underlying majority, Connecticut had left a period of Republican hegemony not for one of undisputed Democratic control but rather for one of competitiveness.

Twentieth-century America was given its modern shape and character by industrialization, urbanization, and immigration, forces which together worked a profound and ramifying transformation of the nation's economy, society, culture, institutions, and politics. Connecticut shared fully in the process and in the experiences of that modernization. By the time of the interwar years, the "land of steady habits"—of hilly farms, small towns, and the old-time Protestant Yankee—was largely myth and memory. Changing the state, factories, cities, and European newcomers had in Connecticut as in other northern industrial states reshaped the social bases of its politics in ways that would underwrite the political upheaval culminating in the Roosevelt Coalition.

Industrialization was basic to the modern contours of Connecticut life and to its altered political culture. In the half-century from the Civil War to World War I, industry had burgeoned and agriculture had declined precipitously. Reorganized to take advantage of the growing urban markets nearby, Connecticut agriculture did continue to provide a living, sometimes a good one, for some of the state's people. Dairying, centered in Litchfield County in northwestern Connecticut, had become the state's most important agricultural activity, while the fertile fields of the Connecticut River Valley in northern Hartford County made tobacco the leading cash crop in 1919. Vegetables ranked as the second crop in value, and small vegetable farms dotted Hartford, Fairfield, and especially New Haven counties near the state's major cities. But with only 5 percent of the state's labor force in agriculture and farm income only 5 percent of manufacturing income, post-World War I Connecticut was fundamentally an industrial state. Twelfth nationally in total value of product and second in manufacturing output per capita, it depended upon manufacturing, especially of durable goods in metals and machinery, for employment and income. More than half the working force had jobs in manufacturing, some five times the number in each of the supporting fields of clerical work and trade, and ten times the number engaged in agriculture.

Connecticut industry was concentrated in, but not confined to, the cities. The five most populous cities accounted for nearly half the state's manufactured goods, roughly the same share as their percentage of the state population. A close third in population, the diversified industrial city of Bridgeport had since the early twentieth century led the state in value of manufactured products, and it remained the "industrial capital of Connecticut" in the interwar years. Waterbury, fourth in size and the center of the Naugatuck Valley brass industry, had edged into second place in value of product during World War I. Third and fourth respectively came New Haven and Hartford, the two largest cities, which were not so dependent as the others on manufacturing. Hartford, the state capital, a national insurance center, and the hub of Connecticut's finance and trade, had a particularly balanced economic life. New Britain, the "hardware city," was a rather distant fifth in industry as in

5

population. Besides the five big cities, Connecticut had an array of lesser industrial cities, located chiefly in Hartford, New Haven, and Fairfield counties in the central and southwestern sections of the state. Other industrial areas included southeastern Litchfield County (part of the Naugatuck Valley industrial region), the New London-Norwich area in extreme southeastern Connecticut, and the textile towns of eastern Connecticut. Because of Connecticut's size, residential patterns, and interspersal of large cities, small cities, and towns, few areas escaped the direct impact of industry and industrialization.[1]

Although Connecticut shared partly in the economic problems of competitive disadvantages and stagnation which beset New England after World War I, her economy differed significantly in structure and consequently in performance from those of her New England sister states to the north and east. Much less reliant on the faltering textile and leather industries, Connecticut, despite a fall of perhaps 10 percent or more in the manufacturing labor force, escaped the hard times experienced most dramatically by Massachusetts in the 1920s. Some older industries expanded, especially light metals and brass goods, and such new enterprises as radio and the aircraft industry (the latter most important for the future) located in Connecticut during the decade. Hartford, New Haven, and Fairfield counties, home of the state's durable goods industries and of some 80 percent of its population and industrial activity, had bright long-range prospects. Even in eastern Connecticut, hit hard by a textile depression, the New London-Groton submarine industry had obvious potential. Connecticut's economy, in fact, had much in common with those of the advancing industrial states to the west and south. Geographical proximity reinforced the structural similarities. Expanding less than the nation but more than New England, concentrating in the durable goods and transportation industries, and oriented largely toward the mid-Atlantic market area, Connecticut despite its problems had the soundest economy in New England.[2]

Population growth and urbanization had accompanied Connecticut's industrialization. The state had an extremely high population growth rate in the late nineteenth and early twentieth centuries, some two-thirds of the increase stemming from immigration. Settling largely in the cities, the immigrants were joined there by native rural folk, pushed by agricultural depression and pulled by industrial jobs. Two-thirds urban in 1920, and the fourth most densely populated state, Connecticut had no single dominating metropolis but did have a variety of medium-sized and large cities. Like its industry, Connecticut's population was largely concentrated in an arc running along Long Island Sound from New York to New Haven and then turning northward through central Connecticut to New Britain and Hartford. The three populous, "metropolitan" counties contained the chief urban-industrial centers: Hartford and New Britain in Hartford County; New Haven and Waterbury in New Haven County; and Bridgeport in Fairfield County. None of these cities was a "big city" in the way of a Boston or a New York—Hartford, New Haven, and Bridgeport all had populations in the vicinity of 150,000, Waterbury counted not quite 100,000 citizens, while New Britain's population was less than 70,000—but they shared much of the flavor and the basic social, economic, and functional characteristics of the nation's urban giants. Those five cities, moreover, held more than 40 percent of the state's population, and their total metropolitan areas included some two-thirds of Connecticut's people.[3]

By the interwar years, the cities had given way to the suburbs as Connecticut's most important areas of population growth and redistribution. The central cities grew by some 12 percent in the 1920s, the outlying suburban areas by 44 percent; and although the movement to the suburbs slacked off in the Depression decade, the metropolitan suburbs rose from one-sixth of the state's population in 1920 to nearly a quarter in 1940. Some of the suburbs attracted many factory hands who moved from the cities to find new jobs or to engage in part-time farming. Nicer, more expensive suburban areas grew primarily because of middle-income people escaping the congested cities. In the often plush commuter towns of Fairfield County, the new suburbanites, many from New York City, were most

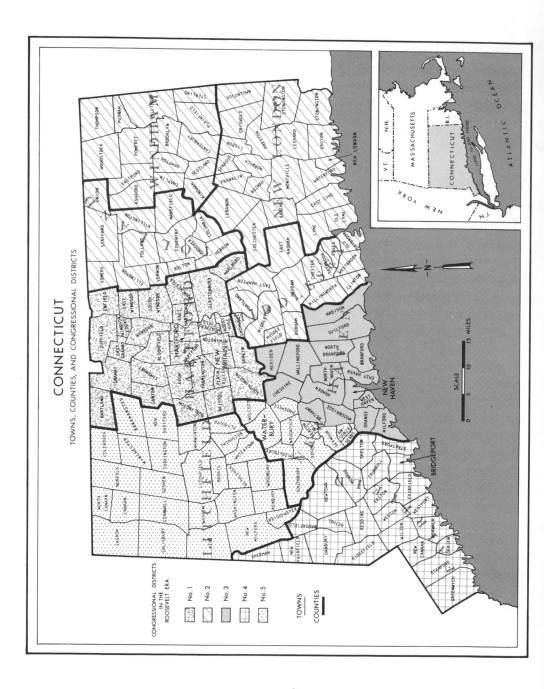

CONNECTICUT

TOWNS, COUNTIES, AND CONGRESSIONAL DISTRICTS

CONGRESSIONAL DISTRICTS IN THE ROOSEVELT ERA

No. 1
No. 2
No. 3
No. 4
No. 5

TOWNS

COUNTIES

8

likely to be businessmen or professionals, least likely to be workers. But despite the variety, the suburbs did generally comprise middle- and upper-income groups in white-collar, business, and professional occupations, and that characteristic, along with their rapid growth, made the suburbs an ever more significant part of Connecticut life and political culture.[4] Together, urbanization and suburbanization had in Connecticut as elsewhere produced by the interwar years a population redistribution of great social and political importance.

As Connecticut had not for decades been a rural, small-town state, so it had not for decades been a predominantly Yankee state. With its thriving industrial economy and its location between the great entry ports of New York and Boston, Connecticut attracted hundreds of thousands of the immigrants who flocked to America. In the mid-nineteenth century only one-tenth of the state's population was foreign born; by 1920 Connecticut's 378,000 immigrants constituted one-fourth of its people. Despite the restrictive national immigration laws of the 1920s, as late as 1940 roughly one of every five Connecticut residents had been born abroad, a proportion which was more than twice the national figure and which was a close fourth in the nation behind New York, Massachusetts, and Rhode Island. In 1940, moreover, nearly three of every five people in Connecticut were "foreign stock"—immigrants or the children of at least one immigrant parent.[5]

Connecticut had many immigrant groups as well as many immigrants. The Irish had been the first of the nineteenth-century immigrants to come in large numbers, and they were at first joined chiefly by Germans and then by French-Canadians. But beginning late in the nineteenth century and peaking early in the twentieth, another, much larger, and significantly different influx of immigrants—the "new immigrants" who thronged to America from southern and eastern Europe—provided the great majority of the newcomers. Italians, Poles, and Jews, the last mostly from Russia, were by far the most numerous of the new immigrants in Connecticut. Italians came in the greatest numbers. Fewer than 1,000 foreign-born Italians lived in Con-

9

necticut in 1880; forty years later there were 80,000, mostly from southern Italy and Sicily, and Italian immigrants and their children represented one-eighth of the state's population. Comparable increases brought the number of Polish and Russian immigrants to 47,000 and 39,000 respectively in 1920. By then, the first and second generations of these three major new immigrant groups constituted a "distinctly alien" one-fourth of Connecticut's people.[6]

Different old-country backgrounds and times of arrival in America bred substantial disparities among the immigrants in social and economic status.[7] Falling between the Yankees at the top and the blacks at the bottom, the immigrant groups were ranged throughout Connecticut's stratified (though not static) society much as they were in the nation's other ethnic areas. Near the top stood the easily assimilable northern and western Europeans, especially the English but also the Scandinavians and Germans. Generally well-integrated both occupationally and residentially, these small groups tended to identify with and share the status of middle-class Yankees. They won relatively easy acceptance into the dominant Yankee society.

The Irish and the French-Canadians fell between those groups and the new immigrants. Second only to the Italians numerically, the heavily urban Irish had carved out their own position in Connecticut by the interwar years. Irishmen rarely held top positions in business and industry, but they pursued diverse occupations and had begun to enter the middle class in significant numbers. Success in politics and the law even gave the group some claim to status. By making public service employment available, moreover, leadership in municipal politics opened up a particularly important avenue to the middle class. More acculturated than truly assimilated, the Irish were nonetheless more respectable and acceptable than the newer immigrants.

Although one of the older immigrant groups, the French-Canadians ranked nearer to the new immigrants than to the Irish in social and economic status. The proximity of their homeland, the province of Quebec, helped to inhibit acculturation and assimilation, for French-Canadians often came south intending to stay only long enough to better their economic lot. Even when they remained, close ties with Quebec helped them preserve a bilingual and a bicultural society well beyond the first and second generations. Too, the nearness of French Canada produced a substantial new influx of unacculturated French-Canadians when European immigration dwindled in the 1920s. Mostly manufacturing workers, French-Canadians settled in the greatest numbers in Hartford and Waterbury, but they were proportionately most important in many of eastern Connecticut's textile towns.

Near the bottom of Connecticut society were the new immigrants from southern and eastern Europe. Largely of impoverished peasant stock, they seemed backward by American standards and were unused to an industrial society. The newcomers as a consequence characteristically took jobs as rough laborers and as unskilled and semiskilled factory hands. Those who became farmers typically fared little better, for they usually located on the poorest soil and lacked familiarity with new management and marketing techniques. Jews provided the chief exception to the concentration of new immigrants in occupations with little status, pay, or security, for many of them found employment in trade and commerce, the professions, white-collar jobs, and skilled artisan work. Still, the newcomers generally constituted an industrial lower class, and numerous Jews were employed as sweatshop workers in urban garment manufacture.

Most of the new immigrants lived in the cities, although Polish and Russian farming communities in eastern Connecticut and Italian truck farmers near the cities helped make even Connecticut's rural-farm population predominantly foreign-stock by the interwar years. Jews were the most urban of the immigrants. More than half of them lived in Hartford and New Haven, where they formed one-sixth of the population. New Haven held the largest Italian settlement. First- and second-generation Italian-Americans accounted for one-fourth or more of that city's population, and perhaps of Waterbury's

11

too. Polish-Americans, also predominantly urban, settled less in the biggest cities than did Jews and Italians. New Britain's "Polonia" was much the largest and most important Polish community in Connecticut—and one of the largest in the nation.

In Connecticut as elsewhere, immigration helped produce major social divisions and strains. The immigrants, especially the new immigrants, tended to live among and associate with their own kind in organized, in some ways almost self-sufficient communities. There a variety of organizations and the ethnic press heightened group consciousness, helped preserve cultural traits and values, and coordinated group life. Religion bound the Jews together and helped shape sundry aspects of their lives, and the Church did the same for the various Catholic groups. To an important degree, the ethnic groups participated in their ingrown social lives out of choice. Removed from their homelands, living in strange cities, performing new jobs, surrounded by different and often hostile peoples, ways, and religions, they naturally sought out those with whom they could speak the old language and at least approximate old customs.

Yet if the immigrant groups wanted to live together and preserve old ways, they were also perforce thrown in on themselves. Yankees resented the immigrants and often sought to exclude them from the social and economic mainstreams. Disliking the newcomers and their ways in any event, and sure that their stereotyping patterns of employment, housing, dress, and education proved their inferiority, Yankees were all the more hostile because they saw in the numerous immigrants a threat to their culture and to their economic and political leadership. Added to the Yankee-immigrant polarities was the considerable tension, even conflict, between the various immigrant groups themselves. The Irish disdained contact and identification with the new immigrants, who in turn released their feelings of resentment and insecurity on smaller, weaker, or lower-status groups. Catholic-Jewish hostility roiled the waters further. Fueled by myriad differences of background, conventions, status, and outlook, then, considerable ill feeling marked intergroup relations. The immigrants found balm as well as meaning in their community lives.

So also with Connecticut blacks, the weakest and most ostracized group of all. Negroes constituted less than 2 percent of the state's people, though the black population doubled to nearly 30,000 between 1910 and 1930. Repelled by conditions in the South and attracted by the prospects of new opportunities, blacks also found their color a liability and their life difficult in Connecticut, as they did throughout the North. Most blacks settled in the cities, especially Hartford and New Haven, where they lived in the poorest housing and by the interwar period found employment almost exclusively as servants or laborers, performing the most menial, dirty, taxing, and ill-paying jobs. Their social status was no better. No matter how excluded and despised immigrants may have been, the blacks were always at least a notch or two lower and prey to the resentment and prejudice of the insecure whites. Like the white immigrants, blacks had their own ethnocentric pride, and like the white immigrants, too, blacks reacted defensively, retreating to their own separate and structured society.[8]

For blacks, but especially for the much more numerous immigrants, the spirit of the 1920s heightened group defensiveness and self-consciousness. That decade saw old Americans rise in an ugly mood to do battle with the immigrants, the citics, the Catholics, the Jews, the blacks, and the drinkers. Connecticut shared in some of the strife. The Ku Klux Klan, which as elsewhere in the Northeast vented its hatreds chiefly on the immigrant groups and the Catholic Church, symptomized the cultural cleavages. Although its membership was never large and although it declined rapidly in the second half of the decade, the Connecticut Klan, and the mood it represented, could only have intensified the newcomers' sense of themselves as religious and social outcasts.[9] The Klan was one more sign, and a highly visible and emotion-charged one, that the state's cosmopolitanism was superficial and not attitudinal—a circumstance that affected virtually every area of Connecticut life.

13

Connecticut had changed enormously since the time when such terms as the "land of steady habits" and the "Connecticut Yankee" had adequately described its life and society. Interwar Connecticut was a modern urban-industrial state where the Catholic and Jewish immigrant groups far outnumbered the Protestant Yankees. Flux and the resulting challenges to the traditional Yankee culture and leadership continued in the 1920s, moreover, and fueled the social and ethnocultural tensions of the decade. The suggestion of placidity implicit in the term "normalcy" thus did not fit 1920s Connecticut either, for that generally prosperous decade was also a rancorous one full of stress and conflict for virtually every element of Connecticut's variegated society. Nor indeed was even the prosperity so widespread and so well-founded as many believed. Those changes and circumstances made the post-World War I hegemony of the business-oriented, rural- and small-town-based, Yankee-dominated Republican party shakier than it seemed; and beginning in the late 1920s a hammering series of events would catalyze a transformation of Connecticut politics and make political patterns more congruent with the underlying political culture.

For most of the 1920s, however, Republican control of Connecticut seemed anything but fragile, and a political upheaval that might overturn that control was hard to imagine. GOP domination was overwhelming. Republicans won all of the thirty contests for statewide office in the decade, each presidential and senatorial election, twenty-four of the twenty-five congressional races, and crushing majorities in the state legislature. In the statewide elections of 1920, 1924, and 1926, furthermore, the GOP captured some two-thirds of the vote.[10]

The Republican hegemony of the 1920s was no sudden or accidental thing. Like so much of the industrial East, Connecticut had been normally a solid Republican state since the realigning election of 1896 had ended a period of political competitiveness and begun one of Republican ascendancy. Threatened in the 1910s, Republican supremacy was reasserted with

14

Warren G. Harding's 1920 landslide victory, which marked both a multifaceted reaction against Woodrow Wilson's last years as president and a powerful reaffirmation of Connecticut's normal Republicanism. But Republicans owed their 1920s domination of Connecticut politics to more than history and the postwar reaction. During the decade the state GOP profited from "normalcy" and evident prosperity under the national Republican administrations, and it had important strengths of its own. The party, indeed the state, was in the hands of J. Henry Roraback, concurrently national committeeman and chairman of the Republican state central committee, who skillfully dictated to the GOP and the Republican-dominated General Assembly. So great was his power, which stretched from Hartford to Connecticut Republicans in Congress, that some called Connecticut "Rorabackia." A Yankee from rural Litchfield County with many important business interests—especially in the burgeoning utilities industry, which greatly benefited from the lax supervision and eager help of Roraback's state government—"J. Henry," large, prosperous, close-mouthed, and powerful, personified as well as ruled his party. Like Roraback, the other major Republican leaders and candidates (all of them clearly J. Henry's subordinates) were conservative, respectable, business-minded Yankees who implemented a minimal "pay as you go" public policy spiced by services for farmers and favors for business. The combination of respectability, general prosperity, fiscal prudence, and pro-business conservatism at the state and national levels ensured for Republicans the support of their chief constituents—old-stock, middle- and upper-class voters, especially from the suburbs, farms, and smaller towns.[11]

To that core vote the GOP added enough ethnic and urban support to give the party its overwhelming majorities. In Connecticut as in other states, ethnic attachments and antagonisms had been at the heart of politics since the nineteenth century. But although the Democratic party had long tended to be the party of the immigrants and the GOP the party of the Yankees, that pattern stemmed largely from the numbers and political proclivities of the Irish. In the nineteenth century

Irish immigrants had found a home in the Democratic party, and by the twentieth century Irish politicians ranked high in its leadership. Apart from the Irish, however, ethnic groups in the 1920s were far from overwhelmingly Democratic. The relatively small northern European Protestant immigrant groups, for example, their politics reflecting their social and economic status, aligned largely with the GOP.[12]

What especially blurred the ethnic basis of state and national politics for most of the 1920s was the voting behavior of the numerically crucial new immigrants. Finding politics a new experience which required some acculturation, and without a middle class to provide leadership, the new immigrants were less active politically and less stable in their partisan allegiances than other groups. Often disaffected by the Yankee and sometimes nativist cast of the GOP, they also had little stake in the Democratic party. The Irish, who dominated the Democratic party in the cities where so many of the new immigrants congregated, were loath to share such rewards of their own hard-earned leadership as party decisions, important nominations, and municipal jobs with the recent arrivals. That alienated many of the newcomers, already at odds with the Irish for other reasons, from the Democratic party. So also did the cluster of ethnic issues arising from World War I that bled away gains Democrats had made among these groups in the 1910s. Republicans frequently capitalized on the opportunities thus afforded them. Since early in the century, for example, New Haven Republicans had substantially eroded potential Democratic strength by giving attention to the city's Italian population. In the 1920s, astute GOP politicians in Connecticut exploited anger at the Wilson Presidency and the Versailles Treaty and also offered "recognition"—a few nominations, some patronage, and a limited hand in party affairs—to new immigrants. Such measures, together with the allure that the Republicans' reputation as the party of industrial prosperity held for the largely working-class new immigrants, helped bring the GOP significant ethnic support for most of the decade.[13]

The Democrats, then, had no monopoly of the ethnic vote.

16

They did even worse among blacks, who, virtually ignored by both parties, continued like their brethren elsewhere to discharge their debt to Republican Abraham Lincoln.[14] If the Democrats' great strength after 1928 rested largely on their ability to win large majorities from the state's ethnic population, their weakness before then resulted from their inability to do so. So, too, with Democratic performances in urban areas. As elsewhere in the North, Democrats in Connecticut had traditionally done better in the cities than outside them, and in the 1920s they won large, often majority votes in big-city municipal elections. But without full support from the urban ethnic voters, the Democrats did not unfailingly carry municipal elections, and they captured a majority of the aggregate big-city vote only once, in 1922, in the four major statewide elections from 1920 through 1926. Such showings in the cities doomed the Democrats to their minority status of the decade.

The Democrats, however, suffered a variety of other ills as well. The state and nation seemed in safe, indeed in indispensable hands, while Democrats were hurt by their reputation as the party of "turbulence and disorder" and by their reputedly extravagant and shameless urban administrations. Able to win only at the local level, moreover, Democrats had instead of a strong state organization a loosely confederated directorate of urban bosses whose political machinations sometimes sapped the party's strength. Three men in particular sat atop Connecticut Democratic politics in the post-World War I years. One of them, Homer S. Cummings, a lawyer from Fairfield County, seemed on the way down and out in the 1920s. Long a power in the state party—he served as national committeeman for the first quarter of the twentieth century—he achieved some national prominence at the end of the Wilson era when he served briefly as chairman of the Democratic national committee, keynoted the 1920 national convention, and ran as a dark-horse candidate for the presidential nomination. But Cummings's power ebbed in the 1920s, and not until he championed Franklin D. Roosevelt's campaign for the 1932 Democratic presidential nomination and the White House did Cummings, who became Roosevelt's Attorney General, regain a large influence in the state.

More important than Cummings to Connecticut's Democratic party in the 1920s were two Irish politicians from the state's largest cities, David E. Fitzgerald of New Haven and Thomas J. Spellacy of Hartford. A dapper second-generation Irish-American who stood barely more than five feet tall, "Little Dave" Fitzgerald was the upwardly mobile son of a New Haven grocer. After graduating from Yale Law School and gaining admittance to the bar when just twenty-one, he entered politics and became Democratic town chairman in New Haven in 1907 at the age of thirty-three. A few years later Fitzgerald became state chairman, a post he held until the early 1920s, and he served four terms as New Haven's mayor from 1918 to 1926. In his four decades in politics he went from ward chairman to vice-chairman of the national committee and was the state's national committeeman when he died in 1942. But for all his talent and his political power and longevity, Fitzgerald, a quiet man, never won the notoriety or achieved quite the importance of his frequent ally and sometime opponent, Hartford's mercurial Thomas J. Spellacy.

Spellacy was for decades the state's most spectacular politician. Known as "T.J." to his associates and usually referred to by politicos as "Long Tom" or "the Long Fellow," Spellacy was an angular, long-faced, rather plain man well over six feet in height. His father, a contractor, had been active in Hartford politics, as were two of his brothers, and shortly after Long Tom completed Holy Cross College and Georgetown Law School he too got into politics. From his election as state senator in 1906 until his last hurrah in 1946, when his protégé John M. Bailey toppled him from the pinnacle of Hartford Democratic politics, Spellacy's career stretched over some forty tempestuous, roller-coaster years of ups and downs and ins and outs. Having what Bailey once called "the smartest political brain I have ever come into contact with," Spellacy, who seemingly knew everything and forgot nothing, could be masterful at manipulating men and political machines and could

18

put on spectacular oratorical displays when necessary. A "natural politician," Spellacy was also a superb administrator, and during his tenure as Hartford's mayor from 1935 to 1943 this brawling Irishman, who proudly called himself an "organization Democrat," won the tribute of the ardently Republican and respectable *Hartford Courant* by virtue of his managerial and bureaucratic talents. Yet Spellacy often wasted his gifts and spoiled his successes. Possessed of a "volcanic personality" and given to towering, pugnacious rages, he could neither stay clear of a political fight nor forgive an enemy. Consequently, he accumulated a long list of devout foes and often dissipated his strength by fighting battles he should have ignored or left to others. Even so, Long Tom, forever scrambling and scheming, charming when he wanted to be and fascinating regardless, managed to remain at or near the top of Connecticut politics for decades.

Spellacy first rose to that position during the Wilson era at roughly the same time as David Fitzgerald. Despite losing races for governor in 1918 and for U.S. senator in 1922 (when Fitzgerald lost the gubernatorial contest), he briefly became national committeeman when Homer Cummings stepped down in the mid-1920s. With J. Henry Roraback and occasionally with Cummings, Long Tom and Little Dave maneuvered themselves through the 1920s, reputedly playing the ancient "double machine" game of the hopeless minority by cooperating with Roraback and the GOP in return for patronage and favors enough to retain their personal power. Such tactics, beneficial perhaps for the two players and the stuff of later political legend, proved no boon to the party. Looking back on this period decades later, John Bailey, the party's enormously successful state chairman in the three post-World War II decades, said "It was a great era, but they never won!"[15]

They, and the party they led, never won in the 1920s above all because of a lack of strong issues and effective strategy. Deprived by the general prosperity of the hard times virtually any out-party politician can exploit, Democratic leaders offered no real policy alternative to the Republicans. Essentially conservative (or at least nonideological) and practical men, their chief concerns were with power, patronage, and their own local followings. In fact, the heavily Irish Democratic leadership failed even to practice ethnic politics imaginatively or thoroughly in the 1920s. After offering relatively cosmopolitan slates headed by Irishmen in 1920 and 1922, the party in the next two elections nominated fewer ethnic candidates, all of them Irish and none at the head of the ticket. Rudderless and foundering, the Democratic party polled barely one-third of the vote in 1924 and 1926.

By the late 1920s Connecticut seemed virtually a one-party state. Connecticut Democrats might have looked with some envy upon their counterparts in neighboring Massachusetts. There economic and social grievances and a campaign built upon important issues, shrewd ethnic tactics, and a popular, progressive, foreign-stock candidate elected Irish Democrat David I. Walsh to the United States Senate in 1926. Although other Bay State Democrats did not fare as well as Walsh, the victorious Walsh coalition of industrial workers, Irishmen, new immigrants, and many Yankees, liberals, and unhappy Republicans showed what might be done in an electorate similar in many ways to Connecticut's.[16] But without the issues or candidates to mobilize their potential strength, Connecticut Democrats seemed far from a breakthrough which would capitalize on the changes of past decades in the social bases of Connecticut politics. Nor did many look in that direction for the party's salvation. Surveying the bleak position of the state Democrats before the 1928 election, one student of Connecticut politics, in offering his advice as to how the party might enhance its prospects, said it must especially "go out of its way to be 'respectable'" in its platform and its candidates.[17]

Instead of respectability, Connecticut Democrats in 1928 got Al Smith and his Brown Derby presidential campaign of "provincial Catholic urbanism."[18] The short-term result was still another Republican sweep of the state. But Smith fared much better than had the two previous Democratic presidential nominees in Connecticut, better indeed than any but Wilson since 1892. More important, the election of 1928 helped touch off a period of political realignment which restored competition to Connecticut politics and which eight years later culminated in the landslide Democratic victory of the Roosevelt Coalition.

The extraordinarily rancorous 1928 presidential campaign brought the ethnocultural stress of the 1920s to the very heart of politics. In Connecticut as elsewhere, Alfred E. Smith, the proud Irish-Catholic representative of the nation's urban, ethnic multitudes, inspired his supporters and appalled his opponents.[19] By arousing such emotions, the bitter, sometimes scurrilous campaign reversed the long-term decline in state and national political participation that had set in following the election of 1896. Connecticut's voter registration climbed by 27 percent and its voter turnout by 38 percent over 1924 levels. As elsewhere, especially notable gains came from urban and immigrant areas.

The election polarized as well as mobilized Connecticut voters, and it brought significant gains to the Democratic party. Much more than in past elections, voting patterns reflected the social cleavages between city and town and between newcomer and Yankee.[20] Winning some 46 percent of the statewide vote and some 55 percent in the five big cities, Smith advanced sharply over recent Democratic showings in urban and immigrant areas and lost ground in native, small-town, and agricultural areas. Consequently, the spread in the division of the vote between the five big cities and the towns with populations under 10,000 was twenty percentage points in 1928; in 1920, 1924, and 1926 it had been only some seven points and in 1922 some thirteen points. The most important and generally the most spectacular Democratic gains came in urban new-immigrant constituencies, as Smith won impressive majorities in Polish, Jewish, and Italian areas carried handily by the GOP in the two previous elections. With new immigrants—many of them, women especially, first-time voters—joining the Irish in returning heavy, solidly Democratic votes, ethnicity was a far stronger correlate of Democratic support in Connecticut than

21

it had been before. The party's new supporters, moreover, enabled Smith to poll more votes than the combined totals of the two previous Democratic nominees for president.

Connecticut, then, experienced what has sometimes been called the "Al Smith Revolution" that altered voting patterns in the industrial North and East and laid foundations for the greater political upheaval of the 1930s.[21] Sparking political interest and participation, the campaign and election of 1928 had important implications for the future. They not only strengthened but also revitalized the Democratic party and helped bring to the fore a "New Guard" of Connecticut Democrats to battle for party control with the "Old Guard"—Little Dave Fitzgerald, Long Tom Spellacy, and their cohorts—of the 1920s. Further, as part of the politics of 1928, Connecticut Democrats nominated a much more cosmopolitan state ticket than they had in recent elections, and in subsequent elections they continued to provide more such recognition to new-immigrant groups than did the GOP. Because the ugly 1928 campaign made Catholics and immigrants all the more defensive and self-conscious, that was a significant change. Most important, the election of 1928 was not simply episodic. Rather, reflecting long-term social changes and the decade's social tensions, it helped begin a major realignment of Connecticut politics. Solidified and reinforced by subsequent events, the Democratic urban and ethnic strength evident in 1928 provided the basis of the powerful Roosevelt Coalition of 1936. But while Al Smith catalyzed and polarized voters in Connecticut and brought new support to the Democratic party, he gave the party neither the respectability nor the substantive issues that it needed to win the state; and as elsewhere Republican prosperity was probably more important to the GOP's victory than was Republican respectability. Despite the impact of Smith's candidacy, more was needed for the transformation of Connecticut politics and for the triumph of the Democratic party.

More came, beginning just a year after the 1928 election, when Connecticut and the nation entered the long decade of the Great Depression. Besides its economic and human impact, the Depression had enormous political implications. It discredited the Republican party, helped Democrat Franklin D. Roosevelt win the presidency in 1932, triggered the New Deal, and gave the Democratic party the issues, orientation, and support that changed it and made it the state's majority party. Each election from 1930 to 1936 marked a further step along that road.

The elections of 1930 and 1932 were characterized more by a negative reaction against the GOP than by an affirmation of the Democrats. Striking the highly industrialized Connecticut economy with particular severity, the Depression provided an intense, widespread grievance against the party in power, especially in the cities and industrial towns and among unskilled, semiskilled, and foreign-stock workers, where it hit hardest.[22] Since the Republican state government proved no more disposed than President Herbert Hoover to take ameliorative action, and since both were identified with the hard times, Connecticut Democrats found their stock boosted by the Depression.

In 1930 that stock rose to virtual parity with the GOP's. Democrats won the governorship, two of the five congressional races, and nearly half the vote for lesser statewide offices. Voting patterns conformed fairly closely to those of 1928: Democratic support came chiefly from the urban and immigrant areas where Al Smith had augmented the party's strength, and turnout was higher than in the midterm elections of the 1920s. Democrats picked up their additional strength primarily in those Yankee and small-town constituencies that had found Smith anathema.

The Democratic gains came in significant degree because of the gubernatorial candidacy of Wilbur L. Cross, the only Democrat to carry the state. Sixty-eight years old in 1930 and just retired as dean of the Yale Graduate School, Cross was a short, dignified but peppery man with close-cropped white hair, glasses, and a mustache. He seemed almost the quintessential "Connecticut Yankee," the apt title of his autobiography. His family went back some three centuries in Connecticut on his father's side and nearly as far on his mother's, and Cross him-

23

self had been born and raised in rural Connecticut and educated at Yale. His upbringing plus time spent as a youth around courtroom and country store provided him with a fund of cracker-barrel wit and stories that he used to good effect in politics. Although 1930 marked his first foray into active politics —his candidacy, supported by the "New Guard" and opposed by the "Old Guard," had come really by chance—Cross had been interested in politics since he was a boy and had been a devout Democrat since Grover Cleveland had appealed to his mugwump insistence on honest government. To a striking degree, Cross always remained faithful to the Cleveland Democrats' philosophy of honest, efficient, economical, limited government. Although generally supporting and sometimes applauding Franklin D. Roosevelt and the New Deal in the 1930s, Cross was in 1930 and remained during his eight years as governor a small-government, states'-rights "Jeffersonian Democrat," always a bit suspicious of the New Deal and occasionally downright opposed to it. Cross's own foremost goal as governor, even at the worst of the Depression, was to rationalize and reform the state government. In 1930, his appeal was that of a respectable Connecticut Yankee, and his campaign focused more on good government, criticism of Republican boss J. Henry Roraback and "Rorabackism," and opposition to prohibition than it did on the problems of the Depression.[23] Cross's image and campaign got him enough small-town support to nudge him into office, while the rest of the Democratic ticket fell just short. Still, if Cross's margin of victory was essentially personal and if his party had yet to advocate activist liberal policies, Connecticut Democrats, thanks largely to the Depression and to Wilbur Cross, had finally won major office again and had begun to consolidate and build on their 1928 advances.

That process continued in the 1932 election, which in Democratic strength and programmatic orientation belonged to the early phase of the realignment period rather than to the latter. The Depression deepened in Hoover's last two years as President. By the summer of 1932, Connecticut business activity, factory man-hours, and net individual income had all fallen to less than half of 1929 levels, while manufacturing employment was down by 37 percent.[24] Connecticut Democrats blamed such conditions on "the evils resulting from a departure both national and local from the Democratic belief in economy of government expenditures and proper limitation of government activities."[25] Not yet the state's liberal party, the Democrats were also not yet its majority party. While Roosevelt buried Hoover nationally by winning nearly three-fifths of the vote, he fell 7,000 votes shy of carrying Connecticut, one of only six states, all of them in the Northeast, to stick with the President. Wilbur Cross barely won reelection, and Augustine Lonergan, an old law partner of Long Tom Spellacy's and a congressman in the Wilson years, became the first Democrat elected senator from Connecticut in half a century; but Republicans elected the rest of their state ticket, won four of the six congressional seats, and carried 50.6 percent of the presidential vote. Nevertheless, Democrats did make gains over 1928, particularly in Yankee and small-town areas, and they did further consolidate their advances of the two previous elections. The stability of voting patterns was striking and important: at the town level, Roosevelt's vote correlated at +.93 with Smith's, and the gubernatorial vote showed nearly the same consistency.[26] Turnout remained high, and Roosevelt won some 30,000 votes more than Smith's 1928 total, while Hoover polled about 8,000 votes fewer than he had four years before. With a solid core vote, based in the cities and in foreign-stock wards, Democrats had come within striking distance of controlling the state because of the reinforcing effects of Al Smith's candidacy and the Great Depression.

By 1936 the Democrats had won control. The transformation of Connecticut politics was completed in the elections of 1934 and 1936, as the New Deal evolved, the Roosevelt Coalition emerged in its full flowering, and state Democrats adopted a far more liberal stance. After 1932 the Democrats profited from a favorable response to Roosevelt and the New Deal as well as from the continuing negative reaction to Hoover and the Great Depression. The 1934 campaign became the first of a parade of campaigns centering on Roosevelt and the New Deal. In response to GOP attacks on the New Deal as wasteful, ruinous, and antithetical to the American form of government, Connecticut Democrats warmly defended the President and his policies. Departing now from their old limited-government strictures, they toured the state in the "Roosevelt Special" and urged voters to show their support of the President and his programs by voting Democratic.[27] The people did so, if by a narrow margin, and Democrats finally captured Connecticut as part of their resounding victory throughout the urban-industrial East. Cross won a third term, but this time the rest of his ticket also won, Congressman Francis T. Maloney won the second Senate seat for the Democrats, and the party won four of the six congressional races. Turnout was extraordinarily high for a midterm election, and the pattern of the vote again closely followed that of elections since 1928.

Connecticut Democrats had profited in 1934 from the popularity and political salience of Roosevelt and the New Deal. The President and his policies would be even more central in the election of 1936, for the continued unfolding of the New Deal was the paramount fact of the intervening biennium. By 1936, nearly the full range of New Deal programs had been enacted. Providing a then phenomenal array of help and benefits for the state's people, New Deal measures also hastened the implementation of state social, labor, and public welfare legislation. From Washington, not Hartford, came the ideas, most of the policies, and much of the money that dealt with the Great Depression. Nor did the New Deal provide only relief and reform; it also helped bring significant economic recovery. From an average of 48 percent below normal in 1932, Connecticut's index of general business activity climbed to an average of 12 percent below normal in 1936 and by November had nearly regained 1929 levels. Gross corporate income, which had fallen 77 percent from 1929 to 1932, rose each year thereafter and stood only 20 percent below 1929 in 1936. By late 1936 factory man-hours exceeded the 1929 normal, while employment was at the 1929 level. Relief rolls had declined sharply. Net individual income, which had fallen to 46 percent of 1929 totals in 1933, climbed to 78 percent of that level in 1936. To be sure, full recovery and, because the labor force was larger, full employment eluded Connecticut as they did the nation. But the New Deal could claim credit for considerable economic recovery, and it could also command support because of its programs to provide relief, security, and often jobs for those who needed them.[28]

The campaign and election of 1936 reflected the impact of Roosevelt's presidency on Connecticut life. They reflected as well the long trauma of the Great Depression and the still older polarities and tensions of Connecticut society. As in other states, the confluence of these several factors resulted in the full-blown Roosevelt Coalition, which in Connecticut gave the President a 57.8 percent landslide victory. Roosevelt's 382,129 votes topped his 1932 total in the state by an astounding margin of more than 100,000, while Landon's 278,685 votes fell 10,000 short of Hoover's 1932 total. Local Democratic candidates ran only slightly behind Roosevelt, and Democrats swept every state and congressional race, won overwhelming control of the state senate, and even made inroads into the malapportioned lower house of the legislature. Marking the maximum strength of the Connecticut Democrats in the New Deal era, the election of 1936 from one perspective culminated the 1928–36 restructuring of Connecticut politics, while from another it stands as the referent for political trends in succeeding elections. For all these reasons, the politics of 1936 deserve close scrutiny.

The campaign turned on the President and the New Deal. Connecticut Democrats campaigned as the party of the people, economic improvement, Franklin D. Roosevelt, and the New Deal, Connecticut Republicans as the party of conservatism and traditional American ways. From the time of their convention, Democrats made emphatically clear their fealty to President Roosevelt and his policies. Nearly half of it devoted to explication and praise of the New Deal, the Democratic state

27

platform nicely marked the distance the party had come from its Jeffersonian tenets of 1932. The GOP campaign, by contrast, showed how little Republicans had changed. The gubernatorial candidate put his party's case plainly: "I am opposed to the New Deal. The Republican Party is opposed to the New Deal. . . ." Speaking for the bitter conservative and business foes of Roosevelt and the New Deal, Republicans accused the New Deal of seeking "to change our historic form of government," of subverting state and individual rights by erecting a bureaucratized, all-powerful central government, of reckless fiscal policies and equally reckless attacks on business, and of other "harmful and un-American tendencies."[29]

Although the campaign focused substantively on the New Deal, political strategy entailed more than economic and governmental issues. Ethnic cleavages were as basic to Connecticut life and politics as were class lines or ideological differences, a fact the state's politicians knew well, and ethnic groups received considerable attention by way of recognition, rallies, circulars, and ward-heeling. As had been the case since 1928, the Democrats had the more variegated ethnic slate, but improved ethnic tactics by the GOP, including the party's first statewide Italian candidates in a decade, caused concern in Democratic councils. Both parties also went after the black vote. Despite the conventional wisdom that blacks would return their traditional Republican majorities, some Democrats thought that the appeal of Roosevelt and New Deal aid gave them a good chance in black areas.[30]

The campaign aroused great interest. When Roosevelt toured the state late in October, crowds totaling upwards of three-quarters of a million people thronged to greet him along his way. The only comparable event in recent Connecticut history had been the wild reception given Smith eight years before in the cities, but Roosevelt attracted enthusiastic crowds outside the cities as well.[31] Previous registration and voting records were shattered. The voter turnout of nearly 700,000 people represented some 64 percent of the adult population, as compared with 45 percent in 1924, 58 percent in 1928, and 59 percent in 1932, and it indicated how the social, economic, and political developments of recent years had invigorated political participation.

Most voters cast a straight party ballot,[32] at least partly because of the state's voting procedures. Voting by machines, required in towns of 10,000 people or more and employed in others, entailed pulling a party lever as the necessary first step. Only then could a voter split his ballot, and to vote for each candidate of the other party required changing the position of two smaller levers. Although Roosevelt ran some 10,000 votes ahead of the state ticket, there was so little ticket splitting that the sources of the President's strength were virtually identical to those of the other Democratic candidates.

Geographically, Roosevelt's support came principally from the urban-industrial sector which swept southwesterly from north-central Connecticut through the industrialized metropolitan areas of the state primarily in Hartford, New Haven, and Fairfield counties. A secondary area of Democratic strength lay in the industrial towns of eastern Connecticut. The strongest Republican areas were extreme western Connecticut (in rural and suburban parts of Fairfield County and in rural Litchfield County with its Yankee farmers and pockets of wealth), many agricultural towns of eastern Connecticut, and the suburbs and small towns, particularly along the shoreline. Of the state's eight counties, only the traditional Republican stronghold of Litchfield County voted for GOP nominee Alfred M. Landon. Returning Democratic votes of 61 and 60 percent respectively, urban-industrial Hartford and New Haven counties paced the Democratic party.

The cities, with record turnouts and stunning, unprecedented Democratic majorities, provided the backbone of the Democratic vote. Roosevelt carried 69 percent of the aggregate vote of the five largest cities—much more than Smith's 55 percent and than his own 58 percent of 1932. Though the President won a narrow plurality outside the big cities, their margins and those of the smaller industrial cities were crucial to the size of his victory and provided most of the additional strength he won between 1932 and 1936.[33] Roosevelt's enormous urban pluralities, in turn, came mostly from working-class voters, who lived where the Depression had hit hardest and the New Deal had helped so much. As reflected in the strong correlations between Roosevelt's vote and low-rental (low-income and working-class) areas in section IB of Table I-1, the Roosevelt Coalition in Connecticut as in the nation depended heavily on lower-income, working-class voters.

Table I-1. ELECTION OF 1936, CONNECTICUT: WARD-LEVEL STATISTICS[1]

	Hartford (N = 15)	New Haven (N = 33)	Bridgeport (N = 16)	Combined (N = 64)
I. Simple correlation coefficients for percentage Roosevelt				
A. With percentage foreign-born	+ .83	+ .75	+ .68	+ .77
B. With average monthly rent	− .89	− .73	− .71	− .71
II. Standardized beta coefficients for Roosevelt vote				
A. For percentage foreign-born	+ .46	+ .51	+ .54	+ .56
B. For average monthly rent	− .61	− .48	− .57	− .45
III. Multiple correlation coefficients for percentage Roosevelt with percentage foreign-born and average monthly rent as independent variables	+ .96	+ .86	+ .88	+ .87
IV. Intercorrelation of percentage foreign-born and average monthly rent	− .61	− .50	− .25	− .47

[1]See Appendix for an explanation of the statistics used in this table and for a discussion of the statistical approach and method used in this study. Tables A-1 through A-6 provide more statistics for each election from 1936 to 1948.

The coalition also relied on Connecticut's foreign-stock voters. To be sure, the ethnic vote was not monolithically Democratic, nor the Yankee vote all Republican; and the various immigrant groups continued to differ, sometimes marginally, sometimes substantially, in their partisan attachments. But foreign birth was a stronger correlate of the Democratic vote in

1936 than even in 1928,[34] and the state's foreign-stock population overwhelmingly comprised those groups—the Irish, Italians, Poles, Jews, French-Canadians—that throughout America aligned solidly with the Democrats. The most heavily Italian districts in Connecticut's big cities voted 75 to 85 percent Democratic, for example, and other ethnic wards returned similarly topheavy Democratic votes. In some immigrant areas, Jewish and Polish especially, Democratic percentages significantly exceeded previous levels. Where Smith had captured 58 percent of the vote in New Haven's most Jewish ward and Roosevelt himself 57 percent in 1932, for example, the President won 73 percent in 1936. In New Britain's Polish ward, which had voted 75 percent Democratic in 1928 and 84 percent Democratic in 1932, Roosevelt carried a startling 90 percent of the vote. Perhaps the most surprising Democratic gains of all, of a piece with the party's advances in white ethnic constituencies, came in the customarily Republican black areas. In New Haven, "political experts openly gasped" at the shift of some twenty percentage points from recent elections that gave Roosevelt three-fifths of the vote in never-before-Democratic Negro ward 19.[35] Nor did the Democrats command the ethnic vote only in the big cities. French-Canadian and Italian voters in smaller cities and industrial towns helped swell Democratic margins, as did Polish and Jewish voters in agricultural areas. In fact, while rent level and foreign birth correlated about equally with Roosevelt's vote in the big cities, foreign birth was much the strongest correlate of his support at the town level statewide. (See section I of Tables I-1 and I-2.) Ethnicity was apparently at least as important as class or occupation to the Roosevelt Coalition in Connecticut.

To an important extent, of course, the lower-class, blue-collar, and foreign-stock votes overlapped. Immigrant groups (like blacks) tended to have the poorest-paying jobs, to live in lower-rent areas, to work in the occupations and industries most affected by the Depression, to dominate relief rolls during the decade, and thus to owe a special debt to Roosevelt and the New Deal; not surprisingly, therefore, the most strongly

Democratic areas were often both heavily ethnic and low-income. What, then, were the relative effects of ethnicity and class on the Roosevelt vote? Which factor was more fundamental to the President's strength? Disentangling, assessing, and comparing the effects of ethnicity and class is a problem whose resolution is crucial to understanding the Roosevelt Coalition and the era's politics and one that has produced different answers.[36] At the aggregate level, the problem can be addressed by means of statistical analysis; and for the Connecticut election of 1936, scatter diagrams, correlation coefficients, and beta coefficients (all explained in the Appendix) indicate that both ethnicity and class independently and strongly affected the vote and that class and foreign birth were roughly equal determinants of Roosevelt's support. At the ward level in the three big cities (see sections I and II of Table I-1), the near equivalence of the two factors is clear. At the town level (see sections I and II of Table I-2), foreign birth was obviously more important; but in the three urban-industrial counties—which accounted for some 80 percent of the state's population and for a similar share of Roosevelt's statewide vote—the difference between the two factors was much slimmer than in the state as a whole. Ethnicity was evidently a more important foundation of the Roosevelt Coalition than was class status, but not by much.[37] Together, as the multiple correlation coefficients show (see section III of Tables I-1 and I-2), those two factors accounted for most of the variation of the vote in the big cities and in the three populous urban-industrial counties.

Connecticut's 1936 voting patterns and the nature of the state's Roosevelt Coalition followed from the recent history of Connecticut's people and politics. The 1920s had been a time of searing ethnocultural tensions. Polarizing the electorate, Smith's 1928 candidacy had highlighted and heightened those tensions and had attracted many immigrant voters to the Democratic party, especially in the cities. In the 1930s, the Great Depression and then the New Deal had given the Democrats powerful new issues, issues which substantially cut along class and occupational lines, added to the party's urban and

Table I-2. ELECTION OF 1936, CONNECTICUT: TOWN-LEVEL STATISTICS[1]

	All towns[2] (N = 169)	Towns in Hartford, New Haven, and Fairfield counties[3] (N = 79)
I. Simple correlation coefficients for percentage Roosevelt		
A. With percentage foreign-born	+ .61	+ .72
B. With average monthly rent	− .32	− .55
C. With percentage rural-farm	− .44	− .46
D. With total population	+ .46	+ .52
II. Standardized beta coefficients for Roosevelt vote		
A. For percentage foreign-born	+ .44	+ .43
B. For average monthly rent	− .30	− .41
C. For percentage rural-farm	− .38	− .19
D. For total population	+ .18	+ .18
III. Multiple correlation coefficients for percentage Roosevelt		
A. With percentage foreign-born, average monthly rent, percentage rural-farm, and total population as independent variables	+ .79	+ .85
B. With percentage foreign-born and average monthly rent as independent variables	+ .64	+ .81
IV. Intercorrelations between independent variables		
A. Percentage foreign-born with average monthly rent	− .20	− .26
B. Percentage foreign-born with percentage rural-farm	− .12	− .44
C. Percentage foreign-born with total population	+ .31	+ .51
D. Average monthly rent with percentage rural-farm	− .11	+ .02
E. Average monthly rent with total population	+ .04	− .09
F. Percentage rural-farm with total population	− .40	− .41

[1]See Appendix for an explanation of the statistics used in this table and for a discussion of the statistical approach and method used in this study. Tables A-1 through A-6 provide more statistics for each election from 1936 to 1948.

[2]The term "towns" refers to the political units of the state and thus includes cities like Hartford and small rural communities. See note 33, Ch. I.

[3]Statistics for the towns in Hartford, New Haven, and Fairfield counties are listed separately because these three metropolitan urban-industrial counties contained some four-fifths of Connecticut's people and are particularly important for understanding the state's voting patterns.

working-class support, and gave ethnic workers further reasons to vote Democratic. Yet ethnicity itself remained central
to Connecticut life, and some of the vitriol of the 1920s lingered on when economic woes took priority over social conflict. Catholics remembered the Democrats' nomination of Al
Smith and the ugly anti-Smith GOP campaign of 1928, and they
appreciated the added political recognition afforded them by
Roosevelt and by Connecticut Democrats in the ensuing
years.[38] Beyond that, the economic experience of the Depression decade sometimes exacerbated old animosities. Desperately scrambling for jobs, Yankee workers often claimed that
immigrants ("greaseballs" and "animals") deprived them of jobs
and income by a supposed willingness to work for any wage
and live in any condition; resenting the public revenues spent
on relief, many Yankee taxpayers believed that so many immigrants were on relief precisely because they were foreigners
without real American talent and enterprise.[39] Although the
two reactions hardly squared with one another, both revealed
the flaring of old antagonisms during the Depression. Voting
patterns reflected the interconnected social and economic divisions of Connecticut's people.

Social tensions, hard times, and the New Deal, then, had
combined by 1936 to change the contours of Connecticut politics. Sharply increasing political participation, they also
brought the triumph of the Democratic party and the formation of a Roosevelt Coalition characteristic of the nation's
urban-ethnic-industrial areas. From 1920 to 1936, the Democratic presidential vote in Connecticut more than tripled, soaring from 120,721 to 382,129, while the GOP vote increased only
from 229,238 to 278,685; between 1928 and 1936, the Republican presidential vote actually declined, from 296,614 to
278,685, while the Democratic total vaulted from 252,040 to
382,129. The 1928 election had polarized the electorate and
won new voters to both parties, though mostly to the Democrats, and then the Great Depression and the New Deal evidently switched GOP votes to the Democrats while accelerating
the massive influx of new voters, ethnic and working-class

34

young people especially, to the Democratic party. In addition to the burgeoning Democratic strength, election returns from 1928 on also showed a greater constancy in voting patterns from election to election than in the preceding decade and a clearer demarcation between old stock and new, between well-off and not, and between city and town.[40] While Roosevelt in 1936 had significant strength outside the cities, among middle-income and white-collar voters, and in predominantly Yankee areas, his coalition in Connecticut as elsewhere in the industrial North and East was urban-centered and based on working-class and ethnic support. In urban, industrial, cosmopolitan Connecticut, mindful of its recent past, the coalition gave Roosevelt nearly three-fifths of the presidential vote.

The dimensions of their defeat shocked Republicans. As early as the day after the election, calls for reorganization were sounded. That meant, as the Republican *Hartford Courant* editorialized, "new blood and a new outlook"—in particular the ouster of dogmatic and unyielding GOP boss J. Henry Roraback and the adoption of a more progressive orientation. Many Republicans believed their party must change before it could rule again.[41]

Yet Democrats should not have been too confident. For one thing, control and direction of the state party were uncertain. Although the party had grown far more liberal and powerful in the 1930s, it held in uneasy alliance competing, often shifting factions and leaders of conflicting ambitions and differing outlooks. Since 1930 the Democrats had been plagued by struggles over party control between the "Old Guard" urban bosses and the "New Guard," which had engineered Wilbur Cross's first nomination over Old Guard opposition. In 1932, the two factions had found themselves at odds again, this time over the party's presidential nomination, with the predominantly Irish Old Guard backing Al Smith to the bitter end while the New Guard, abetted by Homer Cummings, pushed for Franklin Roosevelt. The Old Guard-New Guard rivalry festered on through the decade, fed by Old Guard unhappiness with Cross's patronage disbursements and with his efforts to reform

Connecticut's governmental system. By the mid-1930s, however, that rift was overlaid and complicated by contention between avid New Dealers and more moderate, sometimes conservative Democrats, a division that only partly coincided with the Old Guard-New Guard factionalism. The Old Guard, though remaining resentful about Smith's 1932 defeat at Roosevelt's hands and rarely liberals in an ideological sense, did not oppose the New Deal, understood the needs and wants of their urban constituencies, and quickly saw how Roosevelt's programs and political power bolstered the party—and themselves—locally. On the other hand, Cross, while in league with the New Guard on state issues, remained far more equivocal than many of them about the New Deal.

Further blurring and confusing the Democratic party's fault lines was the growing influence of Senator Francis T. Maloney and his principal ally, state chairman J. Francis Smith. Frank Maloney and Fran Smith made an odd political couple, as apparently mismatched by origin as Long Tom Spellacy and Little Dave Fitzgerald were by size. Smith, the son of a Waterbury lumber dealer, had graduated from Dartmouth College in 1923 and had gone on to Amos Tuck School of Administration and Finance. A handsome, lithe man, Smith for years ranked among the top tennis players in New England. After completing his schooling, he returned to Waterbury, where he took over and expanded the family lumber company and made a name for himself in business, athletic, and civic circles. Then in 1932, when he was not quite thirty years old, Smith was asked by Governor Cross to become secretary of the Democratic state central committee. Two years later, young Fran Smith became state chairman on the retirement of the incumbent. Identified at first with the New Guard, Smith from the beginning made it clear that he belonged to neither of the warring factions and emphasized his independent, practical, business-minded approach to party affairs. Although he once or twice revealed a mild itch for public office, he appeared content with his generally behind-the-scenes role in the party.

Francis T. Maloney, short, stocky, round-faced and bespec-

tacled, seemed very different from Smith. Where the latter
was a dashing man and a natural leader, Frank Maloney was a
quiet, nondescript, stolid "ordinary guy" who might have been
lost in a crowd. It seems strange, indeed, that of the pair Maloney was the public figure. But politics became for Maloney a
vocation, while for Smith it remained an avocation. That in
turn, like Maloney's greater liberalism on social problems, perhaps stemmed in part from the widely different origins of the
two men. Smith was a "lace-curtain," even silver-spoon, Irishman who began life and politics near the top, while Maloney
was "shanty Irish" and began life and politics near the bottom.
Born in Meriden in 1894, Maloney left school at the age of
fourteen to work for a nickel an hour in local factories. At
eighteen he became a restaurant counterman, and then the
next year he became a reporter for a Meriden newspaper, a job
which provided him with political knowledge and contacts. In
the early 1920s Maloney began bigger things. He opened his
own real estate and insurance office and took on the job of
Democratic town chairman in Republican-controlled Meriden. He did well in both endeavors, and by virtue of helping
Democrats win the mayorship in 1921 and 1923 he got into
public office by serving as Meriden's Superintendent of Chari-
ties in the mid-1920s.

In 1929, thirty-five-year-old Frank Maloney began his own
career as an active politician. He ran for mayor of Meriden
and won by a record plurality. Taking office at the outset of
the Great Depression, he earned a considerable reputation by
cutting the city budget and taxes at the same time that he implemented a successful public works and work relief program.
The unlikely but popular combination of economy and welfare spending together with a hard-working, concerned, non-
partisan image reelected Maloney in 1931 with a margin more
than three times as large as his 1929 record. Besides providing
the largest plurality ever in any Meriden election, Maloney's
1931 support was notable for the way it cut through party and
class lines. In fact, several patterns evident in Maloney's
mayorship—a tendency to be liberal on social issues but con-

servative on others, a deliberately nonpartisan and independent approach, and very broad-based support—would mark all of his subsequent political career.

In 1932, the year that Fran Smith became party secretary with the help of the New Guard, Frank Maloney became congressman with the help of the Old Guard. He ran against twenty-two-year Republican incumbent John Q. Tilson, once GOP majority leader in the House of Representatives, in the Third Congressional District, which included Little Dave Fitzgerald's New Haven. Helped by Fitzgerald, though even more by the Depression and his own record, Maloney beat Tilson and went to Washington. Two years later the Old Guard helped Maloney land the Senate nomination over the opposition of Governor Cross's candidate, and at age forty Maloney won the Senate seat in the Democratic victory of 1934. For a decade, until he died of a heart attack early in 1945, Frank Maloney, quiet and apparently unassuming but a good orator and a tough, tenacious infighter, would be one of Connecticut's foremost Democrats.

Maloney soon began teaming with Smith. Despite their contrasting backgrounds, their different routes to political power, and their apparently incongruous personalities, the two Irishmen were rather similar in approach and outlook. Tough, cautious, practical, generally supportive of New Deal social legislation (particularly Maloney) but by no means ardent liberals or New Dealers, neither New nor Old Guard, sure of their own ideas, and acutely jealous of their place and power in the party, they proved a powerful and adept team from the beginning. In addition to building their own strength, they allied with Attorney General Cummings to split Old Guard leaders Fitzgerald and Spellacy in 1936 by successfully backing Little Dave for national committeeman over Long Tom's heated opposition. But in advancing themselves, Maloney and Smith did little to cement their party. Despite the Democratic successes of the 1930s, and in part because of them, Connecticut's Democratic party was an untidy and often unruly amalgam of contending groups and viewpoints whose disunity threatened its power.[42]

Beyond the Democrats' factional problems, there lay the fundamental political fact that the party did not have an iron hold on the state's voters. Although routed in 1936, Connecticut Republicans retained important pockets of real and potential strength. Connecticut had come late to Roosevelt's column, and even in 1936 the President's share of the state's vote fell below his nationwide percentage. Many in Roosevelt's Connecticut coalition owed their allegiance to the President, not to the Democratic party, and to the tangible programs of Roosevelt's New Deal, not to ideological liberalism.[43] Beyond that, a majority based in part on economic improvement since the coming of the New Deal might melt with renewed economic problems, while given real prosperity many people might think twice about the costs and priorities of New Deal liberalism. And a majority based so importantly on ethnicity might prove vulnerable to new Republican tactics or to new ethnic concerns. Future developments would test the strength and durability of the newly formed Roosevelt Coalition in Connecticut.

The first major trial of the Roosevelt Coalition came in the presidential election of 1940. Even before then, however, developments of the late 1930s combined to restore competitiveness to Connecticut politics and to produce a GOP victory in the state's 1938 midterm elections. Like Franklin Roosevelt, Connecticut Democrats found themselves amid a "sea of troubles" soon after the great triumph of 1936.[44] Especially important among their problems were the "Roosevelt recession" and scandals involving state leaders. Mirroring the sharp national downturn of 1937–38, Connecticut's business index plummeted 26 points in the last quarter of 1937 to 23 points below the 1929 normal—a more precipitous drop than at the onset of the Great Depression. By June 1938 the business index had fallen to 33 points below normal, and the number of relief recipients had soared to 12 percent of the state's population. Beset by aggravated economic problems, the state was also rocked by revelations of wide-ranging political scandals. Though the scandals implicated members of both parties, and though Cross, himself not involved, dealt forthrightly with them, they inevitably tarnished the reputation of the ruling Democrats.[45]

The Democrats also suffered in 1938 from acrimonious factionalism. Unhappy with Senator Augustine Lonergan's opposition to many of Roosevelt's initiatives, liberals unsuccessfully fought his renomination. Their chances, slender to begin with, were made slimmer still when the President, influenced by Attorney General Cummings, stayed neutral in the struggle despite his efforts to "purge" some conservative Democrats in 1938. The Connecticut affair involved power as much as philosophy. Senator Maloney, state chairman Smith, and the other organization leaders were, to be sure, more conservative than the challengers. Yet they were at bottom conservative New Dealers. Hardly liberal, most of them, and concerned primarily with power, patronage, and votes, they still endorsed, if largely for political reasons, the fundamentals of Roosevelt's New Deal. Certainly they had no intention of divorcing themselves from Roosevelt's favor and political power, and they took pains to praise the President and the New Deal at the state convention. But perhaps the party leaders wanted to avoid too liberal an image in 1938, when the political momentum of the New Deal seemed on the wane, and they surely saw in the insurgents a threat to their control of the party and to the legitimacy of their own moderate views. With his own renomination just ahead in 1940, Maloney in particular had no sympathy with efforts to discipline wayward senators, for he too had opposed important administration proposals. He, Smith, and their allies, who included much of the Old Guard and part of the New in 1938, thus worked carefully to keep control of the party and turn back the "ultra-liberals" without burning their bridges to Roosevelt. They succeeded in those aims, but the rancorous struggle nonetheless illuminated and enlarged party divisions and weakened the Democrats still further for the 1938 campaign.[46]

40

Compounding all their other woes, Connecticut Democrats had to face a far stronger Republican party than had taken the field in 1936. In the intervening two years, Connecticut Republicans, like those in other states, had gotten the new leaders and new orientation that many had called for in the aftermath of the party's 1936 drubbing. The suicide of longtime party boss J. Henry Roraback, whose touch and power had faded in the 1930s along with his party's fortunes, the involvement of prominent Republicans in the scandals, and dismal GOP showings in the 1937 big-city elections made change all but inevitable. The process was hastened and overseen by an ambitious, hard-driving group of young Republicans centered in Fairfield County and headed by new national committeeman Samuel F. Pryor and by Fairfield County GOP leader J. Kenneth Bradley. Pryor, forty years old in 1938, was a wealthy businessman from Greenwich who proved a quick study at mastering the ways of politics. Unlike many businessmen who venture into politics, Pryor seemed immediately to understand that political progress often came via compromise, indirection, and seemingly endless talk (unlike many veteran party professionals, on the other hand, he did not shrink from quick action or substantial change that seemed necessary). After helping infuse the Connecticut GOP with renewed enthusiam and a coterie of young, aggressive businessmen bent on rebuilding the party, Pryor turned his attention to establishing and maintaining contacts with prominent businessmen and national Republican leaders in New York and Washington.

While Pryor increasingly functioned as a sort of "Mr. Outside" involved largely at the national level, J. Kenneth Bradley was more a "Mr. Inside," taking care of local and state party affairs even though he had his own national connections. Known to insiders as the "boy wonder" of Connecticut politics, Bradley, born in 1903, had been elected to the General Assembly when only twenty-five years old, had become Fairfield County GOP leader when thirty, and had served as majority leader of the state senate when just thirty-two and the youngest Republican there. In the mid-1930s he headed the national

41

Young Republicans. Ambitious, aggressive, talented, eloquent, smooth, handsome, Bradley apparently had the tools of a first-rate politician with limitless potential, but he never matched what seemed his promise. His palpable ambition disaffected some people, his brash aggressiveness others, and perhaps his smoothness, which sometimes seemed merely slickness, still more. Conservative Republican regulars could not forgive his combative though generally limited liberalism. But perhaps Bradley's greatest problem was the reputation he developed for wobbling on his word in a crunch. (Long Tom Spellacy, who understood such matters, said the most important thing in politics was to keep your word.) Still, many of Bradley's liabilities became manifest only with time—he did not wear well—and in the late 1930s and early 1940s he was a powerful figure in Connecticut politics and a pivotal one in the state GOP.

Bradley had in fact been largely responsible for persuading Samuel Pryor to get into politics, and he also helped lure a third major hand in the party's remodeling, Raymond E. Baldwin, back into politics. Baldwin, Bradley's law partner, was in his mid-forties and had served two terms in the lower house of the General Assembly in the early 1930s. There he had quickly established himself as an able, scrappy partisan, and he served as GOP floor leader in his second term. In the mid-1930s Baldwin remained active in local politics and, via Bradley, in touch with larger political currents. On Bradley's urgings, he joined Bradley and Pryor in their effort to overhaul the party. Baldwin's special niche turned out to be that of candidate and public official. Together the three men soon made a formidable triumvirate, with Pryor wheeling in national party affairs, Bradley dealing inside the state, and the personable, popular Baldwin serving as the public symbol of the new Connecticut Republicans. They combined to shape the modern, progressive Republican party in Connecticut and to return the GOP to competitiveness in the state.

With others from Fairfield County, Pryor, Bradley, and Baldwin worked hard to reorganize and reorient the state GOP before the 1938 election. One fruitful tactic was to organize throughout the state a number of "Beefsteak Clubs," so named because of the usual fare at their dinner meetings. The clubs helped build sentiment for what Baldwin, the chief speaker at many gatherings, called a "new" Republican party in Connecticut. Mostly younger men in their thirties and early forties and typically businessmen and lawyers, Beefsteak Club members did not, to be sure, want an entirely different party. They wanted to rid the GOP of its association with "Rorabackism," scandal, and reaction and to make it more attractive and progressive, but they also stressed such bedrock Republican concerns as limited central government, private enterprise, individualism, and fiscal prudence. Holding on to what they believed were their party's first principles, the Beefsteak Club Republicans—or "New Era" Republicans as they came to be labeled—wanted the party to tailor its image and approach to the new realities of politics and public policy produced by the Great Depression, the New Deal, and Franklin D. Roosevelt and his coalition.

They also wanted to nominate an attractive slate of candidates for the 1938 election, and for the two top posts they desired two youngish men who were active in the Beefsteak Clubs and experienced in GOP politics. Baldwin was the choice for governor. For United States senator, the New Era group backed John A. Danaher. Born in Meriden in 1899 (he once lived a few doors away from Frank Maloney), Danaher had gone to Yale College and Law School. In 1922 he had begun practicing law in Hartford and that same year had become an assistant U.S. attorney. In 1932 he had run successfully for secretary of the state. Although short, round-faced, and balding, Danaher was a dignified, thoughtful man whose mien, intelligence, and oratorical skills gave him a commanding presence. In time it became clear that Danaher was more conservative and much more isolationist than were Baldwin and other of his Beefsteak allies, but the strains came after the common cause of 1938.[47]

The New Era Republicans routed the old-line regulars at the 1938 state convention. Baldwin and Danaher easily won

43

nomination, and the platform was notable for its progressive proposals, particularly for labor, and its acceptance of some important New Deal programs. The party did not, to be sure, break with its past. Reaffirming their strong philosophical opposition to Roosevelt and the New Deal, Republicans also fitted their principal issue of 1938, the recession, into a familiar framework by claiming that recovery had been prevented by New Deal fiscal policies, economic controls, and harassment of business. But the New Era Republicans clearly did alter the party and modify its image. As part of that, the GOP constructed its 1938 ticket with a much keener eye than before to recognition politics. Danaher, an Irish-Catholic, was the son of the counsel for the Connecticut Federation of Labor. Republicans for the first time nominated a woman for state office (secretary of the state) and they nominated Francis Pallotti, Republican secretary of the state in the 1920s and a man still popular among Italian-Americans, for attorney general. For the first time in Connecticut history a Polish-American won nomination for major office when Boleslaus Monkiewicz of New Britain received the congressman-at-large nomination. Examining the convention's results, the *Connecticut State Journal* said, with reason: "the Republican Party has been modernized."[48]

The Democrats' troubles and the Republicans' remodeling combined with a strong third-party effort to give the GOP a narrow triumph in 1938. Two Republican advertisements summed up the basic GOP campaign appeal. One urged, "FOR RECOVERY Bring on the REPUBLICANS"; the other proclaimed, "I tell you 'THIS IS A NEW REPUBLICAN PARTY.' . . . Human rights must come FIRST." GOP gubernatorial nominee Baldwin frequently stopped at factories to meet workers and play up the economic problems and the GOP's concern about workers and their jobs.[49] Heading the third-party Socialist slate, Bridgeport mayor Jasper McLevy, by 1938 essentially a conservative good-government man despite his party affiliation, flayed both major parties for their involvement in the scandals. McLevy captured better than one-fourth of the gubernatorial vote, and the rest of his ticket won nearly one-sixth of the vote. Taking more votes from the

Democrats than from the Republicans, the strong Socialist showing helped the GOP to elect its entire state ticket, Danaher, and four of the six congressmen with barely more than half of the major party vote statewide.

The political meaning of 1938 was mixed. Republicans had clearly rebounded from the debacle of two years earlier. More than McLevy and corruption had accounted for the GOP victory, as state voting totals and Republican successes elsewhere in the nation indicated. Monkiewicz proved the efficacy of recognition politics by running far enough ahead of the ticket among Polish voters to make him the only Republican to carry heavily Polish New Britain. The election demonstrated that Connecticut politics were competitive again, and it suggested what the future would make clearer—that there were many "Roosevelt Democrats" who would not necessarily vote Democratic when Franklin D. Roosevelt did not head the Democracy's slate. Republicans nonetheless evidently did owe their victory, if not their resurgence, largely to the protest vote given Jasper McLevy. (Baldwin in fact owed his margin to Republican maneuvering which kept Father Charles Coughlin's 1936 Union party technically alive, for Baldwin was among the Republican candidates who ran on the Union party ticket, and the 3,000 votes he won on the Union line provided him his plurality over Cross.) Despite the disruptive McLevy candidacy, moreover, basic voting patterns did not depart greatly from those of 1936.[50] And Republicans had neither won a majority of the vote nor done very well in the big cities. Still, they had won office again and with it the chance to establish a new record.

Raymond Baldwin worked quickly to make that record. The new governor's notion of "friendly government"—friendly to business and to labor alike—lay at the heart of New Era Republicanism. Largely because of Baldwin's efforts, the 1939 General Assembly proved one of the most active and most progressive ever. Its accomplishments included a balanced budget without new taxes, a Connecticut Development Commission to foster new industry, and the most significant legislation for labor ever adopted by the state. That record again showed how

Connecticut's New Era Republicans had married traditional GOP concerns with important new departures. Looking ahead to the election of 1940, Baldwin held press conferences at least once and usually twice a day, and he went on the radio weekly to preach the gospel of friendly government and to recount the General Assembly's record and the successes of his administration in attracting new industry—and thereby new jobs—to the state. He also made 180 speeches in fifty towns during his first year in office as part of his effort to spread the message of Republican change and accomplishment.[51]

Republicans were fortunate indeed to have Raymond Baldwin as the public leader and spokesman of their renascent party. The Governor, forty-five years old when he took office, was one of the more liberal young Republicans who emerged, not only in Connecticut, after the party's 1936 disaster and who, in insisting on states' rights, insisted equally on state responsibilities and responsiveness. Often sharply critical of the New Deal, especially its methods, its enlargement of federal power, and its economic policies, Baldwin nonetheless endorsed many of its social programs. Baldwin clearly was a Republican and in some ways a rather conventional one, and he was no profound social or political philosopher; but he was an able, palpably decent man who was concerned enough personally and astute enough politically to realize that negativism, dogmatic anti-New Dealism, and a retreat to old verities would no longer suffice, particularly in a state like Connecticut.

Baldwin's personality was as much a boon to himself and his party as was his political outlook. Although born into a family that stretched back some ten generations in Connecticut and included some of colonial Connecticut's most famous men, Ray Baldwin was no frosty or provincial Connecticut Yankee. A big, hearty, enormously personable man with a broad grin and booming voice, he made his governorship friendly in direct human terms. The "education" of growing up in Middletown, Connecticut, where he got to know the area's many ethnic groups and their ways of life and gained first-hand experience during the summers in field and factory work, surely contrib-

46

uted to his political orientation and success. Once in office as governor, Baldwin quickly established himself as his party's, indeed his state's, most popular politician. Eventually he became the only man in Connecticut history to serve as governor, U.S. senator, and chief justice of the state supreme court. Perhaps Baldwin's only liabilities as a politician, belied by his public personality and born in part of a certain political naiveté and personal vanity, were a reluctance to give himself over entirely to politicking and a sensitivity to criticism. Although dedicated to public service, moreover, his lifelong ambition was to be a judge, not a politician. He found much rough-and-tumble party politics to be petty and distasteful, and in the 1940s he often fretted that he was ignoring his family and its needs. Nevertheless, Baldwin was a remarkably successful politician, whose personality, outlook, and programs were instrumental in restoring GOP fortunes in Connecticut after 1936. Without Baldwin, Connecticut politics in the era might have been significantly different.[52]

Baldwin's many assets made him important in national Republican councils almost from the time he became governor. Here he was helped by national committeeman Samuel Pryor, who also rose quickly to national prominence and who had large hopes not only for Baldwin but also for another ambitious, articulate younger man, Wendell L. Willkie. Of a persuasion similar to that of Connecticut's New Era Republicans, Willkie already seemed to Pryor and other eastern Republicans to be a promising opponent for Roosevelt in 1940. Envisioning a Willkie-Baldwin ticket, Pryor helped to organize publicity and support for Willkie even as he worked to achieve national standing for Baldwin. Baldwin himself caused a stir at the Governors' Conference in the summer of 1939, and en route to the San Francisco World's Fair later that summer he made a series of well-publicized and well-received speeches. His star, already high in Connecticut, seemed in the ascendancy nationally.[53]

Matters more mundane than Baldwin's national future concerned the rest of the Connecticut GOP in 1939. Its major efforts went toward the year's municipal elections, which Republican leaders saw as a chance to make organizational progress toward the 1940 election and perhaps to build new support as well. Substantial Republican gains in Bridgeport, New Haven, and Hartford brought the party "unexpected good news" that autumn, though the happiness was tempered by a continued inability to win the cities. But the elections did provide hope, and the returns from New Haven and Waterbury suggested how Republicans might further increase their strength. In New Haven, the party's advances stemmed from its nomination of Italian-American William Celentano for mayor. The first such recognition given an Italian in New Haven by either party, Celentano's candidacy electrified the city's Italian voters. Even though his nomination disaffected Yankee Republicans and enabled the Democrats to make inroads among them, Celentano swept the Italian wards and brought striking Republican gains in the heavily Italian city. A different story with the same moral came from Waterbury with its similarly high percentage of Italian-Americans. There the Republican organization had successfully opposed the renomination bid of the acting Republican mayor, an Italian; and there Democrats scored their most convincing big-city victory. The Republican *Connecticut State Journal* understood the lessons taught by the two elections. Specifically it perceived the growing political importance of the Italians, especially in New Haven but also in other cities. Beyond that, it understood the "need for recognizing all groups" and the necessity of Republicans doing "as good a job for O'Brien, or Monsani, or Cohen as they do for Smith and Jones."[54] Already more shrewdly practicing recognition politics in the late 1930s than it had for a decade, the essentially Yankee GOP had added reason to put forth a cosmopolitan as well as a progressive image.

Connecticut politics on the eve of World War II differed markedly from the politics of the Harding-Coolidge years. The interaction of events in the interwar period with the ongoing changes in the social bases of Connecticut politics had, as in many another state, spurred political participation, altered voting patterns, made politics competitive, and changed political issues and tactics. The most dramatic development was the emergence of the Roosevelt Coalition. The product of ethnic tensions, hard times, and the New Deal, the Roosevelt Coalition —with its urban, lower-class, and ethnic voting strength—gave Democrats a commanding position in the state. Although the Democratic party could not count on certain victory and had to face a reshaped and more appealing Republican party after 1936, the Roosevelt Coalition nonetheless gave Democrats an edge in the new politics of competition.

Another area of change in the interwar years lay in the nature of political debate. With the advent of the New Deal, the two parties had begun to offer contrasting approaches to substantive economic and governmental issues. Democrats had veered from their old Jeffersonian standards to a New Deal position in the mid-1930s. Republicans, too, had changed, after the Roosevelt landslide of 1936 had demonstrated the political futility of old-line GOP conservatism; but despite their record and new orientation, the progressive New Era Republicans differed from New Deal Democrats and maintained traditional GOP concerns with fiscal prudence, free enterprise, and the "American Way" of life and limited federal government. Nor indeed did the defeat of the insurgent New Dealers at the 1938 Democratic state convention mean an end to interparty differences, for the victors had affirmed their support of the President and the New Deal. Both parties had moved toward the center in 1938, but they remained at odds about the chief issue of the era, the New Deal, and they retained fundamental differences of outlook, style, and constituencies.

Political change between the wars had involved more than the rise of the Roosevelt Coalition and the ideological effects of the Depression and the New Deal. As the new immigrants had gained political consciousness and strength, and as politics had become competitive, ethnic politics had grown in importance. Beginning with the election of 1928, the Democratic state tickets and state central committee had become more ethnically balanced than those of the Republicans. As the GOP sought to regain power, it had turned anew to ethnic recognition. In turn, the Republican success with Monkiewicz in 1938 and the lessons of the 1939 city elections made some Democrats, at least, want to open their party further in 1940 by nominating a Polish-American for high office and an Italian-American for Congress.[55] Although persisting intergroup tensions could make recognition politics hazardous, as the Yankee defections from the GOP in New Haven in 1939 had shown, the artfully balanced ticket seemed to have more assets than liabilities. Certainly astute politicians knew they must appeal to ethnic voters and speak to their concerns.

While Connecticut had gone to the polls in the autumn of 1939, Europe had gone to war. World War II would have a profound impact on Connecticut and on the United States. Affecting the state's and the nation's people and economy in many fundamental ways, the war from the outset powerfully influenced politics as well. As the nation witnessed and then entered the war, political dialogue necessarily broadened from its tight interwar focus on domestic affairs. As war-borne prosperity eroded the importance and relevance of many New Deal programs, the context and sometimes the content of 1930s domestic issues changed, and new issues gained salience. And as the war had immediate and important implications for most segments of Connecticut's and America's variegated society, new ethnic concerns surfaced. Having such effects, the experience of war provided the first major test of the relatively new Roosevelt Coalition, built as it was on domestic concerns and, particularly in Connecticut and the other populous urban-industrial states, on working-class and foreign-stock support.

II

EUROPEAN WAR AND A THIRD TERM

The war in Europe and its domestic consequences dominated American life in 1940. So doing, they gave shape to the year's politics and provided the context for the first major test of the Roosevelt Coalition. War-induced economic recovery was a paramount feature of the year, particularly in industrial areas, but the war had much more than an economic impact. After the shockingly swift Nazi conquest of western Europe in the spring of 1940, foreign affairs and national security commanded the nation's attention. Immigrant groups had their own immediate concerns about events in Europe, and Italian-Americans experienced as well special war-related problems at home. The war also had important political repercussions. Probably the major reason for President Roosevelt's pursuit of an unprecedented third term, the international situation after the Nazi spring offensive also aided Wendell L. Willkie in his dark-horse race for the GOP nomination. Foreign affairs and foreign policy figured in the 1940 campaign and election as they had not for two decades, a circumstance which marked an important departure from the two previous Roosevelt elections. The war-related economic and social developments had great political significance too. To be sure, the patterns of life and politics in 1940 stemmed from much more than the impact of the European war and the happenings of a single year. But the ramifying effects of the war were central to American society and politics, and hence to the testing of the Roosevelt Coalition, in the presidential election year of 1940. Certainly that was the case in Connecticut.

51

The Second World War transformed economic conditions in Connecticut, for the state's economy was nicely structured to profit from the needs of war. Munitions makers, chief among them Colt's Patent Firearms of Hartford, Winchester Repeating Arms of New Haven, and Remington Arms of Bridgeport, contributed vitally to the arsenals of America and the Allies. Besides supplying his weapons and ammunition, Connecticut industry could claim to outfit the individual soldier with everything from underwear to raincoat and from rubber footwear to steel helmet. Connecticut factories also produced many of the newer instruments of war that made World War II a struggle of machines as well as of men. United Aircraft's Pratt & Whitney Engine Division in East Hartford and the Electric Boat Company in Groton soon established themselves as the state's principal war plants. The importance of war goods manufacturers to the state's economy, moreover, went well beyond the people they employed and the wages, salaries, and dividends they paid out. Airplanes, engines, and submarines required myriad component parts from metal and hardware factories. Munitions manufacture involved large quantities of ferrous and nonferrous metal products. The plants that produced war materials needed machinery and machine tools. Connecticut factories produced many of those essential goods, too, and they supplied them to defense plants outside as well as inside Connecticut.

The first evidence of how war material demands could fire the state's economy came late in 1939, when war contracts helped yank Connecticut out of the 1937–38 recession. Having begun 1939 at roughly the still depressed national level, Connecticut's business index by the end of the year stood some fifteen points above the national figure and with other economic indicators had surpassed 1929 levels. The true war boom still lay ahead, but by the winter of 1939–40 Connecticut had begun to emerge from the Depression decade.[1]

As they had over that past decade of hard times, economic conditions had direct political importance. Continuing his pace as "the 'speechmakin'ist' governor in Connecticut history" into

1940, Raymond Baldwin seized upon the upsurge as evidence that Republican "friendly government" and fiscal prudence had begun to revitalize Connecticut's economy. Democrats, afraid that Baldwin had "stolen the recovery thunder" that had served them so well in the mid-1930s, retorted that the governor greatly exaggerated his role in Connecticut's economic upswing. Point and counterpoint on this theme continued through the year.[2]

But while Connecticut's politicians had thus sounded the first notes of the 1940 campaign, intraparty matters occupied more of their attention early in the year. Each party had factional difficulties, and each had to decide on a presidential nominee. As usual, Democrats had the fiercer internal struggles, but they had little problem in choosing a presidential candidate. Despite the apparent potency of the unwritten law against a third term, no important Democrat in Connecticut and few in the nation seemed ready to oppose Roosevelt should the President, evasive about his intentions, want renomination. New Dealers naturally supported Roosevelt, and although national chairman James A. Farley's pretensions to the presidency enchanted some of the party's moderate Irish leaders, Connecticut national committeeman David Fitzgerald made it clear that Farley was the organization's second choice. As it did among Democrats everywhere, Roosevelt's proven vote-getting power welded Democrats of all persuasions behind him. In Connecticut, New Dealers, moderates, and calculating organization leaders alike joined in open advocacy of a third term for the President as early as the April Jefferson Day dinner.[3]

With the party solidly behind Roosevelt, Democratic activity chiefly involved jostling for place and power within the state organization. Much of it revolved around Senator Francis Maloney, up for reelection in 1940. Ever solicitous of his own career, Maloney throughout the year worked carefully to blunt liberal criticism of his past defections from some New Deal measures and at the same time to safeguard his reputation as an independent and a moderate which he apparently believed had won him his broad support in the state. The Senator

53

sought as well to consolidate and enhance his position in the state party, and in late April he startled the Democrats by proposing that the senatorial nomination, usually made at the late-summer state convention, be scheduled for the early June convention which would select delegates to the national convention. Setting the senatorial nomination for early June would give the unorganized liberal opponents of Maloney and his chief ally, state chairman J. Francis Smith, only a few weeks to campaign for delegates. Yet even with time to contest Maloney's renomination the liberals by themselves stood no chance of unseating him. The real key to Maloney's proposal lay in an emerging factional contest over the gubernatorial nomination.

That factionalism was rooted in the intraparty conflicts of the 1930s and the continuing struggle for control of the state Democratic party. Opposition to Maloney and Smith came not only from the New Dealers but also from the Old Guard urban leaders who had lost power to them during the Cross administration. A key episode had occurred in 1936, when Maloney and Smith had divided Little Dave Fitzgerald and Long Tom Spellacy by supporting Fitzgerald's selection as national committeeman over Spellacy's objections. But by 1940 Fitzgerald had fallen out with Maloney and Smith, partly because of the power of the Maloney-Smith group, but also because of personal resentments. Feeling that Maloney had not been properly grateful for the boost given him by Fitzgerald's New Haven organization in the early 1930s, Fitzgerald was angered as well by the support Maloney gave Smith's brother for a vacant federal judgeship which Fitzgerald badly wanted for his son. For a number of reasons, then, Fitzgerald had begun to edge back into his old alliance with Spellacy and other remnants of the Old Guard machine. The gubernatorial nomination served as a focal point of contention.

The only major avowed candidate early in 1940 for that nomination was the state's forty-five-year-old public works commissioner, Robert A. Hurley. An engineer and contractor from Bridgeport, Hurley had begun his public career in the mid-1930s when he had risen through leadership posts in the

Works Progress Administration in Connecticut to become its State Administrator. Since 1937 he had effectively headed the state public works department. An ambitious liberal, he had generated considerable publicity and no little support for his candidacy by spring. Hurley was a tall, beefy Irishman who had been a four-letter athlete in college at Lehigh and had played professional football and semipro baseball after his World War I service in the Navy. He brought his athletic competitiveness into politics, but, as his career in the early 1940s would prove, he lacked the political skills to match his combative instincts. Raspy-voiced, seemingly aloof, and without the gift (which Raymond Baldwin had in abundance) for effective self-promotion, Hurley neither came alive nor came across before the public. And if he lacked the flair of a first-rate campaigner, he lacked the deftness and shrewdness of a master of intraparty politics. An excellent administrator but a weak politician, a plodder compared to Baldwin, and often ham-handed in party affairs, Hurley was driven by his ambition beyond his real gifts. Still, he was an able and intelligent man by no means without assets, and he was for half a decade at the center of Connecticut politics. And although he lacked the political touch of so many other Irish Democrats, he occasionally enjoyed a bit of Irish luck. He did in 1940, certainly, and right from the start, when for ideological and factional reasons he began to win support from the New Dealers while for personal and factional reasons he got the backing of Little Dave Fitzgerald and a powerful group allied with him.

While Hurley pushed toward the gubernatorial nomination with mounting liberal and Old Guard support, Maloney and Smith remained uncommitted and wary. They seemed to prefer Wilbur Cross, as yet undeclared, and they knew that the nomination would prove a key to control and direction of the party. Those circumstances provided the background for Maloney's surprise proposal to get the senatorial nomination out of the way at the June convention. Anticipating a rancorous battle over the state ticket, the Senator wanted to protect his own renomination from any unexpected turn of events. But the gubernatorial nomination and the broader issue of party control were basic to the Senator's calculations, for Maloney also wanted the delegates elected for the June convention to serve at the late-summer convention which would select the state ticket. That would restrict the delegate selection process to a few weeks in May, which in turn would undercut Hurley's quest for delegate support and make it less likely that the New Dealers and Old Guard could map out an effective cooperative strategy. Finally, Maloney's plan meant that during the summer the maneuvering for state nominations would entail delegate suasion rather than popular appeal—and delegates could prove vulnerable to the kind of political and patronage clout possessed by Senator Maloney and state chairman Smith. Maloney's proposals could variously serve his interests, and in the end the Senator got his way. Despite their strenuous objections, Fitzgerald and his camp, party professionals above all, finally acquiesced in order to preserve party unity for the coming campaign. But the party's divisions could not be papered over by declarations and smiles, and the gubernatorial nomination yet promised to provoke a fight.[4]

Factional and philosophical cleavages stemming from the politics of the 1930s also plagued the GOP. Old-line conservatives remained restive about the leadership of the New Era Republicans, based in Fairfield County and headed by Baldwin and national committeeman Samuel Pryor. Reflecting the ongoing national struggle between those Republicans who accepted much of the New Deal and those who rejected virtually all of it, the division also involved the narrower though related question of state party control. Because Baldwin and the other state officers could count on renomination, the only major state-level nomination Republicans had to make was for United States senator. In May, the Litchfield County organization began soliciting support for Paul Cornell. A former New York advertising executive who had moved to Litchfield County where he headed Romford Boys School, Cornell had been part of the New Era group in 1938 and had its quiet support in 1940. The early boomlet for Cornell disaffected state chairman Benjamin

56

Harwood, a moderate conservative who served as a bridge between the New Era and conservative wings. Like Harwood, conservatives generally frowned on the Cornell effort, as did those Republicans who disliked party control and key positions gravitating too far toward Fairfield County. No acerbity emerged, for Cornell's candidacy seemed premature, but the Republicans were not united.[5]

Republicans had also to decide on a presidential candidate to support at the national convention. National committeeman Pryor and the New Era group had long perceived in Wendell Willkie an attractive exponent of private enterprise and an articulate critic of the New Deal. The congruence of Willkie's outlook with the ideas and programs of Connecticut's New Era Republicans became even clearer in 1940. Willkie and Raymond Baldwin alike accused the New Deal of hampering free enterprise and retarding recovery, and both wanted a frugal government, a friendly government to foster business, and an active government which nonetheless did not overstep its bounds. Both accepted much of the New Deal program and espoused humane and progressive government; but both obviously were business-minded Republicans, not New Dealers. Pryor, one of the small group that arranged speeches, tours, and media exposure for Willkie throughout 1939 and 1940, continued to work for a Willkie-Baldwin ticket.

As it did elsewhere, Willkie's support in Connecticut went beyond a few active and strategically placed leaders. A Willkie for President Association was formed in early May and soon claimed committees in existence or in the making in 129 of Connecticut's 169 towns. As elsewhere, too, Willkie's supporters evidently came largely from the "station-wagon crowd" and "country-club set" led by bankers, businessmen, and professional people, the kind who thought Willkie a hero of sorts for his well-publicized opposition to parts of the New Deal in the 1930s. Fairfield County was the center of Willkie sentiment in the state. Despite Willkie's support, however, the May state convention selected an unpledged delegation to the Philadelphia national convention. Preventing conflict between Willkie's backers and those of the other major candidates, New York's young Thomas E. Dewey, Ohio's Senator Robert A. Taft, and Michigan's Senator Arthur H. Vandenberg, that decision also allowed Connecticut delegates to support Baldwin as a favorite-son candidate until they determined where power lay at the convention. Willkie thus remained in Connecticut what he was in the nation: an apparent dark horse.[6]

Adolf Hitler had swept through western Europe while Connecticut politicians sparred among themselves and prepared for the national conventions. On April 9, Germany invaded Denmark and Norway. A month later the *blitzkrieg* struck the Netherlands, Belgium, and France. Then in late June, after Italy joined the attack, France fell to the Axis. Throughout the summer the *Luftwaffe* and the Royal Air Force clashed in the monumental Battle of Britain. Rallied by Prime Minister Winston Churchill, the British held out; but their plight was desperate, and it reinforced for Americans the potential menace to their own safety and interests posed by Nazi Germany. The events of the spring and summer catalyzed American opinion, led to a greatly accelerated preparedness program and to increased aid to Great Britain, and profoundly affected the year's politics. The impact was pronounced in Connecticut, not least on the economic and ethnic bases of the state's politics.

On May 16, 1940, with German divisions deep in France and the likelihood of a Nazi Europe ominously plain, President Roosevelt adumbrated a far-reaching National Defense Program to ensure American security. Calling for the production of 50,000 planes a year and for large expenditures for the armed forces, the President asked Congress for $1 billion for defense. That was just the beginning. In the remainder of the year Roosevelt requested, and Congress provided, billions more in defense moneys.

The National Defense Program did more than help safeguard national security; it also underwrote, especially in the industrial states, tangible progress toward national prosperity. Defense orders tumbled into Connecticut. By December, Connecticut led the nation in the value of contracts awarded for aircraft engines (40 percent of the national total), for submarines (70 percent of the national total), and for small arms and ammunition, and it ranked second in production machine contracts. The state stood an easy first in value of defense contracts per capita and second in the total value of war orders.

A few prime contractors—in particular, United Aircraft with 42 percent of the dollar volume of Connecticut war orders, the Electric Boat Company with 29 percent, and Remington Arms of Bridgeport with 20 percent—gobbled up almost all the defense orders. Reflecting that allocation, the Hartford area received some 40 percent of the total value of Connecticut defense contracts, while the Groton-New London and Bridgeport areas won nearly 30 percent each.

But despite the skewed distribution of war contracts to large, established firms, a problem that would persist in Connecticut as in the nation throughout the war, the state enjoyed general and widespread economic gains. Connecticut's size and commuter patterns meant that the defense employment boom was not confined to the immediate environs of the big war plants. Further, if the large contractors did not subcontract as much as they might have, they did perforce spread some of their work around. United Aircraft, indeed, subcontracted nearly half of its orders, and the Electric Boat Company roughly one-fourth. Many of the subcontracts were distributed throughout the state's industrial cities and towns. Too, such industries as brass, copper, hardware, and machine tools, which received few primary contracts, expanded rapidly in order to provide goods vital to the defense plants. The general industrial growth, in turn, invigorated construction and commerce and brought more white-collar and service employment. Reflecting the impact, direct and indirect, of the National Defense Program, Connecticut's index of business activity stood 27 percent above the 1929 norm by November, while factory man-hours and employment stood 36 and 20 percent higher than in 1929. Relief loads declined abruptly, and by October no backlog of eligible men awaited assignment to WPA. More jobs, longer

59

hours, and the wage increases announced by many defense firms in the latter part of the year helped hike the state's net personal income by an astounding 63 percent in 1940.[7]

Connecticut's people obviously enjoyed their new jobs and fatter pay envelopes. Retail sales rose rapidly in 1940, and more new telephones were installed than in any previous year. Flocking in greatly increased numbers to the state's resort and recreation areas during the summer, vacationers and weekenders spent money there in amounts unequaled in years. People ate better, too, and the demand for food helped Connecticut farmers to profit from industrial recovery. And despite the spending, Connecticut's citizens also banked some of their money. Deposits in Connecticut banks rose some 22 percent in 1940, twice the national average. Small deposits especially increased. Because of the European war and the National Defense Program, Connecticut in 1940 had entered the wartime era of unprecedented economic expansion and prosperity.[8]

Other, less happy consequences also attended the incipient war boom, however. People learned early that defense prosperity did not bring unalloyed or universal cheer. Prices began to rise, and by late summer housewives had already begun "complaining bitterly" about meat prices. Rents began to go up, too. Because home construction had stagnated for a decade, urban areas had tight housing markets even before defense jobs began to attract more people to the cities. By autumn there existed a clear need to do something about a worsening housing shortage and rent profiteering, both exacerbated by in-migrants coming to Connecticut in search of war jobs. Another obvious need was for a way to use the state's labor force more effectively and fairly, for Connecticut had already begun to feel the labor scarcity which would bedevil it and other industrial states for the remainder of the war years. Involving a shortage of the skilled and semiskilled workers needed in key defense industries, the 1940 problem stemmed largely from inadequate use of existing manpower. Because of the Depression, the skills of many older workers had grown rusty from disuse by 1940, while young members of the labor force frequently lacked training and prior employment; and neither a state job-training program begun by Baldwin for those reasons nor similar efforts by municipalities and industry turned out enough workers to meet industry's demands. Further, inadequate subcontracting meant inefficient use of the state's employed skilled workers, while the refusal of many employers to hire or train blacks precluded use of a portion of the labor pool. In October, Hartford still had significant unemployment problems among men over fifty, young men, and Negroes.[9]

Yet if the National Defense Program and the defense boom had already brought new problems and highlighted old ones, those problems paled beside the ruddy picture of general recovery. The labor shortage, for example, whatever new problems it bred and old patterns of hardship and discrimination it revealed, was a welcome change from the job shortage of the Depression years. The state had not prospered so for more than a decade. The fact of economic improvement and the prospect of more to come mattered more to most people than the related difficulties.

The war brought different sorts of problems and anxieties to Connecticut's ethnic groups. Poles, Jews, French-Canadians, and many other European immigrant groups were gravely worried about their folk in and near Hitler's expanding domain. But the resulting antipathy toward Nazi Germany, based though it was on old-country ties, did not set those groups apart from the mainstream. In Connecticut as throughout the East there existed a strong pro-Allied sentiment among most Yankees and immigrants alike. Nor did some lingering Irish anglophobia isolate that group. By 1940 the Irish obviously were Americans and accepted as such, even if many old-stock citizens still regarded them as inferiors.

For Italians, the story was much different. The war at first served further to alienate them—more than one-eighth of the state's population—from the rest of Connecticut's people. Italian-Americans, of course, came from one of the Axis nations. But more than that, until Pearl Harbor they and the

61

Italian-language press in America displayed substantial pro-Italy sentiment. For both reasons, Italian-Americans faced special difficulties in 1940 and 1941.

The support enjoyed by Mussolini in Italian-American communities stemmed primarily from the status of Italian-Americans in the United States. As a group, Italian-Americans were recent arrivals in the country, only partly acculturated and largely unassimilated, and still the victims of fierce prejudice and active discrimination. (In a national survey taken in 1939 fully half of those responding said that of all the immigrants the Italians made the worst citizens; no other immigrant group was even close.) Italian-Americans had long found in their close-knit community life a group solidarity and pride that helped to compensate for their marginal position in American society. During the interwar years, Mussolini and his apparently powerful "New Italy" provided them with vicarious prestige and with another way to manifest their ethnic pride. Positive reaction to Mussolini did not usually mean a break with America or an affirmation of fascism. Italian-Americans apotheosized Italy more than they rejected America, and that apotheosis was more sentimental and visceral than ideological. Strongest among the still numerous first generation, support of Mussolini depended importantly on individual acculturation and assimilation and on how far one identified as Italian or as American. For many, the related difficulties of establishing a satisfactory identity as either Italian or American and of resolving divided loyalties proved perplexing and worrisome.

Italy's formal entrance into World War II as Hitler's ally in June 1940 increased tensions among Italian-Americans and further estranged them from the larger American society. In Connecticut as elsewhere in the nation, the Italian-American response to Mussolini's invasion of France reflected the group's divided loyalties and mixed emotions. Though various Italian organizations and their leaders denounced Mussolini and affirmed the Americanism and American loyalty of Italian-Americans, reaction below the level of formal, quasi-official statements was more complicated and revealed that professed

allegiance to the United States did not displace pro-Italy sentiment. Italians regretted Mussolini's actions rather than denouncing them. Many found justification for Italy's bellicosity,
indeed some immigrant males were "elated" by it, and sentiment seemed unanimous that the United States had no business
meddling in European affairs. Still evincing a sense of sepa-
rateness, at most disavowing fascism and aggression but not
Italy, Italian-Americans evidently hoped that strict American
neutrality would obviate a clash between the United States
and Italy and thus the necessity of finally resolving conflicting
loyalties.[10]

External pressures exacerbated the internal stresses of the
Italian-American community. Just after Mussolini invaded
France, President Roosevelt delivered at Charlottesville, Virginia, an angry address which clearly ranged the United States
against Italy and the Axis. Equally distressing to Italian-
Americans, the President also charged Mussolini with having
stabbed his neighbor in the back. The speech reverberated
among Italian-Americans in 1940 and for years to come. Like
those elsewhere, Connecticut Italians felt that Roosevelt's
speech had been "too strong, unfair, and uncalled for," especially since the President had invoked a derogatory image—the
supposed Italian fondness for the stiletto—that Italians had
hoped was fading. Congressman James Shanley of New Haven
(where upwards of one-fourth of the population was Italian)
wrote Roosevelt that Italians hoped he would "correct any
wrong impression that might be directed against us."

Shanley also reported to the President a "wave of sentiment"
against Italians, a sentiment manifested in part, he believed,
by dropping Italians from jobs "out of sheer spite and for malicious reasons." Industry had indeed begun to discriminate
more actively and openly against Italian-Americans in hiring
and firing, and by June New Haven relief rolls reflected that
fact. But the anti-Italian feeling involved more than jobs. Public officials and the media urged "Americanism" and excoriated
old-country loyalties. Immigration officials reminded unnatu-
ralized Italian immigrants that they would be classified as

"enemy aliens" and subject to congressional regulation should America enter the war. Deportation proceedings more than tripled by September. Such actions further underlined the marginal position of all aliens, though of the Italians especially, in the society.[11]

Fears about "fifth-column" subversion heightened the social tensions. Such apprehensions, made credible by the reported successes of Nazi agents in Europe, were by no means confined to Connecticut. Stories of spies and saboteurs abounded in the nation, vigilante-style "rifle clubs" sprang up, and the Attorney General advised Americans that they could help by reporting evidence of sabotage and espionage to the Federal Bureau of Investigation. Congress chimed in with legislation requiring alien registration and fingerprinting. In Connecticut the similar impact of fear and rumor on a variegated people produced a summer-long fifth-column phobia with an understandable Italian focus. By mid-June, entreaties to a jittery public to combat subversion and to report unusual activities produced a hundred complaints a week, half of them originating in the New Haven area, about suspected fifth-column activity, and such reports increased over the course of the summer.[12]

Anti-Italian sentiment thus reached new heights in 1940. The largest of the new immigrant groups, Italian-Americans seemed foreign still, and they now aroused apprehension as well as distaste. Germans, the only other Connecticut ethnic group associated with the Axis (there were only a few hundred Japanese in the state), were far fewer in numbers and much better assimilated. Italians were acutely aware of the feeling against them, which they resented, worried about, and attributed largely to Roosevelt's "stab in the back" speech at Charlottesville. Tension remained so high that Columbus Day (October 12), normally a time of festive public celebration for the Italian population, was strangely muted. In New Haven and elsewhere quiet ceremonies replaced the customary parade and banquets.[13]

Besides its effects on the underlying social bases of politics, the European war had more direct political consequences in

64

the summer and fall of 1940. It crystallized Roosevelt's intention to seek a third term, increased the experienced President's popular support, gave Wendell Willkie added momentum toward the GOP nomination, and shaped party calculations and strategy for the fall elections. Yet along with the impact of the war on national and state politics, there was also a large measure of politics more or less as usual. Old domestic issues and ethnic and economic concerns, affected but not transformed by the war, figured importantly in partisan tactics and voter attitudes, and both parties had to work their way toward November through a maze of long-standing factional and philosophical differences.

The Nazi spring offensive shocked the United States into thinking harder about its security and its stake in the European war. Though still loud, hard-shell isolationists found their numbers and influence dwindling. Americans increasingly favored not only a greatly accelerated national defense program but also aid to the Allies to enhance American safety. Reflecting the shift registered in polls and other barometers of public opinion, June mail to New England congressmen was both heavy and heavily interventionist—of the thousands of letters flooding the congressmen's offices, almost all urged aid to the Allies and a few urged a declaration of war. Not many Americans, of course, wanted war in 1940; but the nation did want to preserve its own security, and growing numbers felt that one necessary means to that end was assistance short of war to Hitler's foes.[14]

The international situation and American attitudes toward it helped shape the third-term intentions and prospects of Franklin Roosevelt. Until the spring of 1940, Roosevelt seems to have been genuinely undecided about his political future. No doubt part of him wanted to return to the life of a rural squire at Hyde Park; no doubt another part of him relished the presidency and disliked the prospect of abandoning it. Whatever the inner conflict, public events propelled the President toward trying for the unprecedented third term. For one thing, no alternative candidate emerged whom Roosevelt thought up to the job. More important, the Nazi successes of the spring and the intensifying world crisis persuaded Roosevelt that his experience and anti-Axis leadership should be offered to the nation again. By late spring, the President had determined to be a candidate. And even as the war helped decide Roosevelt to run again, it also improved his chances and defused the third-term issue Republicans were sure to use against him. Anxious about their nation's security in 1940, Americans looked to the man who had led the nation for more than seven years. New Haven residents indicated in May that the world crisis made Roosevelt's experience more vital to them and softened opposition to a third term, and national surveys similarly showed that the imminence of war strengthened Roosevelt politically. An unparalleled world situation paved the way toward an unprecedented political event.[15]

The war and its political implications affected the calculations of the Democrats who gathered at the Chicago national convention. Meeting in mid-July, the convention renominated Roosevelt, sourly acquiesced in Roosevelt's selection of Agriculture Secretary Henry A. Wallace as his running mate, and adopted a platform emphatic in its New Deal orientation. On foreign affairs, the platform resembled the waffling Republican platform adopted earlier in its substance and its efforts to appease both isolationists and internationalists. The Democratic platform did more forcefully condemn aggression, more straightforwardly pledge aid to the Allies, and more clearly indicate an understanding that the war was a worldwide struggle; but like the GOP's, the Democrats' foreign policy position constituted something of a victory for the isolationists.[16] Perhaps more fundamentally, the two platforms reflected the curious attitude of the nation generally in the summer of 1940, an attitude rooted at once in antipathy for the Axis and in a keen desire to stay out of war. The developing consensus was for aid to the Allies so long as it stopped short of war; yet, without being ready to admit the consequences, Americans seemed to understand that such aid probably would lead to war. Politicians therefore denounced the Axis, promised help

66

for the Allies, and pledged that the United States would not go to war. From the beginning, the foreign policy issue of the 1940 campaign was shaped as much by politics and public opinion as by principle.

Connecticut Democratic leaders returned from Chicago professing satisfaction with the convention. Privately they were less happy. Like most of their colleagues from other states, they lacked enthusiasm for Wallace, and although Farley's stillborn candidacy never won the open support from Connecticut that it did from Massachusetts, some delegates felt that Roosevelt had treated Farley and his aspirations shabbily. Farley's refusal to stay on as national chairman threatened further to hurt the President among Irish party regulars, but later in the summer the selection of Edward J. Flynn of the Bronx to succeed Farley did much to soothe Irish and Catholic feelings. As added balm for Connecticut's Irish Democrats, David Fitzgerald served on a special five-person committee designated by the convention to consult with Roosevelt about Farley's successor.[17]

Far more serious problems involved the party's internal divisions and the gubernatorial nomination. The springtime sparring had turned into clearcut conflict during a bitter preconvention struggle to name a successor to state chairman Smith, who had wanted to quit the post for some time. Backed by Robert Hurley's supporters and the Old Guard, John T. McCarthy, a tall, thin Irishman from Fairfield County and a close friend of Hurley's, won the job. J. Francis Smith, though without a formal position, remained a power in the Democratic party, while McCarthy became the first of a revolving-door series of short-tenured and generally ineffective Democratic state chairmen who served between Smith's six years and John Bailey's three decades.

Once the national convention was over, the Democrats' factional battle, now focusing clearly on the gubernatorial nomination, intensified. As part of their strategy, the Maloney forces tried hard, with some success, to discredit Hurley as a pawn of the Old Guard. In fact, the Old Guard did want to regain ascendancy. Believing Hurley a good vehicle for them to ride back to power, they also hoped he would carefully dispense patronage to party regulars. But that was only part of a complex picture involving sometimes overlapping considerations of power, patronage, personality, and philosophy. Hurley had actually risen to prominence in state politics more closely aligned with the Maloney-Smith group than with the Old Guard and had seemed close to them until early 1940, when he refused to bind himself to their direction. Hurley, moreover, had developed substantial strength of his own, especially among relatively young and liberal Democrats from the cities who wanted a candidate more in harmony with the New Deal than was Wilbur Cross, who had Maloney's support.

Still another factor in the fight over the nomination was the election which lay ahead. Victories in state and local contests opened up the patronage so important to power; and power was the *sine qua non* of politics for men like Fitzgerald, Spellacy, and Maloney. Though hardly liberals themselves, the Old Guard may well have thought Hurley, a New Dealer and an Irish Catholic, a stronger candidate to head the state ticket than Cross, at least in their own urban bailiwicks. Maloney and Smith believed that Connecticut Yankee Wilbur Cross's appeal in the suburbs and small towns made him a far stronger statewide candidate than Hurley. Wanting to run on the strongest possible slate, Maloney evidently wanted a combination of Roosevelt's urban strength and Cross's independent, Yankee, and town support as insurance for his own reelection.

Maloney and his allies could not match the combined power of the urban chieftains and New Dealers, and Hurley won an easy victory. His nomination, and the intraparty politics attendant to it, revealed continuing flux of sides and strength in the state party and showed again that control of the party was for many Democratic leaders as important as its direction. The Democratic party remained in Connecticut an often rancorous alliance of diverse factions, held together by the glue of party loyalty and ambition.[18]

Jockeying for the remaining positions on the ticket had proceeded while major attention focused on the gubernatorial nomination. Those lesser nominations had long been reserved largely for recognition of particular groups or sections of the state. Using as leverage the GOP's nomination of Boleslaus Monkiewicz for congressman-at-large in 1938, Polish Democrats formed one of the groups pressing hard for a spot on the ticket.

Italians were another of those groups, and numerically a more important one. Feeling that a major Italian nominee was virtually a right by 1940 in any event, Italian Democrats wanted such recognition all the more because of the situation of Italian-Americans. They had a powerful argument, for few Democratic politicians, Italian or not, could fail to realize that an Italian candidate was imperative to help repair the political damage done by Roosevelt's stab-in-the-back speech. In its advocacy of Bridgeport attorney Pasquale Vioni for a congressional nomination, Bridgeport's Italian newspaper *La Sentinella* spoke to the political and the social reasons for recognition. Noting the advantages of selecting a candidate who could attract such a crucial bloc of voters—a "master strategic move"— it also argued that in Congress Vioni could prove his (and the Italians') patriotism and Americanism. Perhaps believing that the tensions and fears of 1940 required additional justification for nominating an Italian-American, the newspaper went on to say that "Mr. Vioni's supreme and invaluable asset as a candidate is his sterling Americanism and his skill in imparting to the men and women of his race the patriotic spirit and unquestioning love of benevolent America. . . ."[19]

Although it had seemed earlier that events abroad and consequent domestic strains might inhibit ethnic considerations in slate-making, the persistence of the ethnic politicians and the need to attract Italian and Polish voters in November made such recognition virtually inevitable. The maneuvering for the gubernatorial nomination collapsed whatever resistance remained. Nor did party leaders have to accommodate only the immigrant groups. Women and eastern Connecticut Democrats also demanded recognition, while Democratic strategists wanted a Yankee on the ticket. In the end, all those groups won a place on the ticket, and Hurley, if elected, would be Connecticut's first Irish-Catholic governor.

The convention also adopted a markedly liberal platform. Though devoted largely to state affairs, the platform praised Roosevelt and the New Deal with notable fervor. Maloney and Smith quickly endorsed the ticket, and state chairman John McCarthy began efforts to patch up the party divisions. Armed with an artfully crafted ticket and a liberal orientation, and encouraged more than anything else by their faith in Roosevelt's great vote-getting power, Connecticut Democrats were ready for the campaign.[20]

Selection of a presidential nominee had occupied Republicans in the late spring and early summer. Though conservative Senator Robert Taft had support from some party veterans in the state, strong sentiment for Willkie within the Connecticut delegation had emerged by the time of the Philadelphia national convention. By then the carefully orchestrated and remarkably successful "grass roots" Willkie movement that had lifted the Indianan from near obscurity had taken hold. But Willkie's momentum did not derive only from the superb publicity and organizational work of his backers or from the torrents of pro-Willkie correspondence to delegates they generated. Willkie was a genuinely attractive man whose record and rhetoric appealed to diverse segments of the GOP, especially to moderates and those with ties to business and finance, and whose evident independence (he had called himself a Democrat until the late 1930s) promised to appeal to independents and restive Democrats should Roosevelt win renomination.

Important as Willkie's other resources were, however, his greatest asset by convention time was the international situation. The war in Europe, the heightened national concern with security, and the developing American consensus for aiding the Allies helped Willkie and hurt his opponents. Taft and Vandenberg espoused isolationist views held by decided minorities both in the country and in the party by the summer. Dewey, the front-runner, seemed to take now one side, now the other of the foreign policy question, and he suffered further from his youthfulness (he was thirty-eight) at a time when Americans evidently wanted maturity and experience in their next President. While Willkie obviously lacked governmental experience, he seemed thoughtful, competent, and mature. Alone among the chief GOP contenders he had articulated a clear anti-isolationist, pro-Allied position. Gallup polls charting the fortunes of the GOP candidates revealed how Willkie's rise coincided with the deteriorating international situation. Willkie did not even appear on the list of GOP contenders until late April, when he was favored by just 3 percent of the nation's Republicans. By contrast, Dewey commanded an impressive 67 percent. But by the time of the national convention, after the accelerated Willkie blitz at home and Nazi *blitzkrieg* abroad, Willkie's support among Republicans had soared to 44 percent and Dewey's had plummeted to 29 percent.[21]

Willkie, then, had the momentum when the Republicans gathered in Philadelphia. Connecticut helped put him over the top. Baldwin withdrew his own favorite-son candidacy, seconded Willkie's nomination, and served as a floor manager for Willkie. (The anticipated *quid pro quo* was the vice-presidential nomination.) Samuel Pryor also played an important role at the convention. Chairman of the Arrangements Committee, he was responsible for packing the galleries with boisterous Willkie supporters. Pryor also worked to convert delegates to Willkie. Largely because of Pryor and Baldwin, Connecticut was the only state unanimously to back Willkie from the first ballot until his sixth-ballot victory. Connecticut delegates even led the march in the Willkie demonstration.

Despite all that, Senator Charles L. McNary of Oregon, a Western isolationist and a public-power advocate, was chosen to balance the ticket headed by the Eastern (as many perceived him) internationalist and utility magnate. Baldwin yielded gracefully, and he became a member of Willkie's special twelve-man advisory committee. Heading the seventeen-state Eastern Division campaign, Pryor also continued to serve the Willkie

71

cause. Even Baldwin's record became part of the Willkie campaign. The GOP pointed to Connecticut as the "test state" for Republicanism and argued that the accomplishments of Baldwin's "friendly government" presaged the national success of Willkie's similar ideas.

Most of the Connecticut delegation rejoiced in the convention's outcome. Confident that Willkie could carry the state, Connecticut's Republican leaders believed that the New Era Republicanism of new men and new outlooks introduced in Connecticut in 1938 had been duplicated on a national scale. Willkie's nomination was of course the chief cause of their optimism and satisfaction, but the platform offered much that was congenial to virtually all of the state GOP. Accepting in substance many New Deal programs, it nonetheless took sharp issue with the New Deal's philosophy, its centralizing tendencies, its spending, its failure to achieve recovery, and what Republicans called its encouragement of un-American groups and activities. "Americanism" and an effort to bridge party fault lines also figured prominently in the foreign policy plank. Having to take into account both the mood of the nation and their own interventionist-isolationist divisions, Republicans accused Roosevelt of having both an inadequate preparedness program and an aggressive foreign policy, and declared that "the Republican Party stands for Americanism, preparedness and peace." A qualified victory for the isolationists, the foreign policy plank, like that of the Democrats, reflected calculation as much as conviction.[22]

On returning home, Connecticut Republicans organized themselves for the state campaign. Because no strong candidate emerged to oppose Paul Cornell, the senatorial nomination finally fell to him and thus to the Fairfield County-New Era group without contest. The state convention then routinely renominated the incumbents up for reelection and drafted a platform that recounted the accomplishments of Baldwin's administration and made wide-ranging recommendations stressing a liberal social program and vigorous defense efforts. The document also accused Roosevelt and the New Deal of under-

mining the nation with irresponsible and un-American practices, culminating in an unprecedented grab for a third term.[23]

Roosevelt, Willkie, and issues deriving from their contest
dominated the autumn campaign in Connecticut. Virtually
inevitable in any event, the salience of the presidential race
was heightened by the Democrats' strategy of running deter-
minedly on the President's coattails and by the personal and
philosophical ties of Connecticut's Republican leaders to Willkie. Challenger Willkie carried the attack to Roosevelt, and
before his campaign dissolved into immoderation and chaos,
he concentrated on the related themes of recovery and preparedness. Roosevelt and the New Deal, Willkie argued, had
prevented economic recovery by harassing and restricting business. That had left the nation woefully unready to defend itself,
for a vigorous productive economy provided the surest basis
for national defense. "Only the strong can be free, and only
the productive can be strong," Willkie said. Paul Cornell, who
repeated Willkie's ideas throughout the campaign, made that
his central theme.

The palpable facts of defense preparations and economic improvement undercut those Republican issues. The National Defense Program, aid to the Allies, and, most tangibly to many
Americans, the implementation of the selective service system
during the autumn all made it apparent that the nation had begun to attend to its security. Further, the preparedness program
had kindled the economy. Roosevelt exploited those developments, and the heightened public concern about American
safety, in his adroit campaign. For much of the autumn, the
President portrayed himself as the busy, vigilant, and experienced Commander-in-Chief. Forswearing "purely political debate," he made what were advertised as inspection tours of key
defense plants and military bases—where his "nonpolitical"
talks sharply drew attention to the military and industrial mobilization. By the time he formally began his campaign he could
point to substantial progress in both areas.[24]

Nowhere were defense production and recovery more evident than in Connecticut, a fact which Roosevelt nicely capitalized on when he toured the state on October 30. Eager for Republican ideas and policies to get credit for the state's prosperity, Baldwin claimed, as he had all year, that the state's economic gains had followed from his "friendly," frugal government that had buoyed old businesses and attracted new ones to the state. When Hurley responded with the year-long Democratic litany that Baldwin exaggerated his accomplishments and that credit for recovery properly belonged to the New Deal, to the President's defense program, and to the state's economic structure, Baldwin stressed philosophy instead of figures. Maintaining that Democrats lacked sympathy for private enterprise and understood none but relief and war jobs, he said that sound recovery based on private enterprise and fiscal responsibility lay beyond Democratic comprehension. Here the Governor argued from a stance all Republicans could assume and one in line with Willkie's national campaign. Insisting that prior to the defense boom the New Deal had failed to solve the nation's or state's economic problems, Republican candidates for federal office, like Willkie and Baldwin, contrasted Democratic badgering and shackling of American industry with Republican understanding and encouragement of the central role of free enterprise and individualism in American society.[25]

More than economic principles were involved in this aspect of the GOP's campaign. As Cornell put it, "We here in Connecticut believe in the American form of capitalist production."[26] "American" was a key word; and Americanism in one form or another had long been a central Republican issue and image. Since the coming of the New Deal, conservatives and Republicans had used Americanism in a special way, to denounce the "un-American" tendencies of Roosevelt and the New Deal. Free enterprise, individualism, limited government, and traditional ways lay at the heart of their conception of Americanism. The New Deal provided for them the counter-image of Republican Americanism, and throughout the Roosevelt years and beyond

74

the GOP sought to make political capital from its denunciations of the New Deal as un-American.

Though a few Republicans flirted with charges of communism and all stressed the general threat of the New Deal to the "American Way," Americanism in 1940 was most often and most directly connected with what became perhaps the chief GOP issue: the likelihood of dictatorship in America were Roosevelt to win a third term and thus demolish a sacred, fundamental, and indispensable American principle of government. Willkie outlined the argument in his mid-September "Battle of America" speech, where he said that a third term would have a totalitarian end. Citing New Deal centralization as well, Connecticut Republicans in the most vivid terms accused the President of defying American principles, seeking to subvert the American form of government and American liberties, and working toward one-man rule. To support such charges, the GOP presented scenarios depicting the march of the New Deal to dictatorship and even took out newspaper advertisements comparing Roosevelt's America with Hitler's Germany and Mussolini's Italy. Calling the election a "crossroads" for the nation, Republicans said it would decide whether American democracy and liberty would continue. "The real issue," Baldwin declared in a radio address just before the election, ". . . is whether the form of our American government shall remain unchanged."[27]

If the domestic issues of Willkie and Connecticut Republicans degenerated largely to warnings of dictatorship, their treatment of foreign affairs finally came down to accusations that Roosevelt meant war. The Connecticut campaign reflected the general consensus on preparedness, aid to Great Britain, and no war. Because of their substantive agreement on defense, each party blamed the other for retarding the nation's preparedness program, and each claimed that it could best attend to America's defenses. More important to the campaign than preparedness were Republican charges that Roosevelt intended to take the nation into the war. Willkie had begun his campaign in substantial agreement with Roosevelt's foreign policy; indeed, the challenger had aroused isolationist sentiment in his own party by supporting such measures as selective service and, at first, the destroyer-bases exchange with England. Willkie quickly reversed himself on the destroyer-bases arrangement, however—"dictatorial and arbitrary" he called it—and as the campaign developed he became increasingly critical of Roosevelt. Willkie altered course mostly for political reasons. Attacking Roosevelt's internationalist policies promised both to win support from independents and Democrats opposed to or uneasy with the President's foreign policy and to smooth relations between Willkie and the party's isolationist regulars. The most extreme, and apparently politically effective, of Willkie's charges was that Roosevelt would soon take the nation to war. Connecticut Republicans used this accusation with gusto, too, and their foreign policy issue by late in the campaign was epitomized by one congressman's declaration that "war is imminent and war is the foreign policy of the President."[28]

Taking to the hustings in late October, Roosevelt replied to Willkie's attack in a series of five blistering speeches. The foreign policy question especially needed attention, for the charges of war not only threatened to stampede isolationist and apprehensive Americans toward the GOP but seemed to have special power among such ethnic groups as the Irish, Italians, and Germans, who for the most part did not want the United States to align itself with Great Britain against the Axis. Roosevelt insisted that he had no intention of taking the nation to war. On October 30 in Irish Boston, Roosevelt made perhaps his most famous statement of the 1940 campaign: "I have said this before, but I shall say it again and again and again: Your boys are not going to be sent into any foreign wars."[29]

Connecticut Democrats responded similarly to the GOP accusations. The President, they said, did not intend to and would not lead the nation into war. Yet on the whole Democrats in the state replied surprisingly seldom to Republican charges of war, or of dictatorship, or of the third-term menace. They tried to defuse those issues, to be sure; but they did not dwell on them, and defensiveness did not characterize their campaign. Rather, they campaigned aggressively on their own issues and on their own terms.

Easily foremost among those issues was Franklin D. Roosevelt. From the time of the state convention, Democrats made Roosevelt the center of their campaign. As one newspaperman noted, the Democrats might have hung a banner saying "In Roosevelt We Trust" on their convention stage, so strong was their hope that the President would carry them into office with him again; and that sentiment shaped the Democrats' autumn campaign. All candidates, for state and federal office alike, based their campaigns on Roosevelt and the New Deal. Even Senator Francis Maloney, though careful to come across as an independent, moderate New Dealer, grabbed onto the President's coattails for another ride to Washington. In pursuing this strategy, Democrats spoke both to foreign and domestic matters, though they put more emphasis on the latter. Roosevelt's continued leadership, they asserted, was essential. He had led the nation out of depression and reaction and would shepherd her through the perilous times ahead. Praising the New Deal, saying that it must be continued under its author, and arguing that the critical world situation required Roosevelt and his experience and proved skills, Connecticut Democrats helped keep the President at center stage in the state.

A corollary to the Democrats' emphasis on Roosevelt and the New Deal was their portrayal of themselves as the party of liberalism and the workingman, and of the GOP as the party of reaction and business. Hurley, for example, said that Baldwin's "friendly government" had been friendly only to big business. Arguing that such gains as the "common people" had achieved had come from the New Deal, he advocated a state labor relations act and a comprehensive program for the state's workingmen and farmers. Democratic congressional candidates campaigned in the same vein. They praised the New Deal and

77

listed its benefits; they promised to maintain and even extend liberal legislation for the state's workers; and they lambasted the GOP as the home of uncaring, moneyed reaction.[30]

Keenly aware after the 1930s of the power of the "factory vote" and the perils of Hooverism, Connecticut Republicans took pains to project a much more progressive, pro-labor image than they had in 1936. GOP candidates, especially Baldwin and Cornell, made scores of factory-gate speeches. There as elsewhere they endorsed such New Deal measures as the Wagner Act and Social Security. Praising labor and labor leaders, Baldwin addressed the state AFL and CIO conventions (he was the first Connecticut governor ever to speak at the latter), and GOP incumbents gave as much publicity as possible to praise and endorsements from labor. Baldwin, the chief symbol of Connecticut's progressive New Era Republicans, cited his record and promised more social legislation. Sometimes, Republicans could not still their anti-New Deal animus. Like the national and state platforms, candidates often denounced "the New Deal" even as they accepted much of its substance. One congressional nominee, for example, wanted to "end that dire calamity this November—the New Deal" and then promised to protect and strengthen major parts of it. But on the whole the Republican campaign, like its 1938 predecessor, reflected an accommodation to new realities of public policy and politics. Stung by the labor vote four years before, Connecticut Republicans worked to avert a rerun of that dismal election.[31]

When Willkie toured Connecticut on October 9, he too made special efforts to appeal to labor. Endorsing labor's recent advances, he also warned that New Deal spending portended inflation or national bankruptcy, either of which would undo whatever gains people had achieved from the New Deal. Republican leaders, pleased by the large, generally friendly crowds, professed optimism at the results of his visit.

Others, however, noted a lack of enthusiasm for Willkie. Though his crowds were neither rude nor menacing, as they sometimes were elsewhere, they seemed skeptical of Willkie and enamored of Roosevelt. A New Haven advertising man wrote Baldwin that Willkie had talked over the people's heads and had failed to appeal "to their emotions, to their wants and needs and the things they're interested in having from their government." Another correspondent told Baldwin that people simply did not believe that Willkie could bring more jobs, a judgment that must have disheartened the Governor. Baldwin himself lamented later that it was hard to get the "ordinary 'Joe Blow'" to back Willkie—that there were businessmen and Cadillacs with Willkie signs, but few workers or their cars.[32]

Baldwin and his party similarly could take no joy in the response of organized labor to GOP blandishments. In September, the Connecticut Federation of Labor adopted a report directing "severe criticism" of Baldwin despite the Governor's record and his propitiating speech to the convention (and largely because Baldwin had failed to reappoint a former CFL president as a district unemployment commissioner). The CFL went on to endorse Roosevelt, and later it rated each major Democratic candidate in Connecticut more favorably than his GOP counterpart. Nor did the dramatic late-October endorsement of Willkie by CIO president John L. Lewis bring Republicans the dividends they wanted. Although the Connecticut CIO and its political arm, Labor's Non-Partisan League, stayed officially neutral in the presidential contest, important state CIO leaders made clear their own preference for Roosevelt, and Labor's Non-Partisan League endorsed the entire Democratic congressional slate. Most Connecticut labor leaders, in the CIO as in the AFL, remained in the Democratic camp.[33]

Campaign strategy entailed appeals to ethnic groups as well as to workingmen. Besides the recognition afforded various groups (Democrats as usual had more ethnic candidates), both parties held countless rallies for the state's many immigrant groups. Politicians also sought to attract the vote of specific groups by emphasizing matters of special concern. As it did in other areas, the campaign for ethnic votes sometimes degenerated to ugliness and even scurrility on both sides. Democrats were especially culpable. Democratic national committee campaign literature tried to picture Willkie as an appeaser and a racist and to identify him with the German-American Bund and the Ku Klux Klan. Henry Wallace and other prominent Democrats suggested that a vote for Willkie was a vote for Hitler. Such tactics, used in Connecticut, were designed to keep or attract important voting blocs—Jews, blacks, and immigrants from such overrun or threatened European nations as Poland.[34]

Connecticut Republicans worried about the votes of those groups. They feared, for example, that Willkie's German background, Roosevelt's opposition to Hitler, and New Deal reform and recognition of Jews would make Jewish voters even more Democratic than in 1936. They attempted to salvage what they could of the Jewish vote, largely by trying to fuse Jewish antipathy toward Hitler with the third-term issue. Jews, they said, always suffered most from one-man rule. The GOP tried as well to contend with the effects of New Deal assistance to blacks and with the charges that Willkie was anti-Negro. Working to exploit black dissatisfaction with the lack of civil rights action by the Roosevelt administration and with the evident discrimination in the defense program and armed forces, Connecticut Republicans also emphasized Baldwin's record. The Governor had appointed a twelve-man committee (the chairman and four other members were black) to study Negro unemployment problems, an unprecedented action, and in what one prominent black hailed in a campaign radio speech as "the greatest recognition of the Negro race ever made by any governor in the history of this state," Baldwin had appointed Negroes to draft boards in cities with large black populations. Still, in an election year when Joe Louis was booed in Harlem for supporting Willkie, Republicans could hardly have been sanguine about their chances in black areas.[35]

In seeking the large Polish vote, both parties relied chiefly on their Polish-American candidates for congressman-at-large, Republican incumbent Boleslaus Monkiewicz and his challenger Lucien Maciora. To capitalize on the Poles' close ties with and great concern about their homeland, Connecticut Democrats also made good use of Anthony J.D. Biddle, ambassador to Poland, whom Roosevelt had brought home for the campaign. Making his introductory remarks in Polish, Biddle spoke to an overflow audience of thousands in New Britain on election eve, and his obliquely political speech was followed by a rousing Democratic rally. Republican Monkiewicz claimed that an ambassador had no place in politics and the Roosevelt administration no real sympathy for either Polish-Americans or Poland.[36] But with Maciora's candidacy blunting the help Monkiewicz had given the GOP in Polish areas in 1938, the combination of the New Deal and the international situation made GOP prospects for winning much of the Polish-American vote bleak indeed.

Italians received more attention than any other ethnic group. Not only were they much the largest immigrant group in the state, but the events of 1940 and Roosevelt's Charlottesville speech made Italian ethnicity especially salient. State and national Republicans thought that the Italian vote, shifting overwhelmingly from 1936, might be as much as 80 to 90 percent Republican. While Democrats made "frantic efforts to woo the voters of Italian extraction back into line," Republicans worked hard to see that such a change materialized.[37]

Recognition politics partly accounted for the GOP's bright hopes in Connecticut. Heralding state attorney general Francis A. Pallotti of Hartford as an example of an Italian serving with honor in a high place, Republicans could also expect residual profits from William Celentano's 1939 mayoral nomination in New Haven. In Bridgeport, Italian resentment rather than success promised Republican gains. After Pasquale Vioni had failed to win Democratic nomination to Congress as either the at-large or Fourth-District candidate, Bridgeport's Italian newspaper charged that Vioni had been denied nomination only because he was Italian and claimed that Italians would "act on election day." Just prior to the election, Vioni bolted the Democratic party, and at a large Italian-Republican rally he castigated Democrats for not showing Italians a "fair, proportionate regard."[38]

But it was the war and especially Roosevelt's speech at

Charlottesville that provided the main GOP leverage in Italian areas. Republicans constantly referred, directly and indirectly, to the "stab in the back." Speakers at an Italian-American rally in Waterbury, for example, told their listeners that "Roosevelt has insulted us but we know how to answer it"; Italians could "end the humiliation" by voting against the President. Because a war with Italy as the enemy portended vast complications in their lives, the GOP missed few chances to warn Italian-Americans of Roosevelt's bellicose anti-Axis sentiment. A handbill circulated among Italian-Americans in New London passionately got at the heart of the Republican appeal. The circular said with regard to the stab-in-the-back speech that "This great insult and bad name will be given to you and your children a hundred times a day. . . . " Claiming that Roosevelt was "determined" to "eventually arrive at a declaration of war against Italy," it went on to say that "life for us of Italian origin will be very painful because we will have to bear daily the insult of being a traitor." Indeed, Italians "without doubt, will be put in concentration camps." The handbill concluded: "If you still have in your blood the flame of righteousness and the honor of your ancestors you will not cast your vote for Roosevelt."[39]

Democrats understood the political damage done by the Charlottesville speech and sought to repair it. Flattery was part of their strategy. After delivering a "non-political" Columbus Day address hailing Italian contributions and loyalty to the United States, Roosevelt a few days later began his radio campaign with a speech on hemispheric defense which he opened with a tribute to Columbus. (Trying too hard, he also mistakenly credited Argentinian political philosopher Juan Bautista Alberdi with Italian origins.) During the campaign, the President held back on his anti-Mussolini rhetoric. Similarly in Connecticut, Hurley and Frank Anastasio, Democratic nominee for state treasurer, each made major Columbus Day speeches designed to propitiate Italians and to reverse the political impact of the stab-in-the-back speech, and other Democrats did what they could to appease Italians.[40] But flattery and appeals to Italian ethnicity could not suffice for the Democrats in 1940. Republicans seemed to have much the stronger ethnic case.

The GOP did not, however, have the stronger economic appeal. Roosevelt might have made the Charlottesville speech, but he had also given the nation the New Deal; and if Italians had an intense ethnic consciousness and had flocked to the Democrats in 1928 for reasons of ethnicity, they had been part of Roosevelt's 1936 coalition largely because of their economic status. Democrats consequently emphasized the Depression, the New Deal, and Republican reaction at Italian-American rallies. Hurley, for example, speaking at the Sons of Italy Hall in Bridgeport two days before the election, urged Italians to "remember the hunger and the fear and the suffering" of the Depression. He asked:

> How can any of you forget the great man who came to us in that hour of sorrow: The great Democratic President Franklin Roosevelt?
>
> It was he who gave you work; he saved your homes; he gave you social security; he gave you the wages and hours law to protect your rights as workingmen. I do not think you will be so foolish as to trust your future to those who have never been your friends and will not be now.[41]

A Democratic advertisement in the preelection edition of New Haven's most important Italian newspaper put the Democrats' case as strongly as the New London handbill put the Republicans'. Urging Italian-Americans to disregard the "defamatory statements" made against Roosevelt, the advertisement warned that "were President Roosevelt to be defeated, the Italian population of America will lose its best friend, and so will all the needy and suffering people of the world, and all those who hate war and pray for peace." Further, Roosevelt's defeat would mean the end of Social Security, the Wages and Hours Act, and other New Deal aid, and it would mean a return to "those terrible days when banks were shut down and you lost your jobs, your savings, your houses." And if Roosevelt lost, Democrats said, Italian-Americans would be responsible for his defeat and its awful consequences.[42]

There emerged during the state and national campaigns a

83

clear distinction between the two parties. Democrats campaigned as the party of Roosevelt, the New Deal, and the common people, Republicans as the party of free enterprise (not "business"), Americanism, and the American Way. Despite the judgment of most journalists in 1940 and of many historians since, issues of foreign policy and war did not predominate. Rather, the principal issues and images of each party concerned domestic affairs, and newspaper advertisements of both parties were given over almost entirely to domestic matters. Roosevelt, the chief issue in the campaign for Democrats and Republicans alike, was an issue primarily on the basis of his eight-year domestic record.[43] Defense, foreign policy, and the war were important, of course, especially in ethnic strategies and particularly toward the end of the campaign. They made the politics of 1940 different in shape and substance from the politics of the 1930s. Yet Republicans, Willkie included, ended their campaign warning more of dictatorship than of war and arguing that the chief threat to America lay within, not without. Democrats ended their campaign as they had begun it—lauding the President and the New Deal. The past usually counts more than the future in American politics, and America's recent past of the Depression and the New Deal provided the matrix of the 1940 campaign.

The campaign generated great interest. Political involvement seemed higher even than in 1936, and like the nation Connecticut had record-breaking registration totals in 1940, in all some 870,000. On election day, nearly fifty million Americans went to the polls, some five million more than in 1936, and a greater number than would vote in any election until 1952. Connecticut contributed to the surge in turnout. Capping the rise in voter participation begun in the Al Smith election of 1928, almost 790,000 citizens, nearly 100,000 more than in 1936, cast their ballots. Sixty-eight percent of the adult population voted, as against 64 percent in 1936 and 58 percent in 1928, and the 90 percent turnout of registered voters fell only slightly below the 1928 high.

84

Roosevelt won his third term decisively. Whipping Willkie by some five million votes, the President won 55 percent of the national vote. Handsome as it was, however, Roosevelt's mandate fell considerably below the eleven-million-vote plurality of 1936 that had brought him more than three-fifths of the popular vote. Nor did the President generate quite the same overwhelming victory for his party that he had four years before. Still, by most standards Roosevelt and his party did win an impressive victory, and the voting patterns of 1936 persisted strongly into 1940. The Roosevelt Coalition in the nation as a whole had emerged from its first major test victoriously and largely intact.[44]

It had done the same in Connecticut. Although Roosevelt's share of the vote slipped from 57.8 to 53.6 percent, he and his party swept the state. Reversing the setbacks of 1938, the Democrats carried the presidential and senatorial races and regained the governorship, all six congressional seats, and all state offices contested. Like the won-lost column, voting patterns looked much the same as in the banner year of 1936. (See Tables II-1 and II-2.) Democrats again did best in urban and industrial areas and among foreign-stock, labor, and low-income constituencies; they fared worst outside the cities and among Yankee and upper-income voters. The cities provided the key to the Democratic victory, for outside the five big cities Roosevelt's vote declined from 52 to 48 percent. In 1936 the President and Connecticut Democrats could have won without the big cities; in 1940, in Connecticut as in other urban states, they could not have. Even though Roosevelt's share of the vote actually fell more, from 69 to 63 percent, in the cities than in the rest of the state, the urban vote remained the Republican nemesis. Connecticut Democrats owed their 1940 victory to the continuing strength of the urban-based Roosevelt Coalition forged in the previous decade.[45]

Despite the continuity in voting patterns between 1936 and 1940, however, there were also important differences. Nationally, about one-sixth of the people voting for president in both elections voted for a different party in 1940 than in 1936. Most of them shifted from the Democratic to the Republican side.[46] Connecticut voting patterns also showed significant changes, generally paralleling those in the other urban-industrial states in direction, composition, and cause.

Roosevelt's share of the national vote fell off in all economic and occupational categories of voters, but it declined most sharply among upper-income, business, and professional voters. The result was a wider difference between the votes of rich

Table II-1. ELECTION OF 1940, CONNECTICUT: WARD-LEVEL STATISTICS[1]

	Hartford (N = 15)	New Haven (N = 33)	Bridgeport (N = 16)	Combined (N = 64)
I. Simple correlation coefficients for percentage Roosevelt				
A. Percentage Roosevelt 1940 with percentage Roosevelt 1936	+ .97	+ .91	+ .93	+ .93
B. Percentage Roosevelt with average monthly rent				
1940	− .84	− .68	− .76	− .66
1936	− .89	− .73	− .71	− .71
C. Percentage Roosevelt with percentage foreign-born				
1940	+ .85	+ .59	+ .65	+ .69
1936	+ .83	+ .75	+ .68	+ .77
II. Multiple correlation coefficients for percentage Roosevelt with average monthly rent and percentage foreign-born as independent variables				
1940	+ .94	+ .74	+ .89	+ .79
1936	+ .96	+ .86	+ .88	+ .87
III. Simple correlation coefficients for change in percentage Roosevelt 1936–1940 (percentage Roosevelt 1936 minus percentage Roosevelt 1940)				
A. With average monthly rent				− .35
B. With percentage foreign-born				+ .44
C. With percentage Roosevelt 1936				+ .47

[1]See Appendix for an explanation of the statistics used in this table. Tables A-1 through A-6 provide more statistics for each election from 1936 to 1948.

Table II-2. ELECTION OF 1940, CONNECTICUT: TOWN-LEVEL STATISTICS[1]

	All towns (N = 169)	Towns in Hartford, New Haven, and Fairfield counties (N = 79)
I. Simple correlation coefficients for percentage Roosevelt		
A. Percentage Roosevelt 1940 with percentage Roosevelt 1936	+ .94	+ .96
B. Percentage Roosevelt with average monthly rent		
1940	− .43	− .63
1936	− .32	− .55
C. Percentage Roosevelt with percentage foreign-born		
1940	+ .65	+ .71
1936	+ .61	+ .72
D. Percentage Roosevelt with total population		
1940	+ .38	+ .49
1936	+ .46	+ .52
E. Percentage Roosevelt with percentage rural-farm		
1940	− .34	− .44
1936	− .44	− .46
II. Multiple correlation coefficients for percentage Roosevelt		
A. With percentage foreign-born, average monthly rent, total population, and percentage rural-farm as independent variables		
1940	+ .80	+ .87
1936	+ .79	+ .85
B. With percentage foreign-born and average monthly rent as independent variables		
1940	+ .71	+ .84
1936	+ .64	+ .81
III. Simple correlation coefficients for change in percentage Roosevelt, 1936–1940 (percentage Roosevelt 1936 minus percentage Roosevelt 1940)		
A. With average monthly rent	+ .39	+ .25
B. With percentage foreign-born	− .19	+ .06
C. With total population	+ .16	+ .13
D. With percentage Roosevelt 1936	+ .04	+ .18

[1]See Appendix for an explanation of the statistics used in this table. Tables A-1 through A-6 provide more statistics for each election from 1936 to 1948.

and poor, indicative of continuing and perhaps even somewhat increased class consciousness.[47] Town-level returns suggest that the same pattern obtained to some degree in Connecticut. In seven of the eight counties, Roosevelt's vote correlated more strongly with low-rental areas than in 1936, and the President's losses tended to be associated with higher-rental towns. (See section III of Table II-2.) As he did elsewhere—in Westchester and Nassau counties in New York, for example[48]—the President had particularly large drops in affluent suburban towns. Thus in Fairfield County, Roosevelt's share of the vote declined at twice the state norm in high-income commuter towns like Darien, Weston, and Greenwich where Willkie had generated such an enthusiastic following since spring. Similarly, many of the towns in other counties with disproportionate Democratic declines, and some of the city wards too, were high-income areas.

But in Connecticut, as throughout the North and Northeast, ethnicity better explained deviations from the 1936 vote than did economic or occupational status. Roosevelt and the Democrats lost substantial ground in Italian areas and lost some Irish support, but they often gained in Jewish, French-Canadian, Scandinavian, and eastern European (especially Polish) constituencies. In New Haven and Hartford the vote divided less sharply along class lines than it had in 1936 chiefly because of lower-income Irish and Italian switching to the GOP. (See Table II-1.)

Italians left the Roosevelt Coalition in particularly large numbers. Roosevelt's share of the vote declined by twenty percentage points in New Haven's heavily Italian wards 10 and 11, and his losses in the most Italian areas of Bridgeport and Hartford, while less than in New Haven, significantly exceeded the average for those cities. (The especially large Democratic decline in New Haven's Italian wards doubtless owed something to the GOP's nomination of Celentano for mayor in 1939.) The President seems also to have lost substantial ground among Italians in the smaller industrial cities of western Connecticut. To be sure, the fears and hopes that Italians would vote overwhelmingly for the GOP did not materialize in Connecticut, as they did not elsewhere. Roosevelt carried by 54 and 56 percent respectively even wards 10 and 11 in New Haven, probably the most cohesive and self-conscious Italian areas in the state. But if Italian-Americans remained predominantly Democratic, an important strand of Roosevelt's 1936 Coalition had nevertheless weakened.

Continued strong and sometimes increased support from other ethnic groups helped to mitigate the impact of Roosevelt's losses among Italian and Irish voters. Scandinavian and black areas, for example, held up well for the President. More important numerically, at least in Connecticut, were the French-Canadians, Poles, and Jews. Roosevelt generally gained ground in the heavily French-Canadian towns of eastern Connecticut. In New Britain's Polish ward, the President won a thumping 88 percent, down just two points from 1936, and other Polish areas in the state also held up well for Roosevelt or gave him increased support. Similarly, Roosevelt's strength held firm in big-city Jewish areas and increased in small towns with large Russian (Jewish) populations.

Much of the change (and some of the continuity as well) in voting patterns stemmed from the war and foreign policy. True, domestic issues played a part in shifting votes—hence the Democratic declines in affluent areas. But vote switching arising from the European war, and especially from war-related ethnic concerns, was more important in Connecticut and elsewhere than switching arising from economic issues and class identification. Some isolationists and other voters who feared that Roosevelt would involve America in the war left his coalition or stayed out of it. Ethnic grievances deriving from the war, especially among Italians, caused substantial losses. The war also helped the President, for with the apparent imminence of American engagement Roosevelt's experience attracted new votes and retained old ones that might otherwise have gone to Willkie. Roosevelt's evident pro-Allied internationalism also helped him among some voters, in Connecticut the Poles, Jews, and French-Canadians in particular. Together, then, foreign and domestic concerns, the former especially,

89

caused significant changes in voting patterns from the 1936 election.

But however evident and important the changes were, the dominant aspect of the 1940 election returns was their substantial conformity to 1936 voting patterns. Nationally more than 80 percent of the people voting in both 1936 and 1940 voted for the same party in each election.[49] Analysis of aggregate totals by wards and towns in Connecticut suggests a similar stability. (See sections I and II of Tables II-1 and II-2.) Even more than the differences, then, the similarity between the 1936 and 1940 returns must be accounted for. The war, of course, played some part in freezing party allegiances. Party loyalty accounted for another portion of the continuity in voting behavior.[50] But the war's impact on voting can be overdrawn; and voting habits had undergone great change in the preceding decade, so that party loyalty—particularly among the new Democratic voters of the 1930s—probably was not yet so encrusted as to account for the results of the election. In 1938, certainly, voters in Connecticut and the nation had exhibited no overwhelming constancy to the Democrats. Rather than being shaped by partisan loyalty, the election of 1940 seems instead to have reinforced emerging party identifications and to have more firmly established the Democrats as the majority party.

The chief cause of persisting voting patterns, and thus of the Democratic victory, was the salience of domestic issues and Roosevelt's record in the politics of 1940. Voters do pay attention to, and make connections between, what they have experienced, what government has done, and what political parties and candidates seem to stand for. In 1940, the nation had experienced economic depression for a decade and the New Deal for nearly as long. The issues and party images stemming from that experience had dominated the campaign. Voting patterns, voter surveys, and national polls all pointed to the central importance of Roosevelt himself, domestic matters, and related partisan allegiances. War and foreign policy, though important to voting patterns, ranked lower in lists of reasons for favoring Roosevelt or Willkie.[51] Roosevelt's majorities in Italian areas provided one index of the continuing centrality of domestic economic issues and class lines as voting determinants. Though the state and nation prospered more than they had since the 1920s, most voters remained vitally concerned with maintaining recovery, achieving full prosperity, and, most important, ensuring economic security. Republicans—even Wendell Willkie and Raymond Baldwin—could not persuade the electorate that the GOP would protect the New Deal, protect jobs, protect security. Beyond that, the nascent recovery was identified with Roosevelt. Willkie ascribed his defeat largely to the defense-induced recovery, a factor that he said was "most evident in Connecticut."[52] Voting much as it had in 1936, and for many of the same reasons, Connecticut again endorsed the New Deal.

Yet the election turned on Roosevelt more than on the New Deal. Again in 1940 the Roosevelt Coalition—not the Democratic Coalition or even the New Deal Coalition—carried the election. After nearly eight active, controversial years in office, Roosevelt sought an unprecedented third term, and "emotions, for and against, reached their peak in intensity." Roosevelt remained "that man" to those who distrusted and even feared him and his policies; to more he was, as a correspondent to Baldwin put it, "the working man's hero." Those feelings, based on Roosevelt's domestic record and on the loyalties and antagonisms arising from it, helped account for the stability of the vote. Furthermore, the President's coattails remained long in Connecticut. Baldwin, the GOP's great hope there, finished slightly ahead of his slate, but he could not overcome the handicap imposed on all Republicans by Roosevelt and the state's party-lever rule. Baldwin's loss shocked the GOP, as did the defeat of the incumbent Republican congressman from supposedly safe Fairfield County. Among the Democrats, only Maloney, with his carefully tailored image, ran as strongly as Roosevelt. The results of the election in Connecticut, as in the nation, showed that Roosevelt's name retained its "vote-getting magic," and not only for the President himself.[53]

91

The election of 1940 showed one thing more. It revealed as well the cast of mind that would characterize wartime Connecticut and wartime America. Domestic issues and policies mattered more than foreign affairs. Security mattered most. To a majority of the people Roosevelt meant domestic security —recovery, jobs, federal aid if needed—and he also meant international security—peace, they hoped, but at least reassuring experience and pro-Allied internationalism. The concern for security stemmed largely from the events of the 1930s. That concern, and the emphasis on domestic matters, would persist in public attitudes and in politics through the war years.

III

POLITICS AS USUAL

Connecticut enjoyed its most bountiful Christmas in years in 1940. Cars jammed the streets, and shoppers, smashing holiday sales records, thronged merrily in downtown areas throughout the state. As "money streamed freely from pocket books into tinkling cash registers," people bought goods only dreamed about during the Depression decade. The war remained far off— and could for a time be put as far out of mind. Most Connecticut citizens rejoiced in their newfound plenitude.[1]

The cheer of late 1940 yielded to anxiety, frustration, and often anger in Connecticut and throughout the country during the next two years. Although the war changed recovery into true prosperity, it became plainer in 1941 that the boom brought a complicated and sometimes troubled sort of "good times." Then in December the Japanese attacked Pearl Harbor and the United States entered World War II. From the scenes of battle, Atlantic and Pacific, came little but grim news. At the home front, a host of new war-related problems unsettled and irritated Americans, and old ones lingered. Some groups— in Connecticut, blacks and Italian-Americans especially—had added burdens of their own. For all the yearned-for prosperity, the biennium was far from happy. The troubles, sourness, and prosperity of the society had their political ramifications; and in the election of 1942 they eroded the Roosevelt Coalition as Republicans in the state and in the nation made their best showing since before Franklin D. Roosevelt had captured the White House a decade earlier.

93

In 1941, like many other Americans, Connecticut's people had to adjust to real prosperity, and that proved more difficult than most would have thought during the 1930s. However welcome the new jobs and better pay of a burgeoning economy, they were accompanied by various growing pains and often by an inability to deal with new economic circumstances. The prosperity, though, was undeniable, particularly in Connecticut and other centers of war production. Still first nationally in per-capita defense orders, Connecticut's economy averaged a robust 63 points above the 1929 normal, nearly 50 points better than the 1940 record. As in 1940, the industrial advances translated into general economic gains. The state's employment index shot up from 34 to 90 points above normal, and income payments rose by 26 percent. With the economy booming, moreover, welfare and work relief rolls dropped precipitously.[2]

Old habits and old fears shaped Connecticut's response to its stunning economic growth. Despite the unprecedented demands and unparalleled expansion, for example, the state's economy still had considerable, often avoidable, slack. Government procurement agents continued to turn mostly to manufacturers with a known ability to turn out the desperately needed war goods, and a handful of large plants still monopolized defense contracts. Ridden with the fear of "sub-contractor today—competitor tomorrow," those prime contractors frequently built up backlogs while capacity elsewhere went untapped. To speed war production, to help small plants, and to preserve small, nondefense businesses threatened by war-spawned material shortages and priorities, the state and federal governments worked to get war contracts distributed more evenly. But the efforts brought small results.[3]

Manpower resources also fell short of full mobilization. Afraid that an insufficiency of workers, which by 1941 sometimes extended even to unskilled labor, might curtail federal defense orders, public officials and businessmen did move with more dispatch in this area. The continuing in-migration of workers, many of them recruited, provided part of the solution. But neither in-migration nor the many public and pri-

94

vate job-training programs provided workers enough for the state's prodigious industrial expansion. The state employment service thus worked hard to convince manufacturers to hire older and handicapped workers, members of minority groups, and especially women, potentially the largest source of new wage earners. Some employers did begin to reconsider and even revise their policies, but most were reluctant to change old practices. Women were also slow to adjust. Seeing their husbands bringing home more pay than in the 1930s, many became more selective about jobs, and some decided to resume full-time homemaking. Although the labor shortage did require some relaxation of hiring standards—men over forty, for example, found it easier to get jobs—biases against using women in production jobs and against hiring blacks, immigrants, and Jews proved harder to shake. As in subcontracting, so in employment, war production needs had yet to erode old patterns of economic life.[4]

Like the state's businessmen—in November, the Manufacturers' Association met in an "atmosphere tense with concern" about the seemingly endless problems of industrial mobilization —Connecticut's people learned in 1941 that prosperity, far from ending all their troubles, often bred new problems and new worries. Rapid economic growth brought not only more jobs and better pay but also an array of personal difficulties, such as troubled marriages, emotional strains, and juvenile delinquency. Prices rose rapidly—by some 9 percent in the twelve months ending November 1941.[5] Though income generally climbed faster than prices and though President Roosevelt had already requested price control legislation from the Congress, inflation was rankling. Wartime taxes threatened to eat further into earnings, and the unwelcome prospect of restrictions on consumption loomed ahead. Over all the irritations hung the specter of war and the dread conviction that bust would follow boom.

The latter was especially noticeable, involving as it did immediate, day-to-day patterns of living. Connecticut responded ambivalently to its new prosperity. As in other areas of life, attitudes rooted in the past determined responses to the defense boom. Though people eagerly sought defense jobs, worked as many hours as possible, and relished their higher incomes, they could not dispel a fear that the bubble would soon burst. Here Connecticut revealed anxieties and attitudes evident almost everywhere that defense spending changed hard times to good. Memories of the World War I boom-bust cycle and of the Great Depression kept economic worries alive; indeed, the very fact of the new war-borne prosperity seemed to a depression-conditioned people to spell virtually certain later collapse. In Connecticut, Bridgeport in particular provided a "case study in boom-town jitters," its people an example of prosperity "psychosis." Unable to forget hard times past, Bridgeporters prepared for the hard times ahead. Instead of indulging themselves, most people saved, or paid off debts and mortgages, or bought needed appliances and furniture. Fearing excess capacity, manufacturers expanded reluctantly and then wanted the federal government to underwrite risks. Bankers remembered their worthless real estate portfolios of the 1930s and hesitated to lend money for badly needed new housing. The municipal government, also afraid of overbuilding and fearful as well of increasing the city's bonded debt to finance new community services, moved slowly to accommodate the thousands of in-migrants.[6]

Gnawing uneasiness about changes in the society and about demands on the community arising from economic mobilization exacerbated defense-boom tensions. Arousing "fear and distaste" for a number of reasons, the 100,000 in-migrants who had poured into Connecticut from other states by mid-1941 lay behind such worries. For one thing, they threatened community stability and standards. Cities complained of an upsurge of vagrancy, drunkenness, and vice, and many feared new health problems. In Hartford, in-migrants complained of a "hand-shakeless community" ready to milk them of their money but not to answer their needs. Children from East Hartford's trailer camps were taunted as "trailer trash." Of all the newcomers, blacks were the most unwelcome. Even the

96

state department of labor imported Southern blacks to alleviate a farm labor shortage only as the "last resort" and stipulated that they return South once the season was over.

Economic fears compounded the unhappiness over in-migration. Workers and organized labor sometimes worried that manufacturers recruited out of state to depress the labor market and retard unionization. Because in-migrants typically lacked the skills most needed by Connecticut's factories, many wound up for a spell as reliefers. Long-range economic anxieties were stronger still. In-migrants seemed likely to glut the postwar labor market and to swell relief rolls. Too, a larger population would necessitate additional community services, which in turn would require bonding and an increased tax rate even if the in-migrants departed during the expected postwar slump.[7]

Such concerns and biases inhibited solutions to the problems arising from in-migration. Nowhere were the palling effects of past experience, of a reluctance to change, and of fears about the future clearer in Connecticut than in the state's response to its housing problem. Despite a perilously low vacancy rate that by the autumn of 1941 had fallen well below the "critical" level in the major cities, Connecticut's people from the outset opposed federal defense housing. Fearing higher taxes, instant slums, and a postwar housing glut, big-city mayors led the opposition. Their constituents applauded them. As taxpayers, Connecticut's citizens feared the effects of new services on their pocketbooks; as homeowners, they feared depressed property values and adjacent low-quality housing; as residents, they worried about the sorts of people who might live in the new developments. The vocal middle class in particular feared and resented any threatened change in their quiet, relatively homogeneous strongholds. The prospect that blacks might move into new projects and create a "Negro problem" proved especially worrisome.[8] Such attitudes persisted even as the housing crisis became more acute.

Yet the in-migrants did not suffer alone from the housing shortage. With that scarcity came rent profiteering, especially

97

in the lower-rental homes where in-migrant workers pressed hardest on the housing supply. Some rent hikes had as their purpose the driving out of large families so that the vacated rooms could be rented singly to war workers and landlords could reap larger profits. Other landlords simply evicted their old tenants or refused families with children, and distressing stories circulated of families separated because of their inability to find lodging.

Efforts by the state government to deal with the interrelated housing problems came to nothing. A 1940 commission established by Raymond Baldwin to study housing needs and to combat rent profiteering had little success, and new Governor Robert Hurley let the agency die. Not until July 1941 did the worsening situation and the possibility of federal action finally move Hurley to try to combat skyrocketing rents by establishing fair rent committees which would receive complaints, hold hearings, seek voluntary adjustments, and use publicity against recalcitrant landlords. But landlords seldom cooperated, tenants (fearing retaliation) rarely initiated complaints, and some fair rent committees were reluctant even to use their sole and tender weapon of publicity. With the housing shortage, the problems of rent raises and evictions grew worse.[9]

The strains of economic growth and the inability and unreadiness to cope with change evident in Connecticut in 1941 were by no means exceptional. Nor was the cold and disdainful greeting given newcomers, nor the reluctance even to house them decently. Throughout the war years, boom areas, indeed the nation generally, suffered an array of growing pains and social strains. Few people anywhere welcomed community flux and new faces.[10] Although the war eventually helped make the American people less divided and less parochial, the adaptation to change came hard and slow and was never complete. It took the full-scale emergency of American entry into the war and the plain necessity of at least coping with new patterns of life to bring such accommodation as there was by local government and the general public.

In Connecticut, old social mores, new wartime circumstances, and eventually some genuine progress especially characterized the experiences of blacks and Italian-Americans during the war years. The progress, though, came haltingly, even grudgingly; the difficulties were great from the outset. Long the victims of white prejudice and discrimination in every area of life, blacks in Connecticut as elsewhere found their position no better, and in some ways more frustrating, after the outbreak of the European war. For one thing, they continued to occupy the bottom rung of the economic and social ladder. Nearly four-fifths of the 7,000 employed Negro males in the state in 1940 held low-level service and blue-collar jobs; fewer than 200 held professional and semiprofessional positions, and a third of them were clergymen. Black women, overwhelmingly employed as domestic service workers, fared no better than the men in the job market. Public as well as private employers discriminated; Connecticut had, for example, one black fireman and two black policemen, and discrimination at all levels of government made blacks reluctant even to apply for public-service jobs. The black unemployment rate was twice that of whites. Nor did the pathbreaking special committee established by Baldwin in 1940 to study black employment problems bring much progress, and Hurley did little to follow up on Baldwin's initiatives. The employment committee expired, and the new governor temporized on requests that he ensure fair employment opportunities for Negroes and that he appoint to his new State Defense Council a black who might work to combat job discrimination in defense industry.[11]

Those requests might have won more urgent attention, for blacks were at first largely excluded from the state's industrial mobilization. As in the past, employers claimed that the sensibilities and prejudices of their white employees precluded hiring blacks. Pleading the possibility of friction between workers, United Aircraft, for example, hired no Negroes until the summer of 1941. Only after President Roosevelt's Executive Order 8802 forbade job discrimination in war plants and after a con-

99

gressional subcommittee aired the firm's hiring policies did United's Pratt & Whitney Engine Division begin an "experiment" with blacks in custodial jobs. Job-training programs, too, were discriminatory, and even Negro graduates of the 200-hour state training course had difficulty finding employment. One black man, able to get only "bullwork" despite a year of college and the completion of a technical training course, summed up the situation when he said, "I must have forgotten I was colored when I enrolled."

Still, blacks did begin to make limited employment gains. By the summer of 1941 the labor shortage forced increased hiring of blacks, even by firms which had never before employed them. From January to May Negro job placements in Connecticut were nearly three times greater than the year before, the highest percentage increase in the nation, while white placements rose only 77 percent. To be sure, blacks obtained mostly domestic, maintenance, and unskilled jobs; but if they seldom got better jobs than before, at least they got more jobs.[12]

While blacks' employment problems were acute but improving in 1941, their housing problems were acute and fast becoming worse. All the ills of Negro housing in the nation obtained in Connecticut. Blacks lived for the most part in cramped, dilapidated, overpriced, often unsanitary quarters in essentially segregated areas. So bad were conditions in New Haven that when a low-rent housing project opened in the black district, over half the city's black population applied. Even blacks who could afford to move from the ghetto met frustration. Real estate owners usually would not rent or sell to them, and Negroes had trouble obtaining mortgages when a seller could be found.

The war boom made things worse. Between 1940 and 1943, Connecticut's black population jumped by 50 percent (though only to some 3 percent of the state's population), and the newcomers could go nowhere but the already crowded ghettos. Both to supply needed accommodations and to earn welcome extra money, Negro families took in roomers. Already appalling conditions grew grimmer as Connecticut duplicated patterns evident in other areas where blacks migrated during the war. Horrible crowding often developed, as did related health and vice problems. Knowing that blacks could not find quarters elsewhere, landlords raised rents relentlessly and demanded unexplained extra payments. Bad as the housing situation was for whites, it was worse still for blacks.[13]

Besides exacerbating many black problems, the war helped illuminate the position of Negroes in Connecticut society. Discrimination in war industry and in the armed forces (Connecticut did protest Army quotas for blacks but not other forms of discrimination and segregation, and the state maintained its own lily-white national guard) seemed especially reprehensible in what was billed as a war for democracy. Like their counterparts throughout the nation, Connecticut blacks were stung by their exclusion from defense prosperity and by the denial of democracy in the defense effort. And like blacks elsewhere—as evidenced most vividly in 1941 by the March on Washington Movement, which forced Roosevelt to issue Executive Order 8802 and to create a Fair Employment Practices Committee—Connecticut Negroes made known their feelings and their determination to use the war as a catalyst for social change. Discrimination in war plants and in the armed forces took first priority, but blacks wanted a new day in many other areas as well. Young people were especially restive. Though more vocal than militant, blacks had by the end of 1941 begun more actively to decry injustices and to organize and agitate for change.[14]

For Italian-Americans, the troubles of 1940 persisted. There were growing protestations of Americanism and loyalty from Italians, but the questions of national identification and loyalty continued to roil the Italian-American community, and Mussolini's Italy retained its emotional hold on much of it. Reflecting such crosscurrents, the late-November organizational meeting in Hartford of the antifascist Mazzini Society proceeded "amid storm, stress, and comedy" caused by proponents of Mussolini and Italy. External pressures continued to exacerbate the internal stress. "I am an American Day" ceremonies held in May revealed societal worries about a hyphenated and possibly disloyal population, and investigations and sometimes detention of Italian aliens gave a hint of what might happen should war come. Job discrimination continued; indeed, some important firms refused to hire even second-and third-generation Italian-Americans. Resenting such practices, all the more because they had to answer draft calls, Italians demanded fairer treatment and sometimes caused disturbances at employment offices. Had they been polled, Connecticut Italians would have agreed with those in Boston's North End that the European war was not America's, that Italians had a much harder time getting jobs than did other people, and that American entry into the war would bring further discrimination. Still suspect in the eyes of others, partly because of their own indecision and divisions, Italian-Americans remained on the margins of Connecticut society.[15]

Municipal politics in New Haven and Waterbury reflected the social tensions. In New Haven, an Italian GOP leader persuaded 1939 mayoral candidate William Celentano, who many thought would again be the Republican standard-bearer, that an Italian would suffer at the polls because of Italy's part in the war. Celentano chose not to run, and Italian wards gave the GOP much less support than two years before, while Yankee areas voted more strongly Republican. In Waterbury different circumstances also showed how social antagonisms spilled over into local politics. Patrick Perriello, denied nomination by the GOP in 1939, won nomination for mayor in 1941. He won great support in Italian areas, but Yankee Republicans cut him badly and he trailed the ticket.[16]

Apart from the sparks struck by local ethnic issues and local personalities, Connecticut politics were dull in 1941. Revealing little more than the paramountcy of local issues, general indifference to politics, and continued Democratic hegemony in the cities, municipal elections came and went in the fall. Politicians concerned themselves largely with legislative and intraparty matters. Looking ahead, they also began groping for issues to use a year hence.

Governor Hurley, who would have to run in 1942 without benefit of Roosevelt's coattails, spent 1941 trying to develop an identity that would enhance his reelection chances. Lacking the personality and magnetism that helped make Baldwin such a formidable politician, Hurley, the onetime engineer and contractor, had consciously to build an image and a reputation he hoped would have wide public appeal. At first it appeared that he would run in the New Deal mold, as the successful champion of liberal legislation that he had piloted through the legislature. During the summer, however, he shifted his focus from liberalism to preparedness. With other politicians in Connecticut and elsewhere, he had evidently come to believe that because of the imminence of war political advantage lay in areas apart from New Dealish social programs, that as early as mid-1941 a worried but prosperous public was less interested in the ministrations of Dr. New Deal than in preventive medicine for the national security. Hurley consequently began to nurture a "too busy for politics" image and with appropriate fanfare devoted himself to matters involving defense and war. Concerning himself primarily with his special pride, the new State Defense Council, he worked assiduously to build a reputation as the "defense governor."

For his efforts, Hurley won a decidedly cool reception from many state Democratic leaders. As governors will, Hurley had tried to strengthen his position in the party by use of patronage appointments; but he proved heavy-handed and injudicious in his effort to control the party, and his patronage selections angered both the Maloney wing and the Old Guard. In addition, Senator Maloney and some others also took exception to Hurley's aggressive espousal of Roosevelt's anti-Axis foreign policy. Excoriating isolationists and calling for "all-out aid to the enemies of Nazism," the Governor went beyond the more careful views held by other state Democrats and by Maloney himself, cautious as ever about a substantive matter. Like the party's

103

factional troubles, the foreign policy differences were simmering quietly, but both threatened to boil over in 1942.[17]

Republicans, for a change, produced more intraparty fireworks than did the Democrats. Benjamin Harwood had resigned as state chairman just after the 1940 election, and after a fierce battle J. Kenneth Bradley, Baldwin's close friend and law partner, succeeded him. Bradley, of course, came to his new position with considerable experience in Republican politics; but he had been one of the leaders of the New Era takeover of 1938 and had once advocated "liberalism in large doses," and this background, together with his aggressive ambition, had earned him no little suspicion and enmity from the party's conservative wing. That he came from Fairfield County compounded his troubles with the anti-New Era group, for his accession to the chairmanship climaxed the New Era-Fairfield County drive for domination of the state organization. When Samuel Pryor, who became a vice president of Pan American Airways but remained very influential in state and national GOP circles, resigned as national committeeman in June 1941, Bradley also won election to that post—this time by unanimous vote of the central committee.

Despite its power, however, the New Era group could not impose its views about foreign policy, the great Republican dilemma of 1941. A struggle paralleling the one in the national GOP raged in Connecticut over a foreign policy stand. Like Wendell Willkie, whose increasingly outspoken internationalism had already begun to erode his support in the party, especially in the conservative, isolationist Midwest, Baldwin and Bradley strongly supported aid to the British. Heading the opposition to Willkie and his foreign policy ideas was Senator John Danaher, part of the 1938 New Era coup, who parted with his old allies on international affairs because of his vociferous, anglophobic isolationism. The foreign policy issue moved toward full-scale confrontation in the autumn, and it became all the more threatening to Republican strength when anti-New Era Republicans appeared poised to use it for factional ends. Seeking to resolve the matter, Bradley scheduled a meeting of the central committee for December 10 to thrash out foreign policy with Danaher.[18]

On December 7 came the Japanese attack on Pearl Harbor, and with it the American entry into World War II. Like other Americans, Connecticut residents reacted with shocked, angered confidence to the news of Pearl Harbor. Though stunned, people evinced scant doubt about ultimate victory, and through the ensuing days and weeks the state buttressed its defenses. The already organized State Defense Council saw its volunteer corps triple by February 1942, when it comprised one of every fifteen Connecticut residents. But the war remained far off, the immediate threats few and illusory; and by March the civil defense fervor had flagged substantially. Home-front Americans began to turn their attention to other matters and other worries. From the beginning, they found plenty to divert them from a single-minded focus on the war and its meaning.[19]

One thing that would engage them, at least more than in 1941, was politics. For their part, politicians anxiously tried to gauge the public mood as they scrambled for issues to use in the first wartime campaign in a quarter-century. Pearl Harbor at least helped clarify the foreign policy muddles of both parties. Bradley canceled the scheduled Republican parley, while the quieter Democratic dissension dried up. The anti-Axis internationalist positions of Bradley and Baldwin in the GOP and of Hurley in the Democratic party seemed vindicated substantively and strengthened politically. There remained nothing to debate about America's part in the war.[20]

For a brief season, in fact, the credulous might even have believed that the nation would hear no political debate in 1942. National chairmen Joseph W. Martin and Edward J. Flynn quickly concluded an agreement that Flynn's Democratic National Committee called "the most complete adjournment of domestic politics since the formation of the two-party system." The adjournment proved chimerical. In early January the GOP publicity director declared that Americans had the right and the duty to "engage vigorously in politics" during such a

105

national emergency. Shortly afterward, Flynn accused the Republicans of having more interest in controlling the House of Representatives than in winning the war, and he suggested that only a major defeat in battle would harm the nation more than a GOP Congress. Martin responded in kind. Clearly the nation would not lack partisan politics during the war.

Nor was there any chance that Connecticut politicians would abstain from their calling. Hurley changed easily from "defense governor" to "war governor." He still intended to campaign on his preparedness record, which he embellished just after Pearl Harbor by negotiating a no-strike "Victory Compact" between labor and industry. The Governor's strategy fitted in nicely with the "Support the President" campaign, already outlined by national chairman Flynn, which held that the necessities of prosecuting the war vigorously and of supporting Commander-in-Chief Roosevelt made a divided government hazardous. Hurley simply tied the tail of "Support the Governor" to the kite of "Support the President." Connecticut Republicans also took their cues from national leaders and sought to link politics with the war in a way helpful to them. Insisting that the two-party system was basic to American democracy, more so "in this time of national emergency than at any other time," they said that responsible partisan politics were necessary both to watchdog the war effort and to maintain the American way.[21]

A late-January special election in Connecticut's Fifth Congressional District provided an opportunity for both parties to elaborate and test the partisan positions already staked out. To general astonishment, GOP candidate Joseph Talbot handily carried the supposedly safe Democratic district. The consensus was that the election had been essentially a popularity contest in which Talbot, a young, personable man who had been active in local affairs for a decade and state treasurer from 1939 to 1941, held the advantage—all the more because he was Irish in an area where Irish Democrats had regularly drubbed Republicans. But whatever its causes, Talbot's surprising success greatly bolstered Republican morale. Demonstrating that Democratic appeals to "Support the President" were by no means invulnerable, it gave the GOP a new confidence and enthusiasm about its prospects ten months hence.

Beyond the cheer engendered by Talbot's election, moreover, Republicans had further cause for optimism. With Danaher and Baldwin formally reconciled after Pearl Harbor, though not so close as they once had been, the party had few worries about major disharmony. Baldwin was expected to run again for governor, and Republicans took heart from his personal popularity and from their belief that Baldwin's long-standing internationalism and his 1940 accomplishments in readying the state's defenses would undercut Hurley's principal issues. Most important, Republicans began to see that the war might actually help them. Errors and inefficiency in the war effort, they reasoned, would redound to their profit, particularly when accompanied by overt support of Roosevelt as commander-in-chief. Connecticut Republicans adopted a policy of "watchful waiting" to see what issues the year would bring them.[22]

The waiting ultimately paid off. War intensified some of the problems evident in 1940 and 1941 and brought new ones. Set backs abroad, production bottlenecks, shortages, rationing, and continuing social ills ranked highest. Yet the war also helped some problems toward resolution, while the relentless demand for war goods forced fairer patterns of production and employment. And as had been the case since 1940, the troubles and adjustments accompanied a return to full-fledged, indeed unprecedented, prosperity. The impact of World War II was complex in 1942 as in other years; still, in the atmosphere of 1942, problems were more apparent than successes, immediate concerns more salient than long-term ones, frustration and anger more evident than equanimity.

Pearl Harbor gave Connecticut's economy another strong kick—the business index averaged nearly twice the 1929 normal in 1942—and the still greater war production had sundry ramifications. Partly because of governmental efforts to spread contracts around more, the problems of small manufacturers diminished appreciably. In April, Hurley established a War Industry Commission (like the no-strike Victory Compact, the first of its kind in the nation—and with the Victory Compact, milked for its political appeal) which helped small businesses convert to war production and win defense contracts. Federal War Production Board contract distribution measures helped, too. But more important than such efforts were the sheer magnitude of orders to the state, the plain necessity of distributing contracts better to ensure maximum production, and the ease with which many Connecticut manufacturers could convert. Only Michigan, with its automobile industry, had a higher rate of conversion from peace to war industry. The state's economic health, especially a substantial rise in real wages, also helped Connecticut escape much of the troubled labor relations and work stoppages that plagued other areas. As still another consequence of the war boom, employment continued to mount and welfare rolls to shrivel. The general relief index (1939 monthly average = 100), which had stood at 62.7 as late as December 1940, fell to 9.2 by the end of 1942. In December, the Works Progress Administration employed but 928 workers in Connecticut, as compared with more than 13,000 two years before and with some 30,000 at its Depression peak.[23]

Like the improved contract distribution, the employment gains and welfare reductions resulted partly from more vigorous state action to meet war needs. As improving economic conditions elsewhere slowed in-migration to a trickle, as the draft stepped up its demands on the state's manpower, and as war orders continued to flood the state, Connecticut began more thoroughly to tap all possible sources of labor. Old people and teenagers found a variety of jobs, and the state pioneered programs to train and place handicapped workers and to have housewives and white-collar workers labor part-time in war plants. Women still seemed the likeliest source of new workers. But while the state employment service, now joined by the state Manufacturers' Association, continued to urge the hiring of women, many employers remained slow to cooperate. As before, women were also to blame for their underemployment.

Many married women quit old jobs or refused new ones in the mistaken belief that their being employed would cause their husbands to be drafted sooner. But as the year wore on and as employment needs became more manifest, the inertia began to yield on both sides. By year's end, women held an estimated 40 percent of the factory jobs in Connecticut, twice the prewar proportion. At United Aircraft, fully two-thirds of new hirings were women by November, and there as elsewhere women performed a widening array of production jobs—as riveters, of course, and also as operators of such equipment as lathes, grinders, and drill presses.

Clearly Connecticut had acted more vigorously than in 1941 to meet its need for workers with in-state labor. Here, then, was still another consequence of war production demands and still another example of how the war necessitated new public action and new private accommodations. But parallel with developments in other spheres, war needs themselves and the fear of losing new contracts proved more effective than a sense of equity, or than governmental action in bringing changed practices. And despite the year's efforts and accomplishments, Connecticut's labor requirements remained well in excess of supply, and employers remained reluctant to hire black and some ethnic workers. State action, better anyway at exhortation than at enforcement, had apparently reached its limit. By October, Paul V. McNutt, director of the federal War Manpower Commission, had designated ten Connecticut cities as labor shortage areas, and the possibility existed that further defense orders might be withheld because of the labor stringency. But while federal efforts were needed, particularly from the national perspective of meshing labor demand and supply, even New Dealer Hurley took exception to the prospects of wmc intervention in state affairs.[24]

The social problems evident in Connecticut and elsewhere in 1941 persisted and often intensified in 1942. Family strains, emotional ills, juvenile delinquency, and vice, troubles requiring in the main private, not public, solutions, seemed to grow worse. Nor did problems potentially more amenable to governmental action show progress enough to give much satisfaction to those ensnared in them. Inertia in public attitudes and inadequacy in public policy, especially at the local level, still prevented full and sufficient responses to the demands, dislocations, and difficulties of the war.

Housing remained woefully short. Indeed, in cities like Hartford and Bridgeport the situation grew increasingly acute, despite federal programs and slackened in-migration. In Hartford, for example, summertime estimates of additional housing units needed to avoid "disastrous conditions" ranged as high as 10,000. There and elsewhere, families of three and four people often lived in a single furnished room. Bridgeport's Housing Authority could have spoken for the rest of Connecticut when it reported that public and private efforts had "not at any time been sufficient to construct enough homes, even to provide mere shelter," for the in-migrants. More than that, as public housing came to focus almost entirely on war workers, efforts on behalf of nonqualifying low-income slum dwellers ceased. And the housing shortage contributed substantially to such other problems as crime, vice, health hazards, juvenile delinquency, and the disruption of family life.

State and local action on housing remained inadequate. Estimating that the state's industrial areas needed an additional 30,000 temporary units immediately, Governor Hurley at last named an Emergency Housing Commission in August; but the commission had no real authority and despite extensive study accomplished little. In the area of rent control, too, Connecticut's efforts were plainly unsatisfactory. In March, his patience with Connecticut's faltering efforts exhausted, Leon Henderson, head of the new federal Office of Price Administration, designated several major metropolitan areas as defense rental areas and gave them and the state sixty days to roll rents back to April 1941 levels. But rents and evictions continued to rise, faster than ever in fact, as many landlords made a final grab before the imposition of controls. By July, the entire state had come under federal rent control. Infuriated by the rollbacks and new regulations, which also protected tenants

110

from eviction, landlords fulminated, organized, and protested. The helpless fair rent committees and tenants welcomed federal control, as did Hurley in this case, and after the initial uproar the state seemed to settle into the new system.[25]

For Connecticut blacks, 1942 was another year of troubles; but it was also a year of gains, of both substance and spirit. The advances, minimal in proportion to the problems, came from war needs and black assertion more than from new white attitudes or governmental efforts to abolish Jim Crow practices. The old problems of economic and social discrimination continued. Indeed, manifestations of anti-Negro sentiment spread from the cities to small rural towns, where as elsewhere in rural New England strong opposition developed to importing black farm workers from the South. Residents feared a large influx of blacks, were afraid that the camps for black workers would be a "nuisance" and the blacks a social problem, and worried that blacks might not leave once the season was over. Of four camps proposed for Hartford County's tobacco areas, only one went into operation—and that one because the town involved protested too late.[26]

Negro economic prospects nonetheless continued to brighten a bit in 1942 as blacks increasingly found jobs in defense industries. Firms still did not train, place, pay, or promote blacks on an equal basis with whites, especially in skilled positions, but black men and women did gain more "dirty, heavy, hot jobs" on the production lines. Even such advances as those stemmed almost entirely from the labor shortage and the promotions given whites, with timely assists from the federal Fair Employment Practices Committee, for employers turned slowly and reluctantly to blacks, and the state government did little beyond exhortation.[27]

Blacks continued to protest their treatment and to point out the manifold injustices done them in the war for democracy. The wartime "Double V" theme—victory over the Axis abroad and over racial discrimination at home—of the national black press and black organizations characterized their efforts. As they worked toward victory at home, blacks began to get some

111

white aid. Church organizations, federal agencies, and even some state labor and political leaders campaigned against job discrimination. In New Haven, a large interracial group, paralleling one founded the year before in Hartford, was established to combat discrimination in housing, employment, and job training. Usually, however, blacks acted alone. The combination of lonely protests and little progress toward altering white attitudes and ameliorating conditions might easily have bred militant frustration with the war. Recognizing that, black leaders typically argued that for Negroes to advance they must demonstrate both loyalty and ability by doing whatever they could to forward the war effort. The "Double V" campaign, then, carried a message of loyalty and unity as well as of protest; it aimed not only at ending discrimination but also at combating black indifference and even hostility to the war effort which might worsen the position of black Americans. To that degree, protest activity and even militant rhetoric had a conservative and protective side. These apparently anomalous ideas—militance and conservatism, racial protest and national unity—all stemmed from the plight of blacks in the early war years. A psychological integration behind the war was seen as essential to progress toward economic and social integration.[28]

If for blacks 1942 was another year of mixed frustration and progress, for Italian-Americans it was a year of anguish and of the real beginnings of Italian assimilation into the mainstream of American life. Pearl Harbor forced resolution of the old questions of divided attachments and loyalties. At once, "Americanism" became the central theme of Italian newspapers and organizations. The Italian-American World War Veterans of Connecticut even considered dropping the word "Italian" from their title. Unity, duty, sacrifice, and victory were the supporting subthemes of Americanism. Seizing the "opportunity to prove that their loyalty to State and Nation is equal to anybody's," Italians demonstrated as well as declared their devotion to America. Record numbers sought citizenship as one way to show their allegiance, and in New Haven three-fifths as many citizenship applications were filed in January 1942 as in all of 1941. (Discrimination against aliens in war industry accounted for part of the surge.) Hartford's Italian district responded warmly to an "East Side is on the V Side" rally. Bridgeport Italians formed an "I Love America" committee, sold thousands of "I Love America" buttons, and held a mass rally in support of the war effort. Throughout the state Italian-Americans bought war bonds and stamps, served in a variety of civil defense activities, and contributed their men in disproportionate numbers to the armed forces. Italian-Americans did not, to be sure, want entirely to submerge their Italianness in a homogenized Americanism. Thus the Italian-American World War Veterans decided to retain their name intact, and a speaker at Bridgeport's "I Love America" rally called the United States an "orchestra" not a "melting pot." But if Italian-Americans did not want to renounce their origins, they nonetheless made it clear that "Italian" was the modifier, "American" the basic noun. America's entrance into the war had for them decided the long troublesome questions of identification and loyalty.[29]

Ultimately, that decision helped speed the substantial integration of Italians into American society, but at first the United States seemed to rebuff the reaching hand of its Italian population. Just after Pearl Harbor, President Roosevelt designated Japanese, German, and Italian aliens as "enemy aliens." That status involved a number of restrictions on possessions (including short-wave receivers and cameras) and on personal movement. Further, enemy aliens were liable for apprehension, restraint, and deportation, and they had to possess special identification with photograph and fingerprint. Citizenship applications were held up.

Italians feared that much worse might be on the way, and not without some reason. In urging Italian aliens to register, officials emphasized that noncompliance could bring apprehension, detention, and even internment. That warning lent itself to misinterpretation and did little to allay the fears of "drastic action" against Italian-Americans by the government. Then in April 1942 an immigration official said that an evacu-

113

ation of aliens from strategic East Coast areas, patterned on the Japanese removals in the West, was "about to take place." Despite denials, rumors of a mass evacuation persisted through the summer. Such extreme actions never materialized against Italian-Americans, of course, nor did the ugly nativism that had disgraced the United States in World War I. Still, a number of disquieting episodes occurred. Alien checkups and round-ups, often involving Italians, began after Pearl Harbor and lasted through the year, for example, and wide publicity was initially given Connecticut's only case of "sabotage" when an obviously unstable second-generation Italian-American from New Haven damaged a lathe used to make gun barrels. Pasquale DeCicco, popular acting Italian vice-consul in New Haven for two decades, was arrested, stripped of property, and interned as "an enemy alien dangerous to the public peace and safety of the United States." However mild and occasional by contrast to the treatment of the Japanese, these incidents and others surely proved unsettling to Italian-Americans, already more visible than ever because of the war and still, partly because federal security regulations were misinterpreted, the victims of job discrimination.[30]

Connecticut Italians, aliens and citizens alike and of all generations, keenly felt and deeply resented the enemy-alien designation and the harassment and discrimination it produced or reinforced. Particularly galling in view of their declarations and demonstrations of loyalty, especially the sacrifice of their kin for America, was the stigma attached to that status. The enemy-alien designation seemed an unnecessary and unjust policy which served only to degrade Italian-Americans and to prevent them from taking their rightful and desired place in America. Throughout the year, while the administration sought to explain and justify the enemy-alien policy, Italian-Americans worked to have the odious designation changed. Championed in Washington by Senator Theodore Green of Rhode Island, the movement for a new policy gained momentum in the autumn. The day-to-day life of Connecticut Italians nonetheless remained strained. More FBI raids of Italian homes came early in October. Columbus Day proved as drab and quiet as in 1940.[31] But the Roosevelt administration, politically attuned as ever in an election year, had taken note of the feelings of Italian-Americans and had decided on a change of policy.

War also brought new troubles to the general population. At the home front, the management of the war effort produced a variety of discontent. The Office of Price Administration, the most prominent of the new alphabet agencies, won special and widespread disfavor. Part of the displeasure stemmed from the OPA's surprisingly successful price control program, worked out in its essentials in 1942. Disliking federally imposed ceilings in any event, farmers and businessmen wanted higher prices than they were allowed, while landlords rarely lived happily with rent control. A related source of resentment against administration anti-inflation measures involved wage and salary controls. Organized labor in particular chafed under hourly wage restrictions, even though longer hours and overtime pay brought significantly higher weekly wages. Still, the wage-price stabilization programs were obviously necessary to keep wartime inflation within bounds, and OPA price controls helped many more of Connecticut's people than they aroused. The other part of the OPA program—rationing—caused much more unrest.

Rationing was of course necessary for price and production controls to work and work fairly. Most Americans realized that and at least in principle accepted OPA rationing. But acceptance in principle did not always mean approval in practice. Despite the OPA's efforts, which improved with practice, to devise fair and effective policies, rationing from the outset produced confusion, hoarding, cheating, black markets, scandal, and bitter complaints about unfairness and red tape. The rationing of autos, tires, and sugar, all begun in the first half of 1942, quickly fell into that soon familiar pattern.[32]

But in Connecticut as in other states, gasoline rationing provoked the most inflamed public response in 1942. For one thing, people felt that they and other Easterners had been un-

115

justly put upon. Not until December did gasoline rationing extend nationwide, and meanwhile tales of abundant supplies elsewhere grated. For another, restrictions on gasoline (and tires) challenged "every American's sacred right to drive an automobile as fast and as far as he liked." Even during the Depression Americans had considered driving one of life's necessities, and with the return of prosperity Connecticut drivers had used record amounts of gasoline. Driving, moreover, manifestly was a necessity, not just a pleasure, in Connecticut. Only 10 percent of the state's industrial workers got to their jobs by way of the inadequate public transportation system, and many drove long distances. The war, in fact, increased commuting (and helped make Connecticut more suburban), for the urban housing shortage prevented many of the new workers in big-city war plants from settling in the cities. On top of all that, the involved gasoline rationing system, seemingly forever in flux and part of the equally confusing and exasperating rubber problem, proved susceptible to confusion, unfairness, and spectacular scandal.[33]

For a variety of reasons, then, the public responded to gasoline rationing with special vehemence. Yet that reaction was but a heightened expression of the unhappy response to rationing programs in general. People simply disliked controls on purchases and consumption. They especially disliked such restrictions when they again had money to spend after a decade of depression and deprivation. The desire to compensate for the recent past, to turn wartime prosperity into a consumers' paradise, would last throughout the war, but it was particularly intense in 1942. The attitude was in ways typified by the many New Britain housewives who barely a month after Pearl Harbor believed that their inability to buy all the sugar they wanted ranked as the "most acute result" of the war.[34] However unheroic, such frustrations were at least understandable among a people tired of doing without, addicted to consumerism and to advertising images of the good life, strained by wartime tensions, and, since there was not in America the total mobilization of resources, energy, and spirit of other nations, supplied both with money and time to devote to material goods.

The antipathy toward OPA came also from the way programs were implemented. Many people believed that controls were neither equitable nor efficient. Nor indeed did some programs —sugar and gasoline rationing, for example—always seem even necessary to a public often bombarded with rumors and hazy official explanations. Bureaucrats—those "propaganda-mad crackpots" who conceived "cockeyed ideas" in "irrational thoughtfests"—drew the special ire of conservatives and Republicans for the inefficiency, red tape, and general confusion of jurisdiction and policy that marked many infant programs. For many people, Leon Henderson, the brash, impolitic head of OPA, served as the symbol of his agency's ills. And more rationing was on the way. Along with the rest of the nation, Connecticut turned cranky over a meat shortage in the summer and the prospect of a formal meat rationing program by early 1943. Coffee was scarce by summer's end, and rationing began in November. To meet an anticipated fuel shortage, a program which aimed at a one-third reduction in fuel-oil usage began in October and provoked new complaints of discrimination against their region from New England governors.[35]

Though the OPA was the most unpopular, because the most immediately felt, of the war agencies, and often the lightning rod for public discontent, others earned their share of opprobrium. The American "miracle of production" occurred only after and in spite of a fumbling, disjointed beginning. From the National Defense Advisory Council through the Office of Production Management to the War Production Board, established in January 1942, Roosevelt tried to order and speed America's industrial mobilization. Shakedown difficulties, clashing personalities, the differing views and concerns of government, business, and the military, and an inadequate priorities system hindered the effort. Seeming chaos sometimes followed. Slowly, perhaps imperceptibly to most citizens, the government began to bring matters under control; and despite all the problems, the production of war goods mounted inexorably. Within a year of Pearl Harbor, the United States was producing as much as the Axis nations combined. Still, the chief feature of 1942 was confusion and inefficiency, not order and solution. Perusal of the newspapers told any reader that.

News from the war fronts was even more unsettling, for there the battles were fought, the men killed, the ground won or, more often in 1942, lost. Like events at home, the military actions of 1942 may have been part of "the year that doomed the Axis,"[36] but they hardly seemed so at the time. Through the year's first ten months Americans read of stalemate at best, of humiliating defeat at worst. While his U-boats ravaged the Atlantic, Hitler remained master of Europe and threatened to extend his hegemony into Russia's heartland. Disquieting reports came from the Pacific, too. That clearly was America's war; just as clearly, it was going poorly. In the half year after Pearl Harbor the United States suffered an alarming series of reverses as it desperately sought to halt the Japanese. Finally in May, at the Battle of the Coral Sea, and in June, at the Battle of Midway, the Japanese were checked in their drives south and east. But the public did not perceive the significance of Midway, the turning point of the Pacific war. Not until August did the U.S. Navy take the offensive, when it opened the long and savage contest for the Solomons. The war did not take a clear turn for the better until just after the November elections, when victory at Guadalcanal in the Pacific and the Allied invasion of North Africa started the Allies toward victory. Before that, however, the progress of the war created, if not quite fear, at least uneasiness, dissatisfaction, and a desire to get on with it.

Whether in newspapers or radio broadcasts, then, or in their own personal experience, Connecticut citizens like other Americans found little to cheer in 1942. Even the booming prosperity, which might have taken the edge off many problems, did not quite translate into the bounteous life they wanted. The various troubles at home and abroad, moreover, nearly all seemed part of the same root problem: the management of the war effort. And that, as Republicans had known from the outset, had obvious political importance. In Connecticut, corroboration came in the spring when GOP successes in New Britain and Norwich municipal elections evidently stemmed at least partly from public unhappiness with the war effort and home-front conditions. The Republican tactic of watchful waiting had turned up the strategy for the coming campaign.[37]

Fully to exploit the public disenchantment, Connecticut Republicans naturally wanted the strongest possible state ticket. Most of them wanted it headed by Raymond Baldwin. To their dismay, Baldwin delayed until June his announcement for another try at the governor's office. As he would in subsequent years, Baldwin before his declaration spoke of devoting more time to his family and his private life; but 1942 was not the time for personal desires to override public service, and in any event Baldwin had promised his family two years before that he would win the governorship back. Baldwin's delay and public indecision probably stemmed instead from a desire to enhance his own position in the party by letting public pressure build for him to run again. He had, to be sure, no strong opposition, for even those at odds with the New Era group easily perceived that Baldwin had that essential political virtue: exceptional personal strength at the polls. Nevertheless, some in the party's regular, conservative wing remained cool to the former governor, and over the summer he carefully mended his fences with them.

At the September state convention, Baldwin faced only the brief, futile opposition of a candidate sponsored by the Bridgeport delegation. Arising from antipathy among Bridgeport GOP leaders to the New Era leadership, the opposition to Baldwin was connected with a bitter contest for the Fourth Congressional District (Fairfield County) nomination. Baldwin and state chairman J. Kenneth Bradley had settled on Clare Boothe Luce, the well-known, quick-witted, and attractive playwright and the wife of *Time* publisher Henry Luce, for the nomination. Opposing her was Vivien Kellems, a wealthy industrialist allied with disgruntled conservatives in Bridgeport who resented the power and the policies of the New Era group. Claiming that Baldwin and Bradley had turned over control of the state GOP to moneyed New Yorkers, Kellems and her Bridgeport allies charged more specifically that the support given Clare Luce by Baldwin, Bradley, Samuel Pryor, and others was simply payment to her husband for his substantial contributions to Willkie's 1940 campaign and that she was just a pawn of the Republican power brokers. The campaigns against Baldwin and Luce proved more acerbic than effective, and they collapsed in the end. Baldwin was nominated by acclamation at the state convention, while Clare Boothe Luce received 84 of the district convention's 86 votes in becoming the first woman nominee for Congress in Connecticut's history. But although the attempted rebellion failed badly, it served as a reminder that the New Era group, whose domination of the party machinery owed much to Baldwin's great popularity in the state, still had opposition.[38]

The Republican slate-makers picked a carefully balanced ticket to complement Baldwin. Ethnic groups received particular solicitude. The renominations of Boleslaus Monkiewicz for congressman-at-large and Francis A. Pallotti for attorney general took care of Polish and Italian representation. Irish-Catholic William Hadden of West Haven got the nomination for lieutenant governor, which Republicans hoped would win over anglophobic and anti-Communist Irish Democrats disaffected by Hurley's fervent and long-standing advocacy of aid to Great Britain and Russia. A woman (whose Italian in-laws were deemed an asset) was slated for secretary of the state, while the other spots fell to the party's rural and legislative blocs.

Substantively, the convention focused on the war effort. In the keynote address, Clare Boothe Luce accused Roosevelt of having waged a "soft war" and argued that "the only political issue of any importance today is: who wants to win the war and how quickly." Alleging partisanship and "bungling and muddling" in the war effort, she pilloried as well the administration's handling of the whole range of domestic matters that so irritated the public. The platform also lambasted the management of the war, and hitching an old horse to their war wagon, Republicans called theirs an "American platform." But the war itself dominated Luce's keynote speech, the platform, and indeed the entire convention. "Our business is war!" boomed the first sentence of the brief GOP platform; "Winning the war is the sole objective. . . . " Bradley put his party's plea tersely and plainly: "We are the Victory Party, elect us." Confident of the strength of their ticket, issues, and organization, Republicans felt sure they would be the victory party on the first Tuesday in November at least.[39]

At their convention, the Democrats routinely nominated their incumbent state officers, with the exception of state treasurer Anastasio, who had joined the Army. Selecting a replacement for him produced the only disharmony at the unusually placid convention. With a nervous eye to the Italian vote, especially in New Haven, the New Haven organization and Italian Democrats insisted on New Haven County jailer Nicholas Mona for treasurer. Hurley and others objected to Mona on the grounds that his sole qualification was his Italian background, but without the power to get their way they eventually acquiesced in his nomination. The slate included the now customary Pole, Italian, and woman, though for the first time in years only one Irishman—Hurley—graced the Democratic ticket, and the party actually had more old-stock nominees than did the GOP.

In substance and mood the Democratic convention contrasted with the Republican meeting. The platform, probably the most liberal in Connecticut history to that point, was given over almost wholly to a comprehensive state program. Unlike the Republicans, who pointedly excluded promises in a time of national peril, the Democrats promised something for almost everyone. They promised labor most of all. The platform was firmly rooted in the New Deal past, and given the concerns and the prosperity of 1942 as well as the tenor of the GOP appeal, it was anachronistic. Evidently suspecting that, and clearly worried about how the war might affect voting, the

121

Democrats did not show the "bubbling optimism" of the GOP. Too, their organization was "sleepy" and "inept," and the ire of many Democrats about Hurley's patronage disbursements threatened further to impair the campaign effort, especially in the cities. The Democrats faced an uphill fight, one made all the more daunting by the abstention of their champion campaigner, Franklin D. Roosevelt, who kept himself away from overt politicking.[40]

In the absence of a presidential or senatorial race and with the congressional candidates coming late to the hustings, the gubernatorial candidates monopolized the Connecticut campaign at the outset. They helped give it a predictable and virtually inevitable cast, one forged both in the politics of the 1930s and in the events and political sparring of the first war year. Trying to exploit Roosevelt's magic name and the public concern about the war, Hurley rang all the changes on the "Support the President" and the "War Governor" themes he had sounded through the year. The basic issue, he maintained, was "who can best help our Commander-in-Chief, President Franklin D. Roosevelt, prosecute the war successfully?" Not, he declared, the obstructionist Republican "propagandists of pessimism" who had hindered all that he and Roosevelt had done and who could "offer nothing but criticism and opposition at a time when strength and unity are essential prerequisites of victory." The Governor did not, however, neglect what he held to be the bedrock differences between the two parties. He said the election also concerned "security and well-being" and pitted "penny-pinching reaction" against the "forces of liberalism and progress." Liberal measures were important not only to build morale and help win the war but also to help the "plain people" and to ensure the postwar "peace of security and prosperity" that the people wanted.[41]

Baldwin made the war his central issue. As he had throughout the year, he charged that "politics as usual" had impaired the war effort in the state and in the nation and that in Connecticut Hurley had only continued, with too much partisanship and delay, what Baldwin himself had begun in 1940. While pledging full support to Roosevelt as commander-in-chief—for "We are Americans before we are Republicans"—he continually criticized the war effort and promised a more vigorous, more efficient, less political prosecution of the war. Baldwin did not ignore the domestic side of Hurley's campaign, and the symbol of New Era Republicanism repeatedly spoke of the "new, liberal, forward-looking, progressive Republican Party" and its achievements in Connecticut. But like Hurley, even more so, he related home-front needs and programs to winning the war. Not only must the government do all it could to solve the housing crisis and the many other problems vexing Americans so they could maximize production, but a vigorous, efficient war effort was needed to win the war and thereby preserve both the American way of life and the American standard of living.[42] An advertisement nicely reflected Baldwin's basic appeal to the electorate on the war issue:

> LET'S STOP THIS FUMBLING. Let's give the working man the break he needs, and go to town for victory. ONE MAN ALONE has proved he can do the job . . . Raymond E. Baldwin. *You know* he will see that rationing is fair to the man who's doing America's job. *You know* he will give your women and children a decent place to live. *You know* he will see that POLITICAL high-jinks do not take away your hard-earned wages in privilege-inspired taxes.
> A vote for Baldwin is a vote for VICTORY.[43]

Once under way in October, the six congressional campaigns largely followed the channels charted by the gubernatorial contest. GOP candidates focused mostly on the war effort and lambasted the Roosevelt administration. All voiced particular concern about what Clare Boothe Luce called "that wasteful, procrastinating, bungling and fumbling arsenal of bureaucracy which has been reared in Washington." Besides botching the war effort, Republicans asserted, the inept bureaucrats had produced shortages and inequitable rationing arrangements which caused unnecessary hardships at the home front. Republicans said they would rectify matters and speed victory.

The GOP's congressional candidates, more in the regular

123

mold than Baldwin, also worried loudly about Democratic
threats to the American Way. A few warned about Communist inroads in the Democratic party and in organized labor,
and some again perceived the threat of "dictatorship." By
electing Republicans and reestablishing a strong two-party
system and an independent Congress, the people could at once
straighten out the management of the war and preserve traditional American ways. Failing a Republican victory, said one
GOP congressional nominee, the war might be used "as a cover
under which to destroy either our American system of government, our American way of life, or our American free enterprise economic system."

Still, the war dominated the Republican campaign. Having
lost before when Roosevelt and the New Deal were made the
central issues, and possessing a different and they believed
winning issue in 1942, Connecticut Republicans like those
elsewhere attacked the New Deal only peripherally and hammered at the management of the war. The war and the concerns of 1942 had provided what seemed an opportunity for
political victory unequaled since the late 1920s, and the GOP
did not want to squander its chance.[44]

In the face of the Republican offensive on the war issue,
Connecticut Democrats like their counterparts in other states
found themselves "on the psychological defensive." Though
they perforce claimed, despite news apparently to the contrary,
that the administration had managed the war well, their chief
tactic was to urge support of the President and to label the Republicans obstructionists. But since the "Support the President"
theme had evident weaknesses given the facts of the war and
war mobilization, Democrats tried as well to freshen their image as the party of liberalism and the common people. They
warned that the reactionary, negative GOP would undo the
New Deal, and as proof they cited Republican campaign calls
to curtail social "theories," "experiments," and spending that
diluted the war effort. When Republicans quickly made it
plain that they opposed only new programs and unnecessary
spending, not "facts" like the Wagner Act and other entrenched

124

and popular New Deal measures, Democrats simply labeled that and Republican pledges to support Roosevelt as deceptive lip service and continued their strident warnings.[45]

But the Democratic campaign fitted neither the realities nor the mood of 1942. If the "Support the President" call was of doubtful potency, the New Deal issue was of doubtful relevance in the prosperous autumn of 1942. The Democrats' inability to devise an effective campaign lay not with their strategy makers but rather with the year's events and concerns. It lay, that is, with immediate and salient issues that the Republicans had not created but had recognized and exploited. The war, its management, and associated home-front problems were simply the basic features of 1942 life. Democrats could neither profit from the war by stressing the "Support the President" issue nor ignore the war by emphasizing the New Deal—and yet those seemed, along with constant invocations of Roosevelt's name and an effort to "stretch the President's coattails over" into 1942,[46] the likeliest Democratic tactics. That the Democrats were cornered was revealed by the fate of other potentially important issues that got nowhere. Each party gave general assurances about postwar foreign and domestic policies—about postwar peace and prosperity—but those pledges seemed obligatory, not pressing, they received little attention, and they were so vague as to be vacuous. The war was at hand and needed to be won; the postwar era seemed far off and could wait. Nor at a time of unity behind the war did attacks on prewar isolationists get far. If Democrats tried harder with such themes, that, like their emphasis on Depression-decade issues, stemmed from their problems with current ones.

Yet even those current issues seemed not to arouse the public. From beginning to end the campaign in Connecticut, as in the nation, seemed awash in apathy. Here was still more evidence that the Democrats had little chance of shaping the campaign to their needs, and more evidence, too, of the influence of the war on the politics of 1942. Off-year elections customarily, of course, generate less interest and attract less attention than presidential campaigns, but in 1942 the war and war news made reaching the electorate especially difficult. Besides riveting the public's attention, the war dampened the campaign in other ways. People worked longer hours and had less time for politics. Prosperity made politics, based on economic issues for a decade, seem different and in some ways less important. Party headquarters had less available manpower because of war jobs, absent servicemen, and transportation restrictions. War restrictions eliminated metal campaign buttons, cardboard buttons did not catch on, and little campaign literature circulated. Few major rallies were held, and those attracted few people. A GOP rally in New Britain featuring Baldwin typified the fate of others; it attracted only seventy-two people, mostly party workers. Clare Luce did draw generally good crowds, but that seemed attributable more to curiosity about a famous and glamorous personage than to interest in politics. What was probably the largest rally in the state in 1942 told much the same tale. A turnaway crowd packed Falcon Hall in Polish New Britain for a Democratic rally—because the Polish-American hero of the recent World Series, Whitey Kurowski, was on the platform.

So unsuccessful were most rallies—even free food and refreshments could not ensure a crowd in 1942—that one local leader admitted they were held chiefly to get newspaper coverage. Indeed, both parties, especially the well-financed GOP—leaned heavily on the media in 1942. Yet war news usually eclipsed the campaign in the dailies. Perhaps for that reason radio found special favor. Each party had a radio specialist, and candidates relied on radio to reach the voters. War seemed to be speeding the old-fashioned rally to the fate of torchlight parades.[47]

Because the war so overshadowed and inhibited politics, both parties reserved most of their energy for the last few weeks and sought to spark interest by appealing to specific groups on the basis of special concerns and interests. Democrats courted labor with exceptional ardor—and with apparent success. Despite the assurances of GOP congressional candidates and despite Baldwin's advocacy of several new or expanded programs, in-

126

cluding a long-sought state labor relations act, labor leaders supported Democratic candidates with unusual unanimity. Worried that long working hours and late factory shifts might prevent a large labor vote, they also importuned Governor Hurley to extend voting hours, and Hurley, who shared that concern, called a special session of the General Assembly which decreed that the polls should be open from 6 A.M. to 9 P.M. Still, such efforts did not mean either that the rank and file would get to the polls or that once there they would vote Democratic, especially since labor's support of the Democrats consisted more of rhetoric than of active grass-roots political activity.[48]

Both parties worked hard to corral the votes of the state's many ethnic groups. But while the usual array of ethnic rallies was held, the rallies suffered from the diminution in size and number that afflicted all political gatherings in 1942. Further, the specific foreign policy issues of 1940 that had so concerned the principal ethnic groups were absent or much diluted. In general, ethnic politics, like the campaign overall, had nothing like the intensity of two years before.

Only the effort to capture the Italian vote involved a crucial ethnic issue the enemy-alien designation. In a nationally broadcast Columbus Day address, Roosevelt's Attorney General, Francis Biddle, announced that Italians would be removed from the enemy-alien list effective October 19. Biddle called the changed policy "the exoneration which [Italians] have so well earned." Surely it was. There had been virtually no evidence since Pearl Harbor of Italian-American disloyalty and much proof of their American patriotism. The Columbus Day action of the American government served in fact as formal acceptance of the loyalty Italian-Americans had manifested, of the Americanism they had declared and demonstrated. It was a basic milestone in the assimilation of Italians into American society.[49]

But for all the social importance of the changed policy, it served patently political ends as well. Roosevelt had denounced Italy in 1940, and suffered for it politically; and his enemy-alien policy had stigmatized Italian-Americans in 1941. Now

127

on the great Italian-American holiday, fortuitously a month before the election, his administration embraced Italians as loyal Americans. Democrats hoped to profit from the gesture. Hailing it, New Haven's Congressman Shanley aptly termed it "a pluperfect recognition." Hurley, "overjoyed," also praised the new policy, said he had long urged it, and within ten days added his own fillip: a special four-man committee (including one Italian) to help "the thousands of loyal Italian aliens" get war jobs.

Republicans, too, welcomed the substance of the new policy, but their own political needs led them to criticize its timing and motivation. Not only was it long overdue, they declared, but it only ratified what everyone had long known and what the GOP had long said. Accusing the administration of crass political maneuvering, of "politics as usual," they rehashed the critical words and actions visited upon Italians since 1940 by Roosevelt, and they attacked Hurley for lack of patronage recognition of Italians and for his opposition to Nicholas Mona's candidacy for state treasurer.[50]

For their part, Italians reacted with joy and gratification to Biddle's announcement. Beneath the happiness, however, ran an undercurrent of bitterness at what New Haven's William Celentano called the "great weight" that had pressed upon "both Italian non-citizens and . . . Americans of Italian extraction." The very effusiveness of their reactions showed how deeply the stigma and restrictions of the "despicable designation" had hurt Italians.[51] Roosevelt had changed the enemy-alien policy; but he could not erase its memory or that of the "stab in the back" speech. Again in 1942, Republicans threatened to make substantial inroads into Democratic strength among Italian voters.

Candidates also tried to win the votes of other potentially important blocs that had altered or novel political importance in 1942. Both parties took particular pains to appeal to women, more crucial to politics in 1942 than ever before because of the absence of so many men. The election was, Hurley said, "more than any other in our history . . . a woman's election." But though the war was obviously causing at least a temporary change in women's roles, the messages usually directed to women reflected traditional views about the role and concerns of women. Thus Hurley told how the Democrats were looking out for "our boys" away at war and were sponsoring social legislation in which women had special interest. Women candidates were more likely to emphasize women's needs and abilities in economic and political life, but there were few such candidates, and women were typically addressed as the guardians of family health, welfare, and morality.[52] Still, the social changes under way by 1942 had at least given heightened political importance and thus heightened political attention to women. In this way, as in so many others, politics reflected the culture.

Blacks, too, seemed to receive more attention than in the past. As with the women, this stemmed in large degree from wartime developments, though in the case of blacks politicians spoke more to rising social aspirations. Both party platforms denounced racial discrimination. Democrats even advocated a fair employment practices committee, and in an "unusual" and perhaps unprecedented move a black seconded Hurley's nomination. When a prominent black minister from Hartford was beaten by whites on a train in Alabama, Baldwin, Hurley, and other politicians quickly joined in the condemnations and contributed to a special legal assistance fund. On October 21, Hurley appointed an emergency committee on job discrimination, and a day later he attended induction ceremonies for the first black unit in the Connecticut National Guard. Recounting his own efforts for Connecticut Negroes, Baldwin criticized Hurley for not continuing those initiatives or taking action of his own until the campaign. Connecticut blacks, more numerous than in the past, more assertive, and possibly pivotal in a close election, were winning increased solicitude from office seekers.[53]

Two more groups got considerable attention from the politicians: absentee servicemen and in-migrant workers. Connecticut servicemen were thought to be two-thirds or more Demo-

129

cratic, and Democrats worked hard to contact them and help them obtain absentee ballots. But few GIs seemed interested, and confusion about the different federal and state absentee ballots complicated matters. In-migrants also showed little interest in voting in Connecticut, although most of the 100,000 or more met the one-year residency requirement. Partly because of a recanvass of voting lists, registration actually fell for the first time since 1930, despite in-migration and despite normal population growth. The big cities had the greatest registration losses—losses which suggested the failure of Democrats and labor to mobilize their constituencies.[54]

The registration falloff, and extraordinarily light voting in the October town elections, pointed as well to the political apathy that political analysts everywhere noted in 1942. Because of the likelihood that low turnout would hurt Democratic candidates more than their opponents, the evidence of apathy worried Democratic leaders. This concern about stay-at-home Democrats led Roosevelt's political advisers to persuade the President to make a last-minute appeal for voters to exercise their right and responsibility of the franchise and for employers to grant paid time off for workers to vote. But the President's entreaty came late, was little more than a gesture, and could scarcely assuage the worries Democrats everywhere had about such other political problems as the war news, home-front troubles, superior GOP organizations, and Roosevelt's abstention from partisan politics. Having the added burden of facing a Republican ticket headed by Raymond Baldwin, Connecticut Democrats were far from sanguine about their chances.[55]

The returns bore out the Democrats' fears. As part of the best GOP showing in a national election since 1930, Connecticut Republicans captured every statewide contest, all six congressional races, and control of both houses of the General Assembly. Some observers thought the election had reversed the Democratic trend of the past decade;[56] at least it demonstrated anew that the Democrats had no iron hold on Connecticut politics and that Raymond Baldwin, who had the largest Republican plurality, remained his party's greatest asset.

The Republican victory, however, was impressive more by its completeness than by its size or by any great disruption of voting patterns. The election saw neither the rout of the Democratic party nor the undoing of the Roosevelt Coalition. Winning but five percentage points more of the vote than in 1940, Connecticut Republicans polled only some 52 percent of the state's major party vote—results closely in line with those in the other northern industrial states and in the nation generally. In Connecticut, the GOP captured three of the five congressional districts with less than 52 percent of the vote. The state's voting patterns were sticky, too, and strikingly like those of 1940. At the ward level, the congressman-at-large votes for 1940 and 1942 correlated at +.95; at the town level, the correlation was +.93. (See Tables III-1 and III-2 for further statistics on the 1942 vote.) The returns, then, told two stories: on the one hand, the GOP had reversed the Democratic triumph of 1940 and swept the state; on the other, the share of the vote and the sources of support for each party had changed relatively little.

Not only did the voting patterns closely follow those of the previous election, but such changes as there were did not go far toward pinpointing the reasons for the Democratic setback. Again depending mostly on urban and industrial areas and on lower-income, foreign-stock, and working-class voters, Democrats simply saw their support eroded virtually everywhere. Within the cities, Democratic strength declined somewhat more in Democratic, low-income, and ethnic areas and tended to hold up better in high-income and Yankee wards. (See Table III-2, sections I-Aa, I-Ba, and I-Ca.) Apart from that, and the effects of local factors in some areas, urban voting changes from 1940 lacked clarity and consistency. As one example, Democrats lost still more support overall among Italians; but in New Haven's most Italian ward the Democratic percentage dropped more than six points, well above average for the city, while Hartford's most Italian area had an average

131

Table III-1. ELECTION OF 1942, CONNECTICUT: WARD-LEVEL AND TOWN-LEVEL STATISTICS FOR THE DEMOCRATIC VOTE[1]

	a. Ward level				b. Town level	
	Hart-ford (N = 15)	New Haven (N = 33)	Bridge-port (N = 16)	Com-bined (N = 64)	All towns (N = 169)	Towns in Hartford, New Haven, and Fairfield counties (N = 79)

I. Percentage Democratic congressman[2] 1942 with:
A. Percentage Democratic congressman[2]

	Hart-ford	New Haven	Bridge-port	Com-bined	All towns	Towns counties
1940	+ .99	+ .96	+ .86	+ .95	+ .93	+ .94

B. Percentage Roosevelt

1940	+ .98	+ .95	+ .84	+ .95	+ .92	+ .93

II. Percentage Democratic[3] with average monthly rent

1942	− .75	− .67	− .68	− .63	− .35	− .46
1940	− .84	− .68	− .76	− .66	− .43	− .63
1936	− .89	− .73	− .71	− .71	− .32	− .55

III. Percentage Democratic[3] with percentage foreign-born

1942	+ .89	+ .49	+ .47	+ .61	+ .58	+ .72
1940	+ .85	+ .59	+ .65	+ .69	+ .65	+ .71
1936	+ .83	+ .75	+ .68	+ .77	+ .61	+ .72

IV. Percentage Democratic[3] with total population

1942	—	—	—	—	+ .38	+ .52
1940	—	—	—	—	+ .38	+ .49
1936	—	—	—	—	+ .46	+ .52

V. Percentage Democratic[3] with percentage rural-farm

1942	—	—	—	—	− .37	− .50
1940	—	—	—	—	− .34	− .44
1936	—	—	—	—	− .44	− .46

[1]See Appendix for an explanation of the statistics used in this table. Tables A-1 through A-6 provide more statistics for each election from 1936 to 1948.

[2]At the ward level, the vote for district congressman is used for individual cities; for combined wards and for town-level analysis the vote for congressman-at-large is used.

[3]For 1942, the vote for congressman is used as explained in note (2) above; for 1940 and 1936 the vote for Roosevelt is used for wards and towns.

Table III-2. ELECTION OF 1942, CONNECTICUT: SIMPLE CORRELATION COEFFICIENTS FOR DEMOCRATIC DECLINE AND TURNOUT DECLINE, 1940–1942[1]

	a. Ward level[2]			b. Town level[3]		
	Bridge-port (N = 16)	Hartford and New Haven (N = 48)	Com-bined (N = 64)	Fairfield County (N = 23)	Fairfield, New Haven, and Hart-ford counties (N = 79)	All towns (N = 169)
I. Decline in Democratic percentage of vote for congressman-at-large, 1940–1942, with:						
A. Average monthly rent	− .17	− .37	− .31	− .30	− .35	− .12
B. Percentage foreign-born	+ .23	+ .41	+ .36	− .15	− .11	+ .05
C. Percentage Democratic 1940	+ .23	+ .39	+ .35	+ .13	+ .06	+ .04
D. Turnout 1942 divided by turnout 1940[4]	.06	.21	.17	.02	.10	.10
II. Turnout 1942 divided by turnout 1940 with:						
A. Average monthly rent	+ .01	+ .22	+ .20	− .18	+ .02	− .06
B. Percentage foreign-born	+ .34	− .22	− .15	− .43	− .20	+ .16
C. Percentage Democratic 1940	+ .16	− .31	− .24	− .08	− .06	+ .14

[1]See Appendix A for an explanation of the statistics used in this table. Tables A-1 through A-6 provide more statistics for each election from 1936 to 1948. Turnout by wards measured by total vote for governor in 1940 and 1942; turnout by towns measured by total number counted by registrar as voting in 1940 and 1942.

[2]Bridgeport data given separately because the third-party (McLevy) vote was heaviest there.

[3]Fairfield County data given separately because the third-party (McLevy) vote was heaviest there.

[4]The negative coefficients in this row indicate an equal and positive correlation between turnout decline and Democratic decline.

133

Democratic decline and Bridgeport's a Democratic gain. Results at the town level spoke still less precisely about the dynamics of the Democratic decline. (See Table III-2, sections I-Ab, I-Bb, and I-Cb.) Democrats lost ground in small towns and big cities, in industrial and farming areas, in high- and low-income towns, and in ethnic constituencies of all varieties, and at much the same rate everywhere. In all, the returns revealed little more than widespread Democratic losses, disproportionately heavy in urban Democratic areas.

Some analyses held that those Democratic declines in their big-city bastions were the basic cause of the party's defeat. The Democrats won just 58 percent of the combined major-party vote of the five largest cities, a share down some five points from 1940 (see Table A-2); and that was a critical drop, for it so eroded the Democrats' big-city pluralities that Republican town support was sufficient to give the GOP state and congressional candidates their margins of victory. But since the Democratic share of the vote fell slightly more outside the big cities than within them, the reduced Democratic urban strength, however critical it was, did not of itself wholly explain the election's outcome or fix the source of the Democratic setbacks. Again, voting patterns pointed instead to a general Democratic decline.

If socioeconomic characteristics and geography did not explain the Republican advances, neither in 1942 did the third-party candidacy of Bridgeport Mayor Jasper McLevy. Running slightly ahead of his ticket, McLevy won just 34,500 votes, or 6 percent of the total cast for governor. Though McLevy's total was greater than Baldwin's 26,000-vote plurality and though his ticket-mates polled a few thousand votes more than the winning margins of the other statewide GOP nominees, statistics indicate, and contemporary analysts agreed, that the Bridgeport Socialist vote for statewide offices did not cost Democratic candidates the election. Only in the Fourth Congressional District, moreover, did a Bridgeport Socialist candidate figure in the election, although there, in Fairfield County, he may have attracted enough normally Democratic votes to allow

134

Clare Boothe Luce to win. But while McLevy and his slate may on balance have hurt the Democrats, they evidently did not hand the election to the GOP. Still less did they provide the basic reason for the general Democratic decline.

There was, however, yet another feature of the election returns—low turnout. Only 583,000 people voted in Connecticut, as against 789,000 in 1940 and 637,000 in 1938. Just over 69 percent of the registered electorate voted, down 20 points from 1940 and the lowest percentage since 1926. Nationally, too, turnout fell precipitously, as it plummeted from 50 million in 1940 to only 28 million in 1942. At the national level, the turnout decline seemed fundamental to the results. Seeking to explain why the GOP had done so much better than he had predicted, George Gallup immediately fixed on the strikingly low turnout as the most important aspect of the election. He attributed the turnout drop to the fact that millions of servicemen, migrant war workers, and apathetic, primarily low-income citizens had failed to vote. Most of those nonvoters were Democrats, Gallup said, and he ultimately concluded that had turnout been at the 1940 level the results would also have been essentially the same as in 1940. Gallup's account of the Republican gains was accepted and even embellished by others and quickly came to be the standard interpretation of the election's outcome.[57]

In Connecticut, many political analysts and chagrined Democrats shared Gallup's conviction that low turnout had been decisive. They had good apparent reason to do so, quite apart from the concurring analyses of the national results. Democrats had carried the state rather narrowly in 1940 with the help of Roosevelt's campaigning and coattails—precisely the sort of circumstances that would make them vulnerable to diminished support via turnout decline in the succeeding off-year election, particularly one in which the war so overshadowed politics and made it all the more likely that less motivated and involved "marginal" voters, predominantly Roosevelt Democrats in the era, would not go to the polls. Beyond that, the specific circumstances and impact of the much reduced voting

135

in Connecticut seemed to favor the GOP in almost every way. Not many of the state's 80,000 registered servicemen, overwhelmingly Democratic according to one survey, cast absentee ballots. Few of the in-migrant factory workers, presumably Democrats, voted, and a heavy election-morning rain and the extensive commuting by war workers probably reduced the usual labor vote. Nor did the Democrats have, either from labor or from their own disaffected and warring city organizations, the sort of intensive grass-roots effort so important in mobilizing voters, especially marginal voters in a midterm election that lacked Roosevelt's allure as well as salient economic issues. Even new 1941 registration laws apparently militated against them by removing many more Democrats than Republicans from voting lists. Finally, the returns themselves seemed to indicate that Republicans had gotten out more of their usual supporters than had the Democrats. A variety of evidence, then, supported the view that low turnout was the key to the election in Connecticut.[58]

Yet whatever the situation may have been elsewhere in the nation, the reduced turnout no more than partly accounted for the Democratic losses in Connecticut. As section I-D of Table III-2 indicates, the correlation between turnout decline and Democratic decline was quite weak both by wards and by towns—about .2.[59] And if the reduced turnout among the state's usual voters had little effect on the election's outcome, neither did the failure of the in-migrants to vote necessarily hurt the Democrats very much. Though many of these people were industrial workers from Democratic areas, many came to Connecticut's war plants from the largely Republican farms and towns of northern New England and upper New York State.[60] And no matter where they came from or how they usually voted, few of the in-migrants could have been pleased with their reception in Connecticut, especially with regard to housing. To the extent that they had their own special resentments, the in-migrants probably spent their hostility against the national, state, and big-city Democratic administrations.

Their failure to vote in significant numbers was by no means the certain Democratic hardship so often supposed.

Turnout seems then to have been but one factor affecting the 1942 election in Connecticut, and almost certainly not the crucial one.[61] Reflection on recent elections in the state—those of 1938, of 1940, and of January 1942 in the Fifth Congressional District—might have dissuaded Connecticut political observers from giving too much weight to the turnout factor. In 1938, Democrats had lost substantial ground from their 1936 landslide; yet while turnout fell sharply, the Democratic losses had rightly been attributed to the various state and national problems associated with the Cross and Roosevelt administrations, to the strengthened appeal of the rejuvenated and more progressive Republican party of the New Era group, and to McLevy's third-party spoiler role. Then in the election of 1940, Roosevelt's share of the vote had fallen some four points from 1936, nearly as much as the Democratic decline from 1940 to 1942; yet between 1936 and 1940, turnout had risen, not fallen. Similarly, Democrats fared worse in the Fifth District in November 1942 than they had in January despite a much larger turnout in November.

As those examples suggest, the simple turnout explanation suffered from ignoring long- and short-term political forces and from assuming a stable division of the electorate from election to election. Many voters switch between virtually every election, and marginal voters, predominantly Democratic in the period, were precisely the ones most likely to be affected by current conditions and short-term partisan forces. Had more of the nominally Democratic stay-at-homes voted, in other words, they might well have voted Republican. And national survey data did in fact indicate a significant, if not huge, amount of switching from the Democrats to the Republicans between 1940 and 1942.[62] The Connecticut returns suggest a similar story of voter switching to the GOP. The pattern of the vote was close to but not identical with that of 1940; Democrats lost ground virtually everywhere, with turnout decline explaining very little of the loss; and big-city data show Democratic losses to have been mildly associated with Democratic areas. Such findings imply some general factors working on the electorate at large, somewhat more strongly in Democratic areas, to cause switching and thus the Democratic decline.

Explanations for such a shift are not hard to discover. For one thing, Roosevelt was not on the ballot and did no campaigning. Besides diminishing the vote, the absence of Roosevelt from the Democratic campaign, together with the wartime prosperity, evidently helped Republicans shake loose newly made "Depession Democrats" and "Roosevelt Democrats" from the Democratic coalition. That would help explain the disproportionate Democratic losses in low-income and ethnic urban areas. Also, with Roosevelt off the ballot, most attention focused on the gubernatorial race—an important Republican advantage because of Baldwin's great popularity and the special Connecticut party lever rule.

But the most important factor in the election, as Connecticut Republicans had anticipated since early in the year, was unhappiness with the management of the war. Candidates of both parties, from Connecticut as from elsewhere in the nation, certainly thought so.[63] The long, dreary year of setbacks abroad and problems at home cut into Democratic strength virtually everywhere. And the apathy, supposedly so important to the Democratic downfall, was not always what it seemed. In one of the countless articles discussing political indifference in 1942, a Connecticut political reporter told of a barber who said that people were talking about the war and rationing and other war-related matters instead of about politics;[64] but in fact those were potently political issues, crowding the front pages and being exploited by the GOP. Even if voters ignored the campaign or were not reached by it, the worries and irritants remained, and they were obviously associated with the Democratic party. Beyond switching 1940 Democratic votes to the GOP column, moreover, the anxiety and anger of 1942 probably also produced cross-pressures among normally Democratic voters which many resolved simply by not going to the polls. The decline in turnout, in other words, may have stemmed importantly from purposeful abstention because of cross-pressures as well as from simple apathy; and had nominal Democrats so affected voted, there is no assurance that they would have voted Democratic in 1942. The troubles of 1942, in short, greatly aided the Republicans and constituted the principal factor behind their advances.

Of the war issues, those involving the home front were probably most important in the Republican gains. Had the successful Allied invasion of North Africa and the American naval victory at Guadalcanal come before instead of just after the election, Democrats might have done better. Yet home-front problems and grievances—confusion in Washington, shortages, controls, taxes, apparent inequities, and above all OPA—seemed to political analysts and politicians to bother people more than the early reversals at arms. Added to those general problems were the special war-related grievances against the administration of various groups, the Italians for example, which surely added to the anti-administration vote. Apathy, weak efforts by party and labor organizations, and the concomitant low turnout may have diminished the Democratic vote in 1942, but the problems, dissatisfaction, resentment, and even the prosperity of 1942 reduced it much more. The sour discontent of an again prosperous but frustrated and sometimes angry and worried people was translated into politics, to the detriment of the party in power.

The election of 1942 was a signal success for the GOP, not alone in Connecticut. Republicans did well in gubernatorial races, but the party's most impressive advances came in the congressional elections. Making its best showing since before the New Deal, the GOP picked up 47 seats in the House to pare Democratic control to 222-209 and gained ten places in the Senate. Local personalities, issues, and circumstances bred sometimes significant variations from state to state. Turnout was perhaps more important in other states than in Connecticut. Still, the main features of Connecticut's 1942 politics—Roosevelt's political abstention, weak Democratic organizations, prosperity, and especially the war news and home-front problems—evidently shaped the results throughout the nation.[65]

As in Connecticut, which had more congressional seats go over to the GOP than any state but Ohio, the Republican gains often came at the expense of staunch liberals. As a result, the new Congress would be dominated by a conservative, Southern Democrat-Republican coalition. Despite some analyses to the contrary, however, the election did not denote a rejection of the New Deal or an ideological shift to the right. There had been little real liberal-conservative dialogue in the campaign, nor had the New Deal itself been the point at issue. The election, despite gains by more conservative candidates, was not a mandate for conservatism. Again the main fact about the 1942 election was that it turned on anger, frustration, irritation, worry—not on ideology as not on turnout. The war was the main cause of the Democratic setbacks.

Nevertheless, the effect of the war on Connecticut and national politics should not be overstated or misunderstood. The war caused neither a massive, despairing rejection of nor a unified rallying behind the Democratic party. Although the electoral verdict changed, the overall shift was not great and the pattern of the vote did not depart much from that of previous elections. The war, itself essentially a political issue exploited for partisan ends, altered political appeals more in context and impact than in substance. Thus Democrats tried once more to capitalize on Roosevelt and the New Deal, but found to their distress that Dr. New Deal, little needed, attracted fewer clients than before, that Dr. Win-the-War seemed a quack, and that neither came to the aid of the party's candidates. Republicans, who had criticized New Deal bureaucracy and inefficiency in past elections, could use the management of the war instead of relief and reform measures to buttress their argument. To their great profit, "bureaucracy" in 1942 evoked images of OPA,

140

not WPA. The war did not even eclipse the political salience of domestic affairs. In tone, tactics, focus, often in content, and in basic voting alignment, politics in 1942, in the midst of a terrible war going badly for the nation, had indeed largely been "politics as usual."

IV

PROSPERITY AND PEACE

The Politics of 1944

The sourness that had marked the first war year subsided in the next biennium. People learned to live with wartime frustrations they could do nothing about and to cope better with the problems and flux of wartime society. While the national government improved its management of the war effort, Connecticut and its citizens more actively addressed state problems requiring action. Abroad, the reversals in battle of 1942 changed into what seemed an inexorable tide of victory. At home, the beneficial economic and social fallout of the war continued. Yet the discontent, the aversion to change, and all the problems of 1942 by no means vanished; and by 1944 still other worries had gained eminence. For the society as a whole, the central and overriding anxieties involved postwar prosperity and peace. Born of the harrowing experiences of the interwar and war years, a desire for security, both domestic and international, increasingly preoccupied the public —and its policy makers and politicians. Coming when victory seemed at hand, the campaign and election of 1944 were nicely timed to reflect the concern about peace and prosperity in the postwar era.

Despite a general mellowing of 1942's dyspeptic mood and a growing concern about large future problems, wartime irritations, opa foremost, continued to exercise Connecticut's people in 1943. The impact of shortages and rationing peaked in the first part of the year. The long-anticipated fuel shortage combined with a season of New England's severest weather to produce a harrying winter of critically low fuel supplies and emergency programs to conserve and distribute them. Not until the return of good weather in March did the crisis ease; but as motorists soon learned, petroleum remained short, and the OPA reduced gasoline rations and restricted pleasure driving during the summer. Cutting travel well below the already-reduced figures of the previous year, the much-violated regulations aroused predictable and widespread resentment. Nor did the public respond with equanimity to new controls affecting eating habits. First came rationing of most canned and processed food; then came meat rationing, perhaps the most unpopular of OPA's programs, since a good T-bone seemed as inviolable an American right to many home-front citizens as did a spin in the car. "Meat hungry crowds," shoving and mauling, stormed the meat markets in late March to buy up the last of the unrationed meat, and shortages, the rationing program, and resulting black markets provoked continuing hard feelings. Returning home during a late-summer recess, Connecticut congressmen like their colleagues elsewhere were besieged with complaints about OPA and other home-front vexations.[1]

But while 1943 sometimes seemed like a reprise of 1942, the public attitude toward rationing and the OPA slowly changed, or at least softened. As people adjusted to rationing and credited OPA with success in combating inflation, the public mood veered from condemnation toward understanding. Some groups, labor and consumer organizations chief among them, even gave the agency vocal support. Restrictions on spending and consumption never proved popular, but they gradually became familiar and accepted parts of wartime life. The obvious need for such programs together with better administration helped mute angry outbursts, as did no doubt the feeling of real participation in the war effort that discomfort and minor sacrifice gave home-front Americans.[2] By 1944, moreover, future concerns drew more attention than did present frustrations.

But even though the wrath over restrictive government programs abated, the disenchantment of the first war year had continuing and important consequences. The 1942 elections

143

had sent to Washington a conservative Congress dominated by a coalition of Republicans and Southern Democrats. Obsessed with "bureaucracy," the "Republocrat" conservative coalition was determined to roll back New Dealism. Even before Congress met, the politically sensitive Roosevelt had ordered the end of the Civilian Conservation Corps and the Works Progress Administration. The new Congress went on to abolish the National Youth Administration, cripple the Farm Security Administration, attack the Rural Electrification Administration, and enact over the President's vetoes the anti-labor Smith-Connally Act and the regressive 1943 Revenue Act. While attending to the postwar needs of business, the Congress refused to expand, even for the postwar period, various social security programs. As its "biggest prize," Congress killed the National Resources Planning Board, which had proposed the most advanced and comprehensive programs the legislators rejected. Connecticut's new Republican congressmen, sometimes joined by Senator Francis Maloney, gladly participated in the conservative harvest. One of them happily reported that it was "very near the truth" that Congress was winding down the New Deal.[3]

In their efforts to prune or even liquidate the New Deal, the new congressmen surely exceeded their rather narrow 1942 mandate. Yet few of their constituents, in Connecticut as in the nation at large, seemed to care. It appeared to some contemporaries, indeed, that mid-war America had turned sharply to the right—hence the 1942 GOP gains and the 1943 conservative successes in Washington.[4] The truth was as usual more complex. Americans in 1942 had voted against apparent mismanagement of the war effort and related anxieties and annoyances, not against the New Deal; and the acquiescence in the conservative record of the new Congress did not signify a new and fundamental anti-New Deal sentiment in the country. What the apparent—and indeed partly real—conservative resurgence of 1942 and 1943 mirrored was a desire for streamlining the wartime government where possible and a general feeling that relief and reform measures were unnecessary or misdirected. Immediate frustrations counted more for the mo-

144

ment than old programs to assist the relatively few remaining impoverished people or than new programs to provide help should hard times return. The congressmen probably represented fairly the mood of a prospering citizenry concerned more in 1943 about winning the war and enjoying newfound affluence than about domestic reform and expensive legislation that seemed to help others. But that hardly meant that the voters were as anti-New Deal as the men and women they had sent to Washington. Indeed, it was revealing that the Congress attacked in the main measures that had small and politically weak clienteles—blacks and small farmers, for example—rather than such measures as the Wagner Act or Social Security which had widespread support. From 1943 on, moreover, the people and their elected representatives turned their attention more to combating present problems and preparing for future ones and less to flaying dead horses and straw men. To be sure, the late war years did not witness a return of a 1930s-style reformist mood; but neither did they simply continue the sourness of 1942 or bring the triumph of anti-New Deal conservatism.

The increased willingness to grapple with problems, and also the limits of that willingness, was evident in Connecticut, where Governor Baldwin in 1943 acted differently from his fellow Republicans in Congress. Anxious to combat wartime troubles and to prepare for the postwar future, he requested emergency executive powers, a new and expanded War Council to supersede Hurley's Defense Council, and special commissions on housing, postwar planning, and interracial problems. Some who had supported Baldwin protested that he and other Republicans had been elected by voters "tired of bureaucracy . . . and spendthriftiness" and that Baldwin's proposals would mean more of both.[5] That response, of course, reflected the continuing small-government conservatism of regular Republicanism which marked so much of the state and national GOP. But Baldwin's program was consonant not only with public needs and opinion but also with much orthodox Republican thought. Baldwin shared the GOP conviction that under Roose-

145

velt the federal government had grown far too powerful. He encountered opposition from conservative Republicans because his progressive (and politically astute) outlook balanced an insistence on states' rights with a lively sense of states' responsibilities.

The General Assembly eventually enacted most of Baldwin's requests. Although the legislative session was marked by shameless politicking—in full control for the first time since 1929, Republicans grabbed all the patronage they could—and although Democrats, liberals, and conservatives all criticized the new programs for one reason or another, the General Assembly accomplished more of potential merit than its many detractors conceded. The commissions on housing, interracial problems, and postwar planning involved areas of great importance for the present and future, while the new state War Council had more powers than its predecessor, Hurley's Defense Council, and used them in wrestling with war-spawned economic and social problems.[6]

Nevertheless, the new agencies often suffered from limitations of purpose and perception. If they reflected the growing desire to meet problems, they reflected as well the tendency evident since 1940 to be fearful of rapid change, wary of new departures, solicitous of entrenched habits and interests. The new State Housing Authority provided a good example of such shortcomings. Meeting initially in July 1943, several months after its creation, the Authority took as its first priority determining whether new housing for in-migrant workers was needed. Two months later it reported that sufficient units were built or being built, and thereupon decided to focus on plans for disposing of emergency projects and aiding large-scale privately-financed postwar construction. Disposition, said the state housing administrator, was "the most serious problem to be faced."

The Housing Authority's conclusions arose less from reality than from a continuing antipathy to federal projects and from persistent fears about a postwar housing glut and postwar slums. Vacancy rates did rise a bit during the biennium, but

they hovered near 1 percent and reflected neither severe overcrowding nor the large backlogs of applicants and desperately
short housing conditions reported by some local housing authorities. The chief threat of postwar slums, moreover, lay not
in the war housing but in the tens of thousands of substandard
and decaying prewar dwellings that urgently needed rehabilitation or replacement, and the major housing problem of the
postwar period would be to provide a sufficient number of decent and affordable accommodations, not to dispose of the
war projects. Connecticut's population increased substantially
during the war (10 percent by 1943), and many of the in-
migrants who had contributed to that growth would remain.
Returning veterans and their families would generate still further housing demands. While deferred demand and wartime
savings together with a more suburban population seemed
likely to touch off a postwar building boom, that promised little help for the state's rundown central cities or for people
without financial means to satisfy their needs or their aspirations. The State Housing Authority, then, was a needed beginning toward resolving Connecticut's housing problems; but it
became mired in the same inertia, fear, excessive localism, and
narrowness of vision that had inhibited housing programs from
the outset of the war. Not until October 1944 did the Housing
Authority even begin action on what it rightly called the "imperative need for a comprehensive picture" of Connecticut's
housing situation.[7]

Jobs caused more worry and focused more attention than
did housing. There were two areas of concern: the continuing
need to find more workers for defense industry and the growing anxiety about finding enough jobs after V-Day for Connecticut's hundreds of thousands of veterans and displaced
war workers. The former problem, insoluble by recruitment
efforts, led to often unpopular federal War Manpower Commission controls. The latter spurred myriad public and private
planning endeavors, chief among them Baldwin's Post-War
Planning Board. In both its aspects, the concern about employment revealed important wartime patterns and attitudes.

147

The effort to find workers enough for Connecticut's war industries remained intensive and imaginative in 1943 and 1944. Teachers were recruited for summertime work and white-collar workers for part-time labor; women were sought still more actively than before, and child-care arrangements and better sanitation measures were adopted to help attract or retain women workers; elderly, handicapped, and minority-group workers won more attention. Despite such efforts, however, labor demand remained far in excess of supply; despite those efforts, indeed, the manufacturing labor force actually fell from a peak of 503,000 in March 1943 to 423,000 in September 1944. The decline stemmed largely from in-migrants returning home to take up new war jobs and from the draft calling away Connecticut workers. But the diminution in the manufacturing labor force came also from less obvious causes. Even before the Normandy invasion, for example, prospects of victory sent many war workers searching for jobs with a secure peacetime future, and for a variety of personal reasons women began to return to the home. Since production demands remained high, something beyond the state's recruitment efforts was needed to fill essential factory jobs.[8]

That need, apparent in other industrial areas as well, led to federal War Manpower Commission programs to rationalize the labor market and funnel workers into critical war industries. Most important among the WMC measures were its labor market classification system (most of Connecticut's war production centers received a Class I labor shortage designation, which theoretically meant the withholding of most additional war orders) and its increasing controls over labor turnover and hiring. The WMC programs provoked an unhappy response from the outset. The possibility that new contracts would go elsewhere caused general dismay. For the state's businessmen and Republican public officials, WMC programs seemed yet further examples of New Dealish bureaucratic excess and inequity which increased the powers of the federal government and its "out-of-town bureaucrats" and which seemed to threaten free enterprise. Local government and business, and the state government as well, devised programs aimed at eluding or ending the wmc controls. The brouhaha touched off by the wmc policies provided more evidence still that the war had by no means transformed old concerns and old attitudes. Indeed, by vesting more authority in and focusing more attention on the federal government, the war sometimes intensified fears and ideological struggles of the Depression years.

Sterner and at times impolitic wmc measures in mid-1944 stirred more protest. So, too, did the growing concern about the state's postwar economy, and Governor Baldwin told wmc and War Production Board officials that the wmc regulations threatened to impair reconversion. No doubt reacting to such pressures as well as to some lessening of the labor stringency, the wmc began, as the 1944 election neared, to ease its local classifications and controls. But Connecticut's labor market remained tight, with out-migration still growing and workers again scrambling for non-defense jobs. By November, wmc and wpb officials feared another critical labor shortage should war production needs increase.[9]

The renewed labor turnover of late 1944 reflected worry about postwar jobs. The primary concern of the American people by 1944, postwar employment caused particular apprehension in such war production centers as Connecticut.[10] The state's prosperity was based obviously, and many thought perilously, on war manufactures. The expansion of Connecticut's defense industries and the conversion to war production by other firms had heightened the state's concentration in durable manufactures, had produced a larger labor force, and had made many more people dependent on defense jobs. Only three states (Ohio, California, and Indiana) had a larger percentage increase in factory workers from 1940 to 1943 than Connecticut's 69 percent. In the same period Connecticut war industries gained 218,000 workers, a jump of 111 percent, and by mid-1943 nine of every ten Connecticut industrial workers were engaged in war production.

War production affected income as well as employment patterns. More jobs, longer hours, and higher wage rates yielded

149

substantially greater earnings. Far outstripping the 26 percent rise in the cost of living, weekly wages nearly doubled between 1939 and 1944, and farm income increased similarly. Besides growing, income statistics changed in other ways reflecting the war's impact on the economy. Between 1940 and 1943 labor income (chiefly wages and salaries) rose from 65 to 80 percent of all income payments. Sixty-two percent of labor and entrepreneurial income in 1943 derived from manufacturing, as compared with 40 percent in 1939. And not only had many prewar workers learned new skills, acquired better jobs, and taken home more pay, but blacks, women, and other previously marginal workers had enjoyed more and better jobs and higher incomes. As it had throughout the nation, the war had done an important part of what the New Deal had tried and failed to do.[11]

With Connecticut's employment and new prosperity founded so manifestly on war production, peace portended a trying period of reconversion and readjustment. Many people might have to revert to jobs of lesser status and lower pay. More alarming still, many people might find no jobs at all. The federal Bureau of Labor Statistics projected Connecticut's number of displaced war workers and demobilized veterans at 331,000, nearly half of total employment in 1940. That proportion, topped only by Michigan's, far exceeded the national estimate, high as it was, that discharged servicemen and war workers would total about one-third of 1940 employment. Small wonder that postwar employment caused such worry among the American people as victory came in sight; and small wonder that the worry was doubly fierce in states like Connecticut—where by one estimate postwar unemployment would be at least at Great Depression levels.[12]

For those who followed such data closely, moreover, Connecticut's economic indices might have reinforced fears about the postwar era. Already they had begun to decline, much faster than the nation's, as war production demands slackened. From a record 120 percent above normal in April 1943, the index of general business activity fell to 62 percent above

150

normal by December 1944, and it averaged only 77 points above normal in 1944 as against +109 in 1943. Employment and factory man-hours fell, too, and after rising steadily through the war years, the average weekly wages of factory workers began to fall early in 1944. To be sure, hard times had not returned to Connecticut. Diminished employment figures meant general labor scarcity, not an army of unemployed. Although unemployment claims and payments rose in 1944, in part because of some cutbacks and layoffs in war industries, they had in 1943, with unemployment below 1 percent, fallen "well below previously conceived ideas of what constitutes a minimum." Wages remained far above prewar levels. The index of general relief continued to fall through the summer of 1944. By September 1944 it stood at a minuscule 3.5, and of the 40,000 people receiving public assistance one-third received old-age assistance, and only 7,500, most of them unemployable, received general relief.[13]

Still, the several indications of a softening economy must have proved worrisome, especially in conjunction with the many warnings, indeed the general expectation, of extensive postwar unemployment. Such signs and forecasts had special significance among a people so recently out of terrible depression and in a war production state so keenly aware of its economic collapse in the wake of World War I. As they had dampened the state's reception of the early war boom, so the sharp memories of the past spurred planning for the next postwar period. Most important among Connecticut's planning efforts were two state agencies fostered by Baldwin. Created in 1943, the Post-War Planning Board had as its central task to prepare recommendations for maximum postwar production and employment. By early 1944 the Board's work was well under way. To develop a training and reemployment program for returning veterans, Baldwin in 1943 also established the Connecticut Reemployment Commission, which quickly began programs for helping not only veterans but also displaced war workers acquire new skills and find different jobs. Both state agencies stressed local initiative, and the towns responded.

By late 1944, 103 towns, accounting for more than 90 percent of the state's people, had postwar planning organizations of some kind; and 140 local committees had been formed to assist veterans, with another fifteen being organized. Besides these and other efforts of state and local government, business groups had also initiated studies and preparations for postwar employment.[14] In all, Connecticut had begun an impressive array of programs, public and private, to help make the outbreak of peace as gentle as possible. Those programs, like the many similar ones in Washington, D.C., and in other states, were but one index of the hold economic concerns had on people and policy makers as the war—and with it war prosperity—neared the end.

The first fired after the last war, Connecticut blacks had particularly intense fears about postwar jobs. They had made substantial gains during the war. At the peak of wartime employment, for example, 41 of the state's largest plants, which had employed among them 896 blacks in 1940, counted 6,121 on their payrolls—an increase of some 600 percent. Besides the gains in the quantity of industrial jobs, some blacks also got better jobs, as skilled and semiskilled workmen and sometimes even as foremen and supervisors. Outside the factories, Negroes found more professional, semiprofessional, and white-collar employment, and they began to win more local and state government jobs, too.[15]

Such undeniable signs of progress could not, however, efface the fact of continuing racial discrimination, in employment as well as in other phases of life. Advances came slowly. Recognizing that, advised of the potential political benefits of attention to Negro problems, and pressed by blacks to take action, Baldwin had early in 1943 asked for a statutory commission on interracial problems. In May 1943 the General Assembly established an Inter-racial Commission and also amended the state Merit Act to prohibit discrimination in state service. Three months later Baldwin appointed ten men, including three blacks, to the Commission, which was to study discrimination, especially in

employment, and to report its findings and its recommendations for corrective action to the Governor.[16]

The Inter-racial Commission had from its beginning important limitations of concept and purpose. In asking for such a
commission, Baldwin revealed not only his own growing concern about the plight of Connecticut blacks but also some of
the limits on his commitment to remedy that plight:

> We abhor religious prejudice and race discrimination as being
> un-American, but we cannot accomplish all that we should by
> merely passing laws saying that there shall be no religious preju-
> dice or race discrimination. We must practice what we preach.
> We have many thousand negroes in Connecticut. The best help
> that we can give them is equal opportunity for jobs. In this work
> education plays an important factor. I recommend the appoint-
> ment of a Commission to be composed of both whites and negroes
> to work for the betterment of the negroes, particularly in the mat-
> ter of training for and placement in profitable jobs.[17]

Baldwin's perceptions and hopes were ahead of the general
public's, and his efforts went far beyond those of any of his
predecessors in the governor's office; but his vision, like those
of many white racial liberals of the time, was constricted by
his faith in exhortation, education, and economic gains.

The Inter-racial Commission itself showed more about how
those concerned with wartime race relations conceived of their
task. It revealed as well how the wartime experience affected
that conception and how difficult it was to overcome old ideas
and old habits. By law, the commission had as its ultimate aim
"the removal of such injustices as may be found to exist"; its
first biennial report, however, defined the commission's objective as "inter-group harmony and understanding."[18] From a
concern with melioration, then, the Commission shifted to a
concern with conciliation. Tension of course fed on inequity—
promoting harmony and ending injustice were obviously related; but the changed focus, stemming from the experiences
of the war years, was important.

As in the nation, so in Connecticut, black in-migration,
crowded cities, the general irritations and anxieties of the

time, and the conflict between black desires and white prejudice produced tension between the races.[19] Employment and
housing remained key areas of discrimination and black res-
tiveness, but discrimination was evident as well in private educational opportunities, in recreational facilities, and in public
accommodations. While blacks continued to decry their situation and manifest their intent to change it, and while whites
continued to resist change, rumors and malicious gossip added
to the racial tensions.

Occasionally, as on the public carriers, the tension changed
into friction. In Hartford and New Haven, whites complained
of Negro "mashers" and "muggers" and demanded extra police
protection. The much-publicized complaints in Hartford
prompted a biracial group of social, civic, and labor leaders to
protest the "vicious tendency to inflame anti-Negro feelings"
by blaming blacks for local crime and to urge Mayor Thomas
Spellacy to investigate the city's "basic social problems."
Though meeting with the group and denouncing racial dema-
goguery, Spellacy responded evasively. There the matter
rested in the spring of 1943.[20]

Race riots elsewhere in the nation during the summer of
1943 precipitated new perceptions and catalyzed new action
in Hartford and throughout Connecticut. Commanding front-
page treatment in the state press, the terrible riots in Detroit
and Harlem were the most important events. As throughout
America, private citizens and local government began on the
heels of the violence an intensive reexamination of racial problems. In Hartford, where just before the Harlem riot twenty
blacks had assaulted a white policeman for apprehending a
Negro, the local CIO sponsored a biracial conference on racial
problems. The conference urged the mayor to establish a commission to study the causes of racial friction and to propose
ways to eliminate tension and to prevent further outbursts.
Coming in a changed atmosphere, this request won a more serious hearing. The city's new mayor, Dennis O'Connor (Long
Tom Spellacy had resigned in June after a row with the alder-
man stemming largely from factional politics), soon established

an Inter-Racial Committee. Similarly, though its origins ante-
dated the violent summer of 1943, it was clearly that troubling
season that caused the state Inter-racial Commission to focus
on racial tension rather than injustice. The commission worked
hard at investigation, education, and conciliation, and it found
allies throughout the state in political, religious, civic, and labor groups and leaders who denounced racial injustice and
urged interracial knowledge and cooperation. For their part,
blacks continued to press for an end to discrimination and for
white understanding of the dreadful irony of Negroes fighting
for democracy abroad while being deprived of it at home.[21]

Despite the continuing improvement of black economic status and the increasing concern about black problems and inter-
racial harmony, however, Negro progress remained halting and
the white commitment soft. Following the much-publicized
strike of white transit workers in Philadelphia protesting black
promotions, the Hartford Common Council in the late summer of 1944 adopted companion resolutions condemning the
strikers' anti-Negro motivation and urging the Hartford Police
Board to consider the immediate appointment of six blacks.
Though the sponsor of the resolutions argued not only that
blacks were "entitled" to such recognition but also that such
positive action would help avert trouble in Hartford, the proposal met with evasion from the Police Board and aroused con-
troversy. If that episode revealed something about white attitudes, a late 1944 National Urban League study showed with
depressing clarity the extent of the social and economic problems confronting Hartford blacks. Detailing discrimination in
public and private employment, discrimination and segregation in public and private housing, and the frightful conditions
of life in the North End ghetto, the report laid the persistence
of the bleak situation largely to the "unwillingness of official
and civic leadership to recognize the existence and urgency of
problems facing the community." The 1944 report of the state
Inter-racial Commission revealed conditions statewide similar
to those in Hartford, particularly in employment and housing.
Yet despite its grim findings, the Commission confined its rec-

ommendations to exhortations for education, community action, fairness, and harmony. It did "not think it wise" to recommend new legislation, and it suggested that blacks pursue "positive activities" and high standards of behavior and responsibility.[22] Neither experience nor investigation had advanced the state's programmatic response to the circumstances of its black citizens much beyond Baldwin's 1943 inaugural. Still, through 1944, the wartime pattern of some black gains, of much more black organization and protest, of changing white perceptions, and of growing, if still small, white commitment to rectifying discriminatory practices had continued to develop.

Connecticut's major new immigrant groups also had special concerns during the 1943–44 biennium. Assimilation of Italian-Americans did not instantly follow the events of late 1942. Prejudice continued, and Italian-Americans still felt themselves denied appropriate political recognition, that avenue to and index of acceptance. They especially craved such recognition because of their treatment early in the war years. But in 1943 Democrats and Republicans alike showed a reluctance to nominate Italians for important municipal office. In New Haven, GOP leaders ruled against William Celentano's desire to try again for mayor, though Italians did continue to garner lesser nominations.[23]

Even so, the position of Italian-Americans was clearly improving. Complaints of job discrimination fell off, for example, and Columbus Days in 1943 and 1944 were more nearly normal. For such improvement, Italian-Americans could credit the new national policy toward Italian aliens and their own continuing record of service and sacrifice. They could also thank events in Europe. Mussolini was deposed in the summer of 1943, and in September the new Italian government surrendered to the Allies. A month later, as a "co-belligerent" of the Allies, the Italian government declared war on Germany. Though the liberation of Italy from German control went slowly, Italian-Americans no longer represented a nation at war with the United States.

156

The demonstrated and accepted Americanism of Italian-Americans and the changing status of Italy also permitted Italian-Americans to give their attention freely to the homeland. After responding euphorically to Mussolini's ouster and Italy's surrender, they tried to dissociate the Italian people from fascism and Axis aggression and to help speed American assistance and the return of Italian sovereignty. The continuing attachment to Italy did not contradict the Italian-American desire to be accepted as Americans. Bonds of blood and memory, not unhappiness with America, accounted for the persisting ties to the homeland. Italian-Americans had parents and brothers and sisters and cousins there, and upon Italy's surrender they frankly expressed their anxieties about them. The Connecticut Sons of Italy criticized the Roosevelt administration's Italian relief effort as "inactive [and] inadequate" and helped to coordinate a successful clothing drive. As revealed in such actions and in the columns of the Italian-American press, the situation and treatment of Italy and her people were of paramount importance to Americans of Italian origin.[24]

Jews also had problems in America and worries about their folk abroad. As elsewhere in the nation, so in Connecticut, anti-Semitism flared in the midst of war against the Nazis. Wartime tensions activated the old habit of finding scapegoats in troubled times; and as in the past the Jew provided a handy target. A good deal of the anti-Jewish feeling also stemmed from long-standing interethnic and religious hostility, and in Connecticut much of the anti-Semitism came from Italians and other Catholics. The anti-Semitism took various forms. Rumors circulated that Jews evaded service and combat. Job discrimination in Hartford war plants eased during the labor scarcity, but quota systems in private educational and vocational facilities continued, as did discrimination in housing. Sometimes anti-Semitism became nastier than whispers or discrimination. Anti-Semitic vandalism marked Halloween 1943 in Hartford and Bridgeport. In Hartford at least a hundred

157

storefronts were defaced by swastikas and ugly scribbling, and continuing acts of vandalism there prompted the mayor to request an antidefamation ordinance.[25]

Such demonstrations aroused Jews. The Jewish War Veterans of Connecticut acted with particular vigor to discredit the rumors and denounce the incidents. In September 1944 the group forwarded to Baldwin a legislative program including proposals for a fair employment practices act and for a commission to study anti-Semitism. Meeting late in October, the Connecticut State Council of the American Jewish Congress heard the principal speaker warn against anti-Semitism in the nation and urge the "total mobilization of the strength, energy, and support of every Jew in America" to combat it.[26]

Jews also turned their attention abroad, to the plight of fellow Jews in Europe and to the old dream of a Jewish commonwealth. Palestine seemed to provide the key to both. There Jewish refugees as well as Zionists might settle, and there a Jewish state might be established. Underwritten by Great Britain's 1917 Balfour Declaration, there had been significant Jewish immigration to British-controlled Palestine during the interwar years. As evidence of the horror of Hitler's "final solution" grew in the late 1930s, moreover, there grew with it the desire of Jews for a safe refuge, best of all in a Jewish state. But even as the felt need for such a state waxed, the prospects of one waned. In 1939, wanting to conciliate the Arabs on the eve of the war, Great Britain went back on the Balfour Declaration by announcing a new policy limiting Jewish immigration to Palestine to 75,000 for the next five years and ending it as of April 1944. With all that as background, the question of Palestine fired the burgeoning American Zionist movement of the war years and enlisted as well the support of American Jews generally. Led by the Zionists, Jewish spokesmen and groups lobbied fiercely for unrestricted Jewish immigration to Palestine and for American assistance in creating a Jewish state there. Organized efforts to achieve those goals multiplied, not least in Connecticut with its high proportion of Jews and correspondingly large degree of Zionist activity.[27]

By 1944, Palestine had become an important issue in both diplomacy and politics. The Jewish activity, and its evident support in Congress, caused trouble for President Roosevelt, who found himself caught between policy needs on the one hand and political needs on the other. Whatever the President may himself have thought about the Palestine question, he and the State Department wanted to further American oil interests in the Middle East, in Saudi Arabia in particular; and that concern had led Roosevelt in 1943 to assure Saudi Arabia's King Ibn Saud that the United States would stand for no changes in Palestine's status "without full consultation with both Arabs and Jews." That pledge not only clashed with Jewish hopes but also led Roosevelt to oppose a bill before Congress calling for the free entry of Jews into Palestine with the ultimate goal of establishing a Jewish state there. Not sure how to stymie congressional action that would arouse the Arabs without also alienating Jews and perhaps losing an important source of his political support, the President found assistance in the view of the War Department that conflict between Arabs and Jewish immigrants would materially harm the war effort. Here was the rationale Roosevelt could use to quash the congressional resolution, and use it he did. At the same time, however, he covered his exposed political flank by giving two important Jewish leaders heartening if vague assurances about the future of Palestine. By so mollifying the Jews, Roosevelt's strategy minimized political repercussions. Although Palestine did not vanish from politics—Republicans in Connecticut and elsewhere accused Roosevelt of evading the real issues and of appeasing the Arabs—the President's maneuvering had substantially reduced GOP hopes of winning many Jewish votes because of Palestine.[28]

Polish-Americans had no such domestic troubles as did the Italians and Jews, but they, too, were anxious about their people abroad. And like Palestine and even Italy to some degree, Poland came to have important political and diplomatic dimensions by 1944. Poland, indeed, was a more important problem than Palestine in the 1940s—more important to di-

159

plomacy because so many germs of the cold war lurked in the issue, more important to domestic politics because more votes seemed likely to be deflected by it. As with Palestine, Roosevelt found himself ensnared between two unappealing alternatives: alienating the Soviet Union and jeopardizing Allied unity by resisting Soviet designs on Poland, or alienating Polish-Americans and jeopardizing Democratic strength by acquiescing in Russian desires. The latter alternative, as presidential adviser Harry L. Hopkins said, was "political dynamite" because of the estimated six to seven million Polish-Americans; the former surely was diplomatic dynamite which might rupture the Grand Alliance and endanger postwar peace. To avoid igniting either keg, Roosevelt tried to handle the Polish question with circumspection and conciliation in 1943 and 1944.[29]

If Roosevelt's intentions often were vague, the worries of Polish-Americans were clear enough, as were the related aims of the Soviet Union. Concerned as they had long been about relief for Poland's people, Polish-Americans came to worry most about the integrity and autonomy of their homeland. The Soviet Union early in the war made clear its insistence on retaining eastern Poland, part of pre-Revolutionary Russia over which the Soviets had been granted control by Germany in the 1939 Nazi-Soviet Pact. The Soviet claim was resisted by the fiercely anti-Communist Polish government-in-exile based in London and was opposed as well by the anti-Communist and anti-Russian majority of Polish-Americans. When the Russians broke relations in 1943 with the exile government in London, partly over the territorial issue, anti-Russian activity among Polish-Americans picked up, much of it in Connecticut with its large, nationalistic, and well-organized Polish population. In New Britain, nineteen Polish organizations denounced the "unexampled and undemocratic claims of Soviet Russia," which they said violated "all human decency," and memorialized Congress to oppose the Soviet claims.[30]

Concern mounted still more in 1944 as Russian troops pushed westward across Poland. The advance of the Red Army made Poland's borders only a part of the problem. Now the basic issue became the very organization and government of the nation of Poland, especially after a Moscow-based, Communist-dominated Polish government was formed early in the year. That prompted Polish-American spokesmen and groups in Connecticut and elsewhere to grow louder in their worries about Poland, in their condemnation of the Soviet Union, and in their insistence on firm American action. Scenting political advantage, Republicans, led in Connecticut by Congressman-at-large Boleslaus Monkiewicz, joined in. Soviet threats to the Polish Church, a frequent theme of the *Hartford Catholic Transcript* and other Catholic newspapers, further agitated the devoutly Catholic Poles.[31]

Polish-Americans, then, had by mid-1944 several interlocking fears about their homeland and Soviet domination. Rather than ebbing, moreover, those fears, heightened by Roosevelt's evident reluctance to restrain Soviet influence in the area, mounted in the remainder of the year. Russia's recognition of the Moscow-based Polish government and its refusal or inability to aid the savagely repressed Polish uprising in Warsaw caused Polish-American anxieties to reach a new peak in the late summer and autumn of 1944. Nationally, Polish-American activity was coordinated by the newly formed and broadly based Polish-American Congress, which clearly intimated political retaliation should the administration prove unwilling to be firmer toward the Soviet Union with regard to Poland. Such pressures and activities grew in Connecticut, too. The United Polish Societies of Hartford petitioned Roosevelt for action in the three principal areas of Polish-American concern: aid to Poland; no partition of Poland by Russia; and the full reestablishment of the Republic of Poland, "not any forcefully imposed puppet regime." Still trapped in his diplomatic-political dilemma, however, Roosevelt responded with little more than blandishments and evasion. A mutually satisfactory resolution of the diplomatic and political problems inherent in the Polish issue proved even more elusive than with Palestine.[32]

Not just ethnic groups but Americans generally gave increasing attention to foreign affairs as the war went on. In retrospect, in the perspective of the cold war, relations with the Soviet Union have seemed the basic foreign policy problem of the war years. And certainly Soviet-American relations did concern many at the time. To view the foreign policy making of the war years only in the perspective of the ensuing cold war, however, is to miss what seemed the crucial foreign policy issue to most contemporaries, at least through 1944. That issue was, simply, what role should and would the United States play in the postwar world; and there developed by the mid-war years a strong national consensus that the role should be major and should include leadership in an international organization that would keep the peace.[33]

That consensus, and the direction of the new American internationalism, was like so much else in the war years rooted in past experience. As they had after World War I, Americans in the 1940s determined to avoid the errors which they believed had dragged them into a world war. Since the "isolationist" policies of the interwar years had failed, the lessons of the recent past pointed toward adopting Wilsonian aims of an international organization and collective security. As they approached the question of postwar foreign policy and international relations, moreover, the American people and policy makers, remembering the aggression and appeasement of the 1930s, were "concerned primarily with the problem of armed aggression and the techniques of preventing its recurrence." Proposals of the "idealist" internationalists—men like Wendell Willkie and Henry A. Wallace—for a meliorative, innovative, truly multilateral internationalism therefore found little favor. Motivated principally by practical self-interest, Americans wanted simply to "make sure that *there are no more world wars.*" As Senator Joseph Ball of Minnesota, perhaps the Senate's staunchest internationalist, observed, the nation was "mostly concerned with . . . preventing another war," not with a "changed and utopian world."[34]

Congress and the administration developed postwar foreign policy plans within this basic national consensus and the framework of international cooperation to keep the peace. By mid-1944, with victory apparently in sight and with the presidential election looming ahead, there had emerged the contours of a bipartisan postwar American internationalism based on a world organization dominated by the major powers and concerned chiefly with the maintenance of peace. The new internationalism was actually as nationalist as it was internationalist, for it aimed to "make the world safe for the United States" and to maintain American leadership and freedom of action.[35] The nationalistic orientation stemmed partly from the inertial drag of an isolationist heritage and the difficulty of moving too far, too fast. It arose chiefly from the preoccupation with security that the recent past had bred in Americans. Although most Americans worried more about postwar jobs than about the postwar world, peace was obviously essential to the secure enjoyment of prosperity. International security was thus at once a major aim in itself and a precondition for genuine domestic security. (Conversely, for many policy makers, national and worldwide prosperity seemed an essential precondition to world peace—a view also powerfully reinforced by the troubled 1930s.) Having grown together from the terrible experiences of the interwar and war years, the interrelated longings for prosperity and peace dominated American hopes and gave direction to national policies in the war years and beyond.

As it turned out, the "new internationalism" of the war years proved as much a prisoner as a product of the past. Not only did it depart less from previous foreign policy than the nation believed, but it also provided less security than Americans wanted and often proved of doubtful relevance in the greatly changed postwar world. Prizing peace, stability, and American security above all, the internationalist consensus of the war years raised to rigid preeminence the "Munich lesson" that totalitarian aggression must be halted forcefully, helped shape often dubious American perceptions of and responses to the Soviet Union, and led to ignoring or misconstruing ferment in the former colonial areas of the world. For those reasons,

163

moreover, the nationalistic internationalism at its heart sometimes became unilateral interventionism. To be sure, peace should not have been despised as an end nor the United Nations as a vehicle; and certainly wartime Americans believed that their new internationalism was realistic and promised peace and security. But the past did not always speak clearly and relevantly to the present. The internationalist consensus of the war years, understandable though it was and new in some ways though it was, carried with it limitations and weaknesses not apparent to most people at the time.

The wartime internationalist consensus did nonetheless signal an important change in national policy. Like most new departures, it encountered opposition and had important political ramifications. A central issue in the politics of 1944, it affected political activity well before the election, particularly within the GOP, which remained divided on foreign policy. Domestic policy differences and intraparty politics complicated matters for Republicans, who had to decide on a presidential nominee as well as on a foreign policy stance. Democrats by contrast had for the most part little trouble accommodating themselves to the cautious internationalism of their president, who most Democrats expected would be renominated. Connecticut's politicians followed with few detours the different paths of their parent parties toward the election of 1944.

Wendell Willkie was at the center of Republican contention as the GOP groped toward its 1944 decisions on foreign policy and a presidential candidate. Following his defeat in 1940, Willkie had set out to rally the country and his party behind an internationalist foreign policy. His advanced internationalism and also his growing domestic liberalism soon disaffected many Republicans, especially in the GOP's conservative, prewar isolationist wing headed by Senators Taft and Vandenberg and centered in the Midwest. Willkie's attacks on elements of his own party, his decidedly tenuous relations with the GOP organization, and his virtual abstention from the 1942 campaign cost him further support among party regulars, suspicious of him anyway because Willkie was a renegade Democrat who had joined the GOP only just before the 1940 election. Though Willkie remained strongest in the East, his popularity among regular Republicans even in Connecticut was "highly questionable" by mid-1942.

Willkie's standing in the GOP declined further in 1943 as he became increasingly forceful in his calls for internationalism and liberalism. Shortly after the phenomenal sales success of his internationalist book *One World*, a group of internationalist Republicans formed the Republican Postwar Policy Association to urge a strong foreign policy position on the party. Afraid that the group had as its chief aim the renomination of Willkie, Republican national chairman Harrison Spangler, a staunch regular, appointed a Republican Postwar Advisory Council, dominated by prewar isolationists and not including Willkie. Pressured by the course of public opinion and by the internationalist Republicans, the Council in September 1943 called for "responsible participation by the United States in post-war cooperative organization among sovereign nations to prevent military aggression and to attain permanent peace with organized justice in a free world." Hedged about though it was, the declaration placed the GOP within the emerging mainstream foreign policy position and formally ahead of the Democratic party, which had adopted no such policy statement. It fell far short of Willkie's position, even on the power of the projected organization to maintain peace. By late 1943 Willkie clearly had little influence in party councils. While he called upon Republicans to be "the great American liberal party" on domestic and international issues, the "normalcy group" of Robert Taft and his allies gained strength, and popular support for nominating New York Governor Thomas E. Dewey for president was growing fast.[36]

Wilkie also continued to slip badly in Connecticut, which had been so important to his 1940 nomination. Besides losing public support, he aroused growing opposition from important Republican leaders, including most of the state officers and congressmen. Some, especially Senator John Danaher, disliked

Willkie's internationalism. Others, many of whom had supported Willkie in 1940 because of his business background and
orientation, had become disenchanted with his domestic liberalism. Still others, concerned largely with organization affairs,
distrusted Willkie's loyalty to the party and feared what he
might do about patronage and related matters. Though not
really united, these sometimes overlapping groups reflected
the renascent strength of traditional, regular Republicans. It
seemed likely that they could come together behind the safe
and regular Thomas Dewey. Further, Willkie lacked open
support from the men who had led his 1940 drive in Connecticut. A leader of the party's internationalist wing, Baldwin had
remained personally and philosophically close to the 1940 candidate. Perhaps despairing of Willkie's chances, however, the
Governor did not publicly commit himself, and he devoted his
attention to influencing Republican policy. Samuel Pryor, still
important in the state GOP, and state chairman J. Kenneth
Bradley both stayed carefully aloof from Willkie. By March
1944, with his foes increasing in number and volume and his
friends growing fewer and quieter, Willkie seemed "doubtful"
at best in Connecticut, one of the states where his prospects
had once looked brightest.[37]

His fortunes at such low ebb among Republican leaders by
early 1944, Willkie knew he had to prove his popular strength.
The Wisconsin primary in April provided the major testing
ground of his candidacy; and Willkie finished a dismal, disastrous fourth and last behind Dewey. At bottom, the Wisconsin
vote reflected the general truth that Willkie had run too far
ahead of his party, indeed of his country, on domestic and international issues. As *Time* magazine put it, Wisconsin Republicans in rejecting Willkie had voted for "realistic internationalism" and for "100-proof, Regular Republicanism." Unable to
speak for or lead his party, which thought it could win in 1944
on more traditional terms, Willkie withdrew his candidacy.[38]

In Connecticut as elsewhere, Willkie's withdrawal clarified
matters. Led by several state officers and gaining support
among lesser party leaders and rank-and-file Republicans, the

Connecticut Dewey movement burgeoned. By early May, Pryor and Bradley seemed to favor the New Yorker. Even Baldwin, against Dewey's candidacy to the end, admitted that he was the likely nominee. By the time the national convention opened, Dewey had the nomination in hand, and the Connecticut delegation voted for him on the first (and only) ballot.[39]

The platform aroused more interest than Dewey's predetermined nomination. Hoping to use his still important national following as leverage, Willkie had after Wisconsin turned his efforts toward influencing Republican policy, especially on international affairs. Refusing even to invite Willkie to address the convention or platform committee, the GOP's leaders entrusted the foreign policy plank to Senator Vandenberg, whose draft sounded internationalist while committing the party to little. It endorsed "responsible participation by the United States in postwar cooperative organization" but opposed joining a "world state"; it said that the organization should prevent military aggression but that "peace forces" should do it. Willkie and his followers sought unsuccessfully to have the plank clarified and strengthened. The brief contest highlighted the continuing division of opinion among Connecticut Republicans. Together with New Jersey's Governor Walter Edge, Baldwin led the fight for stronger language, while Danaher, a member of the platform committee, defended the official position.

Like the foreign policy plank, the Republican platform was a "catch-all for votes." As in 1940, the GOP endorsed much of the New Deal but criticized its methods and accused it of encroaching on liberty and private enterprise. Postwar reconversion and prosperity received major attention, as they did also in Dewey's acceptance speech. Republicans also tried to tailor their platform to as many specific groups as possible—labor, business, farmers, veterans, Jews, blacks—by advocating policies (a free, independent Jewish state in Palestine for Jews, a permanent FEPC for blacks, for example) desired by those groups. In all, the platform revealed something of Republican philosophy, something of Republican political needs, and most Connecticut Republicans evinced the usual enthusiasm about the

167

convention's work and their party's chances. By mid-July, moreover, Dewey had satisfied many former Willkie adherents, including Pryor, by declaring that he supported a world organization and the use of "force if necessary" to keep the peace.[40]

Connecticut GOP leaders returned from the relative harmony and confidence of the national convention to state party troubles that had plagued them all year. In the spring, long-brewing personal discord between Bradley and Baldwin had threatened to disrupt the GOP and touch off a larger confrontation along its factional lines. Bradley and Baldwin had fallen out in 1943, when state chairman Bradley had too aggressively pushed the organization's patronage demands on the Governor. Although the patronage dispute ended in compromise, Baldwin "deeply resented" Bradley's actions, as he did the chairman's use for partisan purposes of his access to Baldwin and the Governor's office. Nor was that all dividing the two men. Baldwin disapproved of Bradley's remaining active in their law firm while occupying such a high party position. He disapproved, too, of Bradley's retaining both top party posts— state chairman and national committeeman; that, Baldwin believed, smacked of the "Rorabackism" that the New Era group had supposedly expunged back in 1938. At the heart of the tensions between Baldwin and Bradley lay the fact that the Governor, solicitous of his own reputation, wanted to keep himself and his governorship unsullied by obvious partisan party politicking. As state chairman, and by nature a political operator, Bradley had different priorities and standards from Baldwin's. The two longtime friends had not become estranged to the point of enmity, but the personal political discord severely strained their relations.

Such ill feeling between the state's foremost Republicans could scarcely remain a contained, private matter, especially given its political dimensions. Baldwin's evident determination early in 1944 that Bradley relinquish one of his leadership positions guaranteed that it would not. GOP leaders in Hartford County, long unhappy with Fairfield County's domination, seized on the feud and the two-job question to agitate for

Bradley's ouster from one of his offices. At this juncture Samuel Pryor interceded by arranging a mid-May emergency "peace conference" of party leaders, who seemingly agreed that Bradley would retain both posts until after the election. The conference thus averted bloody infighting, and soon afterwards the national convention ended the year-long contest over the presidential nominee. The only other potential source of disharmony had been the renomination of Senator John Danaher. But opposition to Danaher and his isolationist record had been linked to Willkie's candidacy and had faded with Willkie in the wake of the Wisconsin debacle. After the national convention, Connecticut Republicans seemed united behind Baldwin, Bradley, Danaher, and Dewey.[41]

Then early in July Baldwin jolted the party by announcing that he would not seek reelection. His declaration was much more genuine and much less designed for political advantage than his indecision of 1942. For a number of reasons, the Governor was disheartened by politics. Several things rankled: the year and more of fighting with Bradley and the organization; his failure to swing Connecticut Republicans behind either Willkie or Willkie's policies, and the larger failure of the national GOP to support either; the refusal of the Connecticut delegates even to give him favorite-son support at the national convention—the Governor had nursed hopes of the vice-presidential nomination and had wanted recognition at least. In all, Baldwin evidently felt he had had enough of the jostling and disappointment of politics, and after his second term as governor he believed he had done his duty. Added to all that were personal considerations. The Governor wanted to spend more time with his family than politics and public service allowed. He also wanted to support his family in better style than government permitted, and he had in hand an offer to be general counsel of the Connecticut Mutual Life Insurance Company at twice his gubernatorial salary. His declaration, then, was made neither lightly nor disingenuously.

Still, a week later Baldwin reversed himself. Party and public pressure caused him to change his mind. Although the organization regulars chafed at his patronage decisions and disagreed with his positions on many issues, they still knew that Baldwin was the party's greatest single asset in Connecticut. Beyond that, they feared that were Baldwin not to run there might be a divisive struggle for the gubernatorial nomination. Bradley and the others therefore quickly organized a draft-Baldwin movement which soon became general and genuine. An outpouring of public support for Baldwin, which entrenched him as the state's foremost Republican and which no doubt salved his bruised ego, turned the trick. Calling it his duty to do so, Baldwin said he would stand for renomination and reelection. Evidently ready at last, Republicans looked ahead with confidence to the campaign and election.[42]

Connecticut's Democrats had no such troubles as did the Republicans in deciding upon a presidential candidate or a foreign policy stance, but they had more serious internal difficulties. Factionalism, muted during Governor Hurley's tenure, had flared anew on the heels of the disastrous 1942 elections. Rending the party throughout the biennium, the battle for control peaked in the summer of 1944 before ending as it had begun, with the liberals in uneasy control.

The first skirmish came in December 1942, when the state central committee selected a new state chairman and national committeeman. After the defeat of his friend and ally Robert Hurley, chairman John McCarthy had decided to relinquish his post, while the national committee position had come open when David Fitzgerald had died in November. Ending Little Dave's three decades at or near the top of the state Democratic party, Fitzgerald's death came after a lengthy illness that had much reduced his influence. In New Haven, John Golden, a tough, portly Irishman who was also a Rotarian and a successful businessman, had taken control of the party. When the state central committee met in December to select the party's new leaders, three fairly clear factions existed: the liberal Hurley-McCarthy group, nourished by state patronage during Hurley's incumbency; the more conservative Maloney-Smith forces, frozen out of party leadership councils in that period; and the pragmatic big-city bosses, disgruntled about Hurley's patronage policies and distrustful of Maloney's desire to dominate the party. Philosophically as well as practically at odds, the Maloney and Hurley groups squared off in what both saw as an important preliminary to party control in 1944. Though displeased by Hurley, the city leaders could not countenance a Maloney victory, primarily because control of the state organization would give the Senator, already sure as the only Connecticut Democrat in Washington for the next two years to monopolize federal patronage, a stranglehold on the state party. Hartford, New Haven, and Bridgeport therefore threw their support to the Hurley group, and the central committee elected Hurley as national committeeman and John Dowe, Windham County Democratic leader and outgoing state comptroller, as state chairman. The outcome further enhanced the power of the liberals (New Dealer Hurley apparently had Roosevelt's support) and preserved that of the city leaders.[43] The New Dealer-city machine bond remained essentially one of convenience, but in the perspectives of the era's national politics and of the state's voting patterns it had a certain logic.

State chairman Dowe set out to rally and unify his party, but the Democrats remained dispirited and fragmented, their organization a shambles. The 1943 municipal elections, which Democrats had hoped would reinvigorate the party, instead dealt them another blow. The big-city results were most disheartening. McLevy, as usual, buried Democrats and Republicans alike in Bridgeport. In New Haven and Waterbury, Democrats escaped with surprisingly narrow victories. And from Hartford came the worst news of all, for Republicans carried the city for the first time since 1935.

Connecticut Democrats, then, had little cause for optimism as 1944 opened. Nor were they alone in their doldrums, for throughout the nation, and especially in the East, a continuing Republican trend seemed evident, and Democrats apparently lacked the organization, unity, and vitality to counteract it. But Democrats everywhere believed, or at least hoped, that they

171

still held the trump card of American politics—the likely candidacy of Franklin Roosevelt and the "magic Rooseveltian coattails." (Wanting to nullify that magic, Connecticut Republicans had in 1943 unsuccessfully tried to separate the presidential electors from the state and local slates.) The shared belief that the President was their only hope to return to power in 1944 welded Democrats of all persuasions behind Roosevelt earlier and even more solidly than four years before. Connecticut Democrats turned their Washington's Birthday banquet into a fourth-term rally, and they enthusiastically and unanimously committed themselves to Roosevelt in a late-May convention.[44]

The unity behind Roosevelt's candidacy did not, however, dispel the party's contentious factionalism, and Democrats divided bitterly and sometimes confusingly over the state nominations. With an eye to those nominations, Maloney had begun late in 1943 yet another attempt to take party control. Learning from his defeats of 1940 and 1942, the Senator worked assiduously to ally with or overpower the city leaders. He used various tactics, chiefly the carrot and stick of patronage, and he seemed to make substantial progress through early 1944. As spring came, others began to show signs of life. Because Senator Danaher seemed far more vulnerable than Governor Baldwin, most interest and activity centered on the senatorial nomination. Hurley's supporters began to work for him; Hartford's Long Tom Spellacy indicated his availability; old warhorse Homer Cummings in Fairfield County pushed his former Assistant Attorney General, Brien McMahon; and Chase Going Woodhouse, liberal head of the Connecticut Federation of Democratic Women and former secretary of the state, seemed interested. Although the plethora of senatorial hopefuls and the possibility of various new factional and personal alliances caused no little confusion, some clarity began to emerge by early summer. Just when Baldwin had apparently decided to retire from politics, Hurley announced that he would seek the gubernatorial nomination. Soon signs appeared of an alliance between Fairfield County liberals McMahon and Hurley. Their combined strength prompted the Maloney group, strangely slow to decide upon candidates, to put forth New Britain attorney Leo J. Gaffney for governor, and Spellacy said that Hartford would back Gaffney. Although Maloney still had not settled on a senatorial candidate, open struggle between his faction and the Hurley-McMahon-Cummings group had developed by the time of the national convention.[45]

The national convention provided no respite from the factionalism, which affected the Connecticut delegation's course on the most important matter to be decided, the choice of a running mate for Roosevelt. That issue, moreover, also laid open the fault lines of the national party. Conservatives, Southern Democrats, city bosses, and many moderates found the outspokenly liberal Vice President Henry Wallace anathema. Like Willkie, Wallace had taken positions too advanced on foreign and domestic policies for his party or his country in 1944, and he seemed eccentric as well. Roosevelt knew that; and without discouraging Wallace he encouraged several others, including James F. Byrnes and Harry S Truman. Warned that Byrnes, a conservative South Carolinian and apostate Catholic, would hurt the party among workers, blacks, and Catholics, Roosevelt and party leaders apparently decided on Missouri's Senator Truman. Still masking his intentions, however, Roosevelt sent the convention a message endorsing Wallace as his personal choice but leaving the decision to the delegates. Confused by the President's maneuvers, the convention was not sure what he wanted or what it should do.

The upshot was that the vice-presidential nomination, which was of crucial importance to the future of the party and, as it turned out, of the nation, was determined by politics and intraparty factionalism. The Connecticut delegation supported Wallace, but as much because of the byplay of the struggle for local control as because of the delegates' liberalism. Maloney opposed Wallace. Homer Cummings, though he preferred Senate leader Alben Barkley, helped defeat a Maloney proposal to bind the state to Wallace for only one ballot, and Connecticut supported the hopeless Wallace cause until Truman had the nomination sewn up. Cummings's success and

173

Maloney's failure gave a large hint about the relative strengths of the contending factions over the state nominations.[46]

The national convention had little trouble deciding upon a platform, except for the compromise civil rights section, whose weakness prompted the NAACP's gibe that it was a "splinter" rather than a plank. Foreign policy, the great Republican dilemma, proved relatively easy. Democrats called for an international organization "based on the principle of sovereign equality of all peace-loving states . . . for the prevention of aggression and the maintenance of international peace and security" and "endowed with power to employ armed forces when necessary to prevent aggression and preserve peace." More forthright and explicit than the Republican plank, the Democratic position was nonetheless clearly within the narrow national consensus on postwar internationalism. The brief platform went on to hail Roosevelt's record in peace and war and to advance sundry programs for specific groups. Like the Republican platform, it had peace and prosperity as its main themes.[47]

Back home from Chicago, Connecticut Democrats escalated their internecine struggle. As the contest became more heated, it boiled down to those two fundamentals of politics, philosophy and power. The McMahon-Hurley group based its quest for delegate support partly on McMahon's and Hurley's solidly New Deal and pro-Roosevelt stance. Yet whatever the substantive differences between the factions, and they were real, power was basic to the party battle. That was so especially on the Maloney side. Long dependent on federal patronage for his intraparty strength, Maloney evidently saw the governorship, with its rich patronage resources, as a key to enhancing his power in the state organization. At the same time, Maloney feared that a liberal Connecticut Democrat in the Senate might erode his own federal patronage. The apparent alliance of old foes Spellacy and Maloney also stemmed from considerations of power. Trying to work back into control in Hartford, Spellacy would have liked the senatorial nomination if he could get it, and on the gubernatorial nomination he deferred to the anti-Hurley sentiment of Tony Zazzaro, powerful

174

leader of the Italian East Side. In the Hartford caucus only fast-rising John Bailey, long a Spellacy lieutenant but now staking out his own position, cast his lot with Hurley.

As the state convention neared, the Hurley-McMahon team appeared stronger and better organized than its opponents. Though Gaffney seemed to be running fairly well for the gubernatorial nomination, the Maloney group had blundered by not early finding a strong senatorial candidate. Fearing that an easy McMahon victory (the senatorial nomination came first at the convention) would send the power-conscious delegates scuttling to Hurley, Maloney felt he had to halt McMahon's momentum. Just before the convention Maloney, unwilling to endorse Spellacy's hopeless try for the Senate, threw his support to Chase Woodhouse, and Spellacy gave his to another candidate. Maloney and Spellacy felt that they might thus stop a first-ballot McMahon victory and then hammer out a compromise choice and salvage their situations.

But Cummings and McMahon had done their own work too well. By the eve of the convention, McMahon held an insurmountable lead. Just forty years old, McMahon, a handsome, burly, dark-haired Irishman, had quickly gotten far in politics, and he aimed to go farther. Born in Norwalk in 1903 to a moderately well-to-do contractor, he graduated from Fordham and from Yale Law School and then began to practice law and take part in politics in his hometown in the late 1920s. He soon caught Homer Cummings's eye, went to Washington to serve as special assistant to Attorney General Cummings, and in 1935, when only thirty-one, he became Assistant Attorney General in charge of the Criminal Division. After earning something of a reputation as a "racket buster" and some mention as a possible senatorial candidate in 1938, McMahon resigned from the Justice Department in 1939 to return to his private law practice. For several years he was out of the public eye, but not because he shrank from attention. Though born James O'Brien McMahon, he took to calling himself Brien because it was more distinctive, and he enjoyed the reputation as a dandy earned him by his sophisticated tailoring and eye-catching accouterments. He was a cool, calculating, able man, ready to counter convention if need be, whose only apparent hero was Franklin D. Roosevelt. Above all, McMahon was ambitious, and in 1944 he badly wanted to go to the United States Senate.

McMahon's preconvention lock on the senatorial nomination spelled defeat for Maloney in the 1944 party struggle. Nevertheless, having invested so much, the Senator played his hand out. Wanting to make a stand where he had some chance, Maloney abandoned his opposition to McMahon before the balloting and concentrated his efforts on the gubernatorial nomination. But the Senator's new tactic could not stem the tide. As he took the rostrum to nominate Gaffney for governor, the predominance of jeers in the noisy greeting given him forecast the vote. Hurley won nomination by a vote of 640½ to 489. In contrast to his previous struggles with Maloney, Hurley had the support only of New Haven among the big cities, but strong backing from the smaller cities and towns gave him his margin. Although turning many long-standing party alliances upside down, Maloney had met another bitter, humiliating defeat. The New Dealers seemed still in command, and Homer Cummings had made a spectacular political comeback. A few days after the convention, the Cummings-Hurley-McMahon combine flexed its muscle again by having its man, the virtually unknown Adrian Maher of Fairfield County, selected as state chairman.[48]

The party's factions managed to come together on the platform and the ticket. Given over chiefly to national affairs, the platform lauded Roosevelt and said that the President and his party could best speed victory and ensure postwar peace and prosperity. Its state proposals largely reiterated those of 1942, though the party did not repeat its call for an FEPC and attendant legislation. Unlike the 1942 platform, the 1944 document, its emphasis on peace and prosperity echoed by McMahon and Hurley in their acceptance speeches, dovetailed with the dominant public concerns.

Completing the ticket caused the Democrats more trouble

than writing a platform, the more so because lesser nominations had been shunted aside during the long battle over the major offices. Slate making at least did not irritate the factional sores, for the Maloney group took part in it and won two of the five remaining nominations, but other problems arose in the haste and confusion. Supported by the Hartford-based Pulaski Federation of Democratic Clubs, Hartford Polish-American attorney Joseph Ryter won the congressman-at-large nomination. To placate New Britain, which had seen local candidates Lucien Maciora and Gaffney rejected for congressman-at-large and governor, party leaders selected Italian-American Charles Prestia of that city for secretary of state. But awarding the nomination for secretary to New Britain and the Italians meant depriving women of their anticipated spot, and ethnic, geographical, and factional considerations had accounted for the other positions. Excluded even from the slate-making conference, the women openly expressed their resentment, born in part of their progress and rising expectations of the war years. Upon Prestia's nomination they sent up a cry of "We want a woman" and warned that the party would regret its action. Chase Going Woodhouse said that she was "bitterly disappointed" in the irony of women being forgotten by the party even as they worked and served in the war effort and were reckoned a crucial political force. Though urging the Democratic women to down their bitterness and to work for Roosevelt's re-election, she also counseled them to press for the nomination of women for Congress and the General Assembly.[49]

One further aspect of the convention merited attention. Among the Hurley and McMahon supporters was the new state CIO Political Action Committee. The national CIO-PAC had been formed in July 1943 in direct response to the Smith-Connally bill. Its roots lay in the light turnout and Republican gains of the 1942 election, which had persuaded labor leaders that endorsements were no substitute for hard political work in producing a large labor turnout for liberal candidates. The PAC program, designed to elect Roosevelt and a pro-labor Congress, included efforts to influence candidate selection. PAC

177

head Sidney Hillman had enjoyed a virtual veto power over the Democratic vice-presidential nomination—Roosevelt had reportedly said to "clear it with Sidney," a phrase the GOP would embellish and belabor in the autumn. At the Connecticut Democratic convention the PAC proved more a presence than a power, though it did swell the Hurley-McMahon ranks. Days later, however, the Democrats nominated CIO candidates for Congress in the Fourth and Fifth Congressional Districts. Candidate selection was but part of the PAC program, and the state PAC had begun an energetic campaign of voter registration, education, and mobilization. It announced that it would go "all-out" for the election of Roosevelt and Connecticut Democrats.[50]

Despite its labor support, the Democratic party came out of its rancorous convention in sorry shape. Efforts to appease the aggrieved groups soon began. Democrats for the first time nominated women for Congress—Woodhouse in the Second District and Margaret Connors, a liberal young lawyer, in the Fourth. The party's reigning leaders also tried to solve the perennial and now exacerbated problem of harmony and unity. But throughout the autumn, factionalism in Hartford continued to worry Democrats, while promises of full support from Maloney and the Maloney-controlled Waterbury organization seemed empty. As ever, unity was a real problem for the fractious and fragmented Democratic party.[51]

The Republican state convention came next, but not before the GOP had set off its own brief fireworks. The issue of Bradley's leadership positions, apparently resolved in late spring, had come to life again, and at Baldwin's insistence Bradley resigned as state chairman in early August. To his later regret, Baldwin endorsed West Hartford's Harold Mitchell, the forty-three-year-old Speaker of the General Assembly's lower house, who was championed by the conservative, anti-Fairfield forces, as the new chairman. Though Bradley stayed on as national committeeman, the affair marked a shift in the locus of power and a turning point in Connecticut Republican politics. The

178

Baldwin-Bradley-Pryor triumvirate and Fairfield County control had come to an end. The state organization belonged to the forces, centered in Hartford County, which had so long chafed under the New Era-Fairfield County domination of the party. Baldwin seemed aligned with them, for the moment at least, and not with Bradley or with Pryor, who had sided with Bradley. The latter two men retained considerable importance in Fairfield County and in the state's national and congressional politics, but they had little voice in the state organization. And while Baldwin had insisted on Bradley's ouster for his own personal reasons, Mitchell's accession to the chairmanship was part of the resurgence of regular, conservative Republicanism that had undone Willkie earlier in the year.[52]

Much the same story emerged from the state convention. In contrast to the brawling of the Democrats, the GOP presented "primarily a spectacle of well-behaved middle class America." Self-assured, perhaps even self-indulgent, Republicans evinced that mood of confident conservatism, of reluctance to change, that had defeated Wendell Willkie. Although Baldwin had won the party's deference by his electoral prowess, he had not wedded it to his domestic and foreign policy positions, and the New Era group had lost its grip on party decisions. The uncontested renomination of Senator John Danaher, who had drifted far apart from Baldwin since the Beefsteak Club days of 1938, revealed much of that. In a year when America's postwar foreign policy seemed a major political issue and when it was evident that Brien McMahon would run almost solely against Danaher's isolationist record, the clubby GOP unanimously renominated an outspoken America Firster who had recanted nothing and changed little. Accepting his nomination, Danaher scarcely mentioned international issues and devoted himself to a scathing denunciation of Roosevelt's domestic policies. Such was the party's mood that even Baldwin dropped his insistent internationalism and acquiesced in a fuzzy foreign policy platform plank acceptable to the Danaher group. The Governor did, however, declare himself for a "sound liberal program" to ensure postwar employment, prosperity, and se-

179

curity, and he saw that his progressive approach to state affairs was written into the platform.

Renominating an incumbent and already balanced slate, Republicans had no trouble with recognition politics. They took special pains to capitalize on the discontent of the Democratic women. Secretary of the state Frances Redick, renominated "by rising vote in tribute to the women of the state," said that Republicans were "not afraid to treat women as human beings and citizens." (Earlier in the summer, Clare Boothe Luce had become the first woman to give a major address to a national party convention. The GOP seemed primed to emphasize their recognition of women in the campaign, but perhaps because Democrats nominated more women for Congress and for the General Assembly, Republicans did not pursue the issue with much vigor in the autumn.) Confident that their state ticket had more appeal than that of their opponents, and sure, too, that Roosevelt would not run as strongly in Connecticut as he had before, the GOP adjourned.[53]

By emphasizing peace and prosperity at their state and national conventions, both parties had shown their perception of the public's principal concerns. Polls, more important to politicians in 1944 than ever before, underscored the importance of those matters. A late-August report of the Opinion Research Corporation, for example, told Connecticut Republicans that anxiety about domestic international security, skillfully exploited by Roosevelt in past elections, remained uppermost in the nation's mind. In 1944, the report went on, security meant speedy victory, lasting peace, and postwar jobs.[54] During the summer and fall office seekers in both parties, from Roosevelt and Dewey on down, stressed those three concerns. Peace and prosperity—security in the form of victory, a lasting peace, and plentiful postwar jobs—dominated the politics of 1944 in state and nation.

Of those issues, victory figured least in the campaign itself. By the autumn of 1944, the end of the war seemed imminent. The long-awaited Allied invasion of western Europe had come

180

in June at Normandy, and American and British armies were sweeping eastward across Europe to meet the Russians. In the Pacific, too, victory seemed near, all the more after the U.S. Navy completed its destruction of the Japanese fleet late in October in the Battle for Leyte Gulf. Reflecting the swelling public confidence that the war soon would be over, Connecticut cities like those in other states had already begun plans for V-Day celebrations. The obvious nearness of victory made it a secondary political concern.

But the good war news and the attendant optimism did not remove the issue of victory from the autumn's politics. Having suffered in 1942 because the war was going poorly, and wanting in 1944 the political profit that might accrue to the party that had led the nation to the edge of victory, Democratic candidates everywhere recited the triumphant progress of the war and warned against changing a winning team with the end so near. Yet the very imminence of victory had ironic political liabilities for the Democrats, for summertime national polls indicated that should the war be over or nearly so by November, the President would seem less necessary, would lose support, and might well lose the election. One solution to this dilemma was for Roosevelt to emphasize his continuing role as commander-in-chief and for Democrats generally to insist that critical war decisions remained; another was to look beyond the war and to insist that only Roosevelt and his party could ensure postwar peace and prosperity.[55] In the event, the Democrats took both tacks, though as the campaign wore on postwar peace and prosperity became clearly the party's foremost issues. Republicans came to the same emphasis more easily. They could scarcely hope to win votes from the successful prosecution of the war by a Democratic government, and those polls, after all, indicated that the GOP would do better the more voters thought about the postwar era. Postwar peace and prosperity thus became the overriding issues around the country in 1944.

The 1944 campaign came not only when victory seemed assured but also when the major Allied powers were meeting at

Dumbarton Oaks in Washington to discuss the United Nations organization. It came, too, at the crest of internationalist sentiment among Americans, and despite an agreement between Secretary of State Cordell Hull and John Foster Dulles, representing Dewey, to keep the issue of international organization apart from politics, the question was too important and the political pressures too great for the matter to be nonpolitical. Republicans especially, and the GOP presidential candidate most of all, had to establish their internationalist credentials since many people still identified the party with isolationism. Dewey therefore endorsed an international organization and "effective cooperative means," including the use of force, "to prevent or repel military aggression." Neither presidential candidate initially satisfied Wendell Willkie, who retained an important following and whose support therefore seemed possibly decisive in an election the polls showed to be close. When Willkie fell ill and then died early in October, internationalist Republican Senator Joseph Ball stepped in and asked the candidates three questions, most important among them whether the American representative to the Security Council of the proposed United Nations Organization could commit the nation's troops without further congressional authority. Dewey remained silent on that question, and Roosevelt seized the opportunity to win over Willkie's following by answering affirmatively. Though Dewey soon went nearly as far as Roosevelt, Ball and other internationalists announced their support of the President. Significantly, the key question involved the use of military force.[56]

The Connecticut campaign reflected the salience of the foreign policy issue. It reflected, too, the centrality of military force to American internationalism. The senatorial race, which revolved almost entirely around foreign policy and which aroused more interest than any other state contest, revealed both those things. Democratic challenger McMahon hammered away from August until November at Danaher's isolationist record, especially the Senator's opposition to prewar preparedness measures. Danaher tried to dodge McMahon's attack by stand-

182

ing behind the ambiguous GOP platform plank and denouncing Roosevelt throughout the campaign for secrecy, deception, and unilateral executive action in the conduct of foreign policy since the late 1930s. Pressured by McMahon, however, and, no doubt, by his reading of public opinion, the Senator modified his position and in late October issued a seven-point program advocating a world assembly and American readiness to use force if necessary to stop aggression.

But Danaher satisfied neither McMahon nor the internationalist groups which opposed him as they did other prewar isolationists in the nation. McMahon, of course, saw in Danaher's record of opposing preparedness an issue that promised to take him to the Senate. Yet substance as well as political tactics was involved in the negative reaction of the internationalists to Danaher's apparent change of heart. For one thing, the equation McMahon made between isolationism and pre-Pearl Harbor opposition to preparedness made sense given the nature of the wartime internationalist consensus of averting war by force. For another, Danaher defended rather than renounced his record. Still further, the Senator evidently preferred international "cooperation" to organization, "peace forces" to military forces, and some sort of congressional control over American troops. Like Dewey, Danaher allowed his opponent to be the champion of an international organization whose touchstone was the ability instantly and decisively to quash aggression; and, like Dewey, he suffered politically for it.[57]

As discussed on the hustings, and not just in the presidential and senatorial campaigns, the internationalism of late 1944 boiled down to cooperative military intervention to stop war. Democratic candidates embraced that position and denounced GOP isolationism. Republicans edged nearer and nearer the Democratic prescription for peace. GOP calls for international justice, the rights of small nations, and peaceful means of solving problems and GOP criticisms of executive secrecy and deception in foreign affairs, however potentially important, seemed transparently partisan in motivation and did not speak to the public concern for peace and security. Although many saw the election of 1944 as the great referendum Wilson had so badly wanted a quarter-century before, only Wilson's desire for collective security found significant favor or expression in 1944 America.

Domestic security received parallel attention in the national and state campaigns. Dewey devoted his first major campaign address chiefly to domestic matters, employment especially, and throughout the campaign he raised standard Republican charges that the New Deal's failure to end the Depression before the war came had proved its inability to provide jobs. Denouncing Republican reaction, Roosevelt in his few campaign appearances recounted New Deal programs, advances, and concern for the workingman. Both candidates accepted the notion that the government had an obligation to ensure jobs for the American people.

Connecticut's own special fears about postwar employment had not subsided by the autumn of 1944. Pessimistically noting in August the "staggering" problems of reconversion, the Post-War Planning Board estimated unemployment of some 280,000 persons (roughly one-third of the anticipated labor force) if production reverted to 1940 levels. The board advanced a comprehensive set of recommendations to ease the postwar economic transition, and business and other government agencies gave still more attention to preparing for contract termination, reconversion, and readjustment. In mid-September, Baldwin called a conference to discuss reconversion, and on its recommendation the Governor established a new special state committee on reconversion.[58]

Reconversion and reemployment dominated the gubernatorial campaign. Wanting to capitalize on the concern about postwar jobs and economic security, Baldwin campaigned largely on his actions and plans in those areas. Hurley in response repeatedly attacked the Governor's programs as dilatory, insufficient, and riddled with politics. Anyway, he said, postwar prosperity was a problem to be tackled primarily at the national level, where Roosevelt would do more than Dewey.[59]

The jobs issue intensified in early October, when a Senate

184

committee headed by Nevada Democrat Patrick A. McCarran recommended a ban on reconversion in government-owned plants in eleven northern and eastern states, including Connecticut, so that the South and West could develop large-scale industry. Although McCarran's seven-man committee was bipartisan and included six Westerners and one Southerner, Baldwin and other Republicans quickly labeled it another bureaucratic New Deal plot designed to regiment business and to deprive Connecticut workers of jobs. In Bridgeport, the cop distributed 23,000 pamphlets on the report, 20,000 of them at factory gates. Democrats, fearing that the affair might seriously hurt them, especially if workers believed Republican claims that prewar plants might be shut down, criticized the report, explained its origins, and denounced Republican distortions. But the cop would not let go of the issue.[60]

The issue of economic security involved more than the gubernatorial race, Connecticut's postwar plans, and the McCarran report. Democrats used the worry about jobs and prosperity to warn that Republican reaction would mean a return to Hooverism and depression. In running yet again against 1920s-style Republicanism and the Great Depression, Democrats also sought to rekindle the passions and reinforce the attachments of the two previous presidential campaigns. Again they stressed the importance of reelecting Roosevelt and maintaining the New Deal, and again they portrayed themselves as the party of labor and the workingman, the cop as the party of business and reaction. As part of that, Democrat congressional candidates assailed the records of the 1943-44 Congress and of their incumbent opponents.[61]

Republicans knew from past elections and current polls that they had to improve their standing in labor constituencies. Their task was made more difficult by unprecedented cooperation between the AFL and CIO in working for Roosevelt, by solid union endorsements of Connecticut Democrats, and by the unusually strenuous grass-roots political activity by labor, especially the CIO Political Action Committee. Besides attacking the McCarran report, Republicans also renewed their pledges to support labor and its achieved gains. The congress-men defended their records, while Baldwin recounted his and pledged more legislation beneficial to labor, including a state labor relations act. Danaher closed his campaign with a spec-tacular appeal to labor when his father, state labor commis-sioner since 1939 and active in state labor circles for decades, dramatically resigned his post on election eve and took to the airwaves on behalf of his son.[62]

The Republican campaign also emphasized the party's more customary themes. Criticizing New Deal methods, Republi-cans argued that only through untrammeled private enterprise could full production, full employment, and thus true prosper-ity be achieved. More often and more stridently, the GOP stressed "Americanism" and traditional American ways. Baldwin said that with the GOP "the American system, the American way of life, the American way of doing things will go forward"; Congressman-at-large Monkiewicz urged a return to "the Amer-ican way of self government" and the "American way of life"; Second District Congressman John McWilliams said that "the issue in the election this November is Americanism"; and others spoke in nearly identical terms.[63] As before, the Ameri-can Way meant partly an economic system—individualism, op-portunity, unhindered free enterprise—and partly a system of government, without excessive centralization, executive power, spending, or planning. As before, too, Republicans argued that the Democrats and the New Deal threatened the Ameri-can Way. But where in 1940 the GOP had warned of an Ameri-can dictatorship, in 1944 the fourth term was hardly an issue nor was dictatorship the threat emphasized by Republicans. Rather, the GOP decried the awful menace of communism and sought to link it with Roosevelt and the Democrats.

In pressing that argument, Republicans focused especially on imagined Democratic ties with American Communist party head Earl Browder and on alleged Communist sympathies of CIO-PAC leader Sidney Hillman. Worried about the political ef-forts of Hillman's PAC and told by their poll that they could profitably attack the PAC in nonlabor constituencies, distrustful of labor "radicalism" and unhappy with labor's increased power, the GOP made Sidney Hillman, a Lithuanian-born Jew who had helped found the leftist American Labor party in New York, their special target. Republicans called him a Communist agent who with PAC money and votes was trying to buy a share of the Democratic party, and, claiming that Roosevelt had said to "clear everything with Sidney," they cited the convention incident as proof of labor and radical influences on the New Deal. Clare Boothe Luce suggested that PAC really meant "Party of American Communism."[64]

The Communist issue figured prominently in the Republicans' state and national campaigns. Speaking in Connecticut, GOP vice-presidential nominee John Bricker said:

> Insidious and ominous are the forces of Communism linked with ir-religion that are worming their way into our national life. These forces are attempting to take a strangle hold on our nation through the control of the New Deal. These subversive forces of class hatred and pressure politics under the leadership of Sidney Hillman and Earl Browder must be driven from high places in our American political life. First the New Deal took over the Democratic Party and destroyed its very foundation. Now these Communistic forces have taken over the New Deal and will destroy the very foundations of the republic.[65]

Bricker continued in that vein throughout the autumn. Briefly early in the campaign and then more insistently as it closed, Governor Dewey also made such charges. In Connecticut, Republicans from the local to the state and national levels joined the chorus, as did much of the state's press. Even Baldwin toward the end argued that the Democratic party welcomed Communist support.[66]

No candidate campaigned harder on the issue—or gave it wider publicity—than Clare Boothe Luce. By virtue of her personal renown, ready and acid wit, and media connections, Luce naturally drew attention. In 1944, moreover, she was involved in a bitter campaign for reelection to Congress, made speeches for Dewey throughout the Midwest and East, and was the target of a concerted effort by Democrats and labor to unseat her. From her speech accepting renomination until election eve she spoke of the Communist peril to the nation:

> You have heard me say however, over and over that 100,000 Communists [underground in the Democratic party] do constitute a grave danger to the Democratic Party and the nation, now that they are so deeply entangled in the fabric of the party, and now that so many of them hold key positions in labor posts, and in government. And I repeat tonight, that if the Democratic Party wins this election, the Communist Party in America will claim credit for it, and will insist that a Democratic victory has given them a mandate from the electorate to go on taking over more and more key positions in bureaucratic Washington and in the labor movement.[67]

Arguing that the only consistent theme of Roosevelt's foreign policy was "appeasement of Soviet Russia," she also gave an early rendition of GOP cold-war themes by worrying about America "selling out" to communism in Europe and China. And she accused her opponent of "fraternizing" with "avowed Communists" and using them in the campaign.[68]

Democrats worried about such Republican charges. A deeprooted fear of communism and a related distrust of the Soviet Union, only partly allayed by the wartime alliance, had long pervaded American society. Had they so analyzed it, Democrats would have realized that charges of Communist encroachment abroad and infiltration at home implied threats to the security that Americans so badly wanted. But the Democrats had a more specific worry. They feared that the issue might seriously erode their strength among Catholics, especially the Catholic working class so crucial to the Roosevelt Coalition in the North, for fervent opposition to communism had long been part of Church dogma, and Catholic anticommunism had increased sharply (with noticeable political ramifications among Irish-Catholics) in the late 1930s.[69] During the war, the Church's apprehensions about Russia, international communism, and internal Communist subversion figured prominently in the *Hartford Catholic Transcript* and Catholic newspapers elsewhere.

Recognizing the political danger in the Communist issue, Democrats belittled and denied the Republican accusations. Roosevelt disavowed Communist support and condemned Republican "fear propaganda" and "red herrings." Connecticut Democrats responded similarly. With a nervous eye to the Catholic vote, Hurley added that the Catholic magazine *Commonweal* had absolved Hillman of any Communist connections, and in Fairfield County, Democratic challenger Margaret Connors likened Luce's campaign to the red-baiting methods of the German Nazis in the 1920s.

But the Republicans simply increased their attacks as the election neared. The preelection issue of the *Hartford Catholic Transcript* carried a half-page "Message to Americans About a Menace to America" in which Irish-Catholic Lieutenant Governor William Hadden enumerated the alleged links between Communists and state and national Democrats and painted a frightening picture of the effects of a Communist-Democratic victory on American religion, free enterprise, and government. Republicans flooded at least one eastern Connecticut town with "red menace" literature. Congressman McWilliams said that the election "may be our last chance to choose between Republicanism and Communism." A lurid advertisement in a Bridgeport newspaper warned of "HORDES OF COMMUNISTS, fellow travelers and collectivist well-wishers" working to undermine the Democratic party, federal government, and nation. Republicans thought they had found a powerful issue, and Democrats feared their opponents might be right.[70]

The campaign also had its full share of ethnic politics. Republicans hoped to profit from Irish-Catholic anticommunism and from what remained of Irish anglophobia and Irish nationalism. Both parties endorsed a Jewish homeland in Palestine, while Democrats sought as well to capitalize on Jewish sensitivity to rising anti-Semitism by accusing the GOP of bigoted attacks on Jewish immigrant Hillman.[71] Smaller ethnic groups also won attention where they were concentrated, and the campaign closed with the traditional array of ethnic rallies.

Blacks won considerable attention. The campaign revealed

189

both that politicians thought the Negro vote important and that blacks might use that perception for their own ends. For example, two Negro leaders agreed to head a committee supporting Hurley and Roosevelt after extracting assurances from state Democrats that blacks would receive full consideration, especially in appointments to state and local boards handling reconversion and reemployment. Hurley called for a state fair employment practices act, McMahon for a permanent FEPC. In his campaign, Baldwin criticized Hurley's tepid efforts for blacks and emphasized his own Inter-racial Commission, his 1940 employment committee, and the increased use of Negroes in state jobs. National issues also had some prominence. While the GOP accused the Roosevelt administration of neglecting black Americans and pointed to the power of Southern Democrats within the Democratic party, Democrats argued that Roosevelt had done more to combat discrimination than had any president since Lincoln.[72] By 1944, then, blacks and their concerns received far more political attention than in previous decades—a development paralleling the greater militance of blacks and the greater recognition of black problems (and of the growing strength and importance of the Negro vote). And while that attention was largely rhetoric and gesture, it had substance as well and in any event paralleled the tactics employed for white ethnic groups.

The principal ethnic appeals in 1944, however, went to the two major new immigrant groups so concerned about their homelands. In Connecticut as elsewhere in the East, it seemed likely that Poles and Italians would defect from the Democratic party in significant numbers. Republicans pressed those issues that promised them gains. In Connecticut, Congressman-at-large Monkiewicz again carried the GOP campaign to the Poles. Stumping the state and attacking Roosevelt's policies toward Poland, he sought to turn to political advantage the several fears of Polish-Americans about Poland. Luce, too, made Poland an important issue and called Poland the great symbol of freedom whose fate would be that of Europe and, ultimately, of the United States.[73]

Obviously disquieted by the GOP effort to win over Polish votes, Democrats argued that Roosevelt had been and would remain Poland's great friend and benefactor. But for that argument to take hold, Roosevelt himself had to demonstrate his concern and his intentions. The President did so, and with customary political adroitness, albeit in a manner that revealed him as fox rather than as lion. Concerned as he was about the Grand Alliance, Roosevelt would not press on Stalin the demands of the anti-Communist London Poles and of Polish-Americans for Polish sovereignty and territorial integrity. Indeed, his sternest message to Stalin before the election was to ask the Soviet leader to "pipe down" his denunciation of Dewey's support of the London Poles in order to prevent further politically damaging attention from being drawn to the Polish question. For the rest, Roosevelt sought to assuage Polish-Americans with vague and even deceptive assurances about their homeland. On Pulaski Day (October 11), he met with a delegation from the influential Polish-American Congress. Though still avoiding firm commitment, he gave the group "new hope" by agreeing that Poland must "be reconstituted as a great nation." Later in the month, Roosevelt met again with Charles Rozmarek, chairman of the Polish-American Congress, and again gave Rozmarek to understand that the President could handle Stalin and the Polish matter once the war was won. Rozmarek then announced that he would vote for Roosevelt, and Democrats made the most of the endorsement. Combined with Dewey's decision not to exploit the Polish question, Roosevelt's efforts went far toward mollifying Polish-Americans and persuading them that the President was the best chance for Poland.[74]

Roosevelt also used his office in ways Democrats hoped would appease Italian-Americans. Late in September he and Prime Minister Churchill anounced a new program for Italy, one designed to increase home rule, speed relief and reconstruction, and aid Italy in joining the war against the Axis. On Columbus Day, the President promised home rule for Italy as soon as liberation was complete and pledged "wholly adequate" relief when Germany had been defeated. Shortly before the election, the United States, the Soviet Union, and Great Britain gave full diplomatic recognition to Italy, and the Post Office Department announced limited parcel post service to Italy.[75]

The Italian press found such action insufficient, and Republicans sought again to exploit Italian-American unhappiness with Roosevelt. Deploring conditions in Italy, they especially criticized relief policies. A Bridgeport Italian leader, Louis Richards, called Italian relief funds a "miserable pittance," while Clare Luce accused the administration of "permitting the people in Italy to starve." (Consistent with the rest of her campaign, she also warned of Communist designs on Italy.) Attorney General Pallotti and other Republicans used older issues, too, including what Richards called Roosevelt's "false promises" not to send Americans to fight on foreign soil. "We Italians," declared a speaker at a New London GOP rally, "have had the spectacle of our own boys being sent to Italy to kill, in many instances, their own brothers, fathers and cousins." Emphasizing also their political recognition of Italian-Americans, Republicans suggested that their party offered brighter prospects for Italy and Italian-Americans alike.[76]

Democrats countered that Roosevelt had liberated Italy from the fascists, and they hailed the administration's policies to improve conditions in Italy and to hasten Italian sovereignty. Picturing himself as a great friend of Italian culture and of Italian-Americans, McMahon warned that to change administrations would jeopardize Italy's liberation and recovery. Hurley reminded Italians of the administration's change of the enemy-alien policy two years before. A new Italian-American Democratic Federation was founded in mid-October, and important Italian-Americans from within and without Connecticut campaigned for the Democratic ticket. Democrats stressed New Deal gains.[77]

But despite such efforts, Democrats remained apprehensive about the Italian vote, and with good reason. To the still rankling episodes that had sent many Italians to the GOP in 1940 and 1942 had been added the lesser but real irritants of 1943 and 1944. Though the immediate concerns of Italian-Americans for their homeland were much less grave than those of Polish-Americans, many Italian voters had developed an animosity toward Roosevelt for a variety of reasons and had voted against him in the past. Campaign talk and executive action could not do as much with the Italian vote as with the Polish vote.

The campaign of 1944, in Connecticut as in the nation, did not produce quite the same sharp, class-oriented party dichotomy on which the Roosevelt Coalition had thrived. Foreign policy, far more important than in the recent past, cut across class lines. Republican ethnic strategies and charges of communism threatened further to blur class divisions by appealing to segments of the working class. Nor did the issue of Roosevelt himself dominate the campaign as it had in the past. Even Republican charges that Roosevelt, obviously old and tired, compared poorly with the fresh, dynamic, efficient Dewey faded after the President's brilliant speech to the Teamsters in late September. Still central to the campaign, the issues of Roosevelt and the New Deal had not the overwhelming salience they had in 1936 and 1940.

Perhaps partly for those reasons, the campaign lacked the excitement of the two previous presidential contests. Other factors also dampened the campaign. Beginning unusually late, it suffered from competition with war news and war work, from travel and gasoline restrictions, and from a scarcity of ward heelers and volunteer party workers. Because rallies, again sparsely attended, tended to be "pep meetings for party workers," both parties considerably increased their reliance on radio to reach mass audiences. New Haven's Democratic town chairman lamented that radio had killed political rallies, and on that at least his GOP counterpart could agree.[78]

Yet the outward manifestations of apathy were not wholly reliable. Registration was heavy, particularly in the cities, and totaled a record 968,000. As the campaign closed, moreover, crowds increased perceptibly, voters seemed more aware and involved, and the press and radio were flooded with political

193

reports and advertisements. The apparent closeness of the election may have spurred interest, for polls gave Roosevelt only a narrow lead in Connecticut and showed the other major races to be tight as well. With the outcome in doubt, in the rest of the nation as well as in Connecticut, Connecticut was watched as a harbinger of the national trend.[79]

Those who watched Connecticut as a bellwether were rewarded on election night. The state reported a Roosevelt victory of 52.7 percent, and almost every other urban-industrial state fell into the President's column with similar margins and with similar voting patterns. In all, Roosevelt carried thirty-six states with 53.4 percent of the national vote.

The President owed his fourth-term victory to the enduring strength of the coalition that had reelected him twice before. It was not, to be sure, precisely the same coalition. As usual, there was a significant amount of voter switching from the previous presidential election, and the composite picture of national politics did not coincide precisely with that of 1940— the President lost considerable strength among restive white Southerners, for example, and more than in previous elections he relied on big-city pluralities for his margins in the popular and electoral vote. Still, there was less change in the composition of the vote between 1940 and 1944 than between any other pair of presidential elections in the New Deal-Fair Deal era.[80] Despite the events of the war years, the President retained the support of substantially the same combination of most workers, ethnics, urbanites, and Southerners and of many middle-class and farm voters that had elected him before. As before, too, Roosevelt's presence on the ticket helped other Democrats, for the party tightened its hold on the Congress. The only good sign that Republicans could find in what had become their quadrennial catastrophe was a continuing downward trend in Roosevelt's margins and in Democratic congressional majorities. But the shimmering GOP majority glimpsed by some observers in 1943 had proved a mirage, shattered by the champion campaigner and his party.

194

In Connecticut, the real GOP majority of the 1942 election also evaporated. In winning nearly 53 percent of the vote, Roosevelt carried Connecticut by 45,000 votes and helped the Democrats surge back to control. McMahon ran nearly as strongly as Roosevelt in ousting Danaher from the Senate, and the rest of the Democratic state ticket won by some 20,000 votes. In a departure from the two previous presidential elections, however, the Democrats failed to sweep all major contests. Luce's victory in the Fourth Congressional District and Joseph Talbot's in the Fifth gave the GOP two of the state's six congressional seats. More important and more impressive was Raymond Baldwin's arresting display of personal strength in running some 70,000 votes ahead of Dewey and 45,000 ahead of the state ticket to retain the governorship with 51.6 percent of the major party vote. Jasper McLevy, again a candidate but again a negligible factor, polled but 16,500 votes for governor.

Baldwin's victory and the unusual amount of ticket splitting suggested that Republicans might have done better had they not renominated Danaher. The two most popular candidates were Roosevelt and Baldwin, and many voters wanted to support both. Given this situation and also the Connecticut party-lever rule, Danaher's unpopular association with isolationism evidently caused a significant part of the electorate to pull the Democratic lever and split for Baldwin rather than pulling the Republican lever and splitting for Roosevelt and McMahon.[81] How important this effect was cannot be determined; but it surely reduced the party-line GOP vote and may have cost Republicans some of the close contests. The Democratic victory, though not Roosevelt's, was probably more fragile than it appeared.

Despite the reduced Democratic strength as compared with 1940, the Roosevelt Coalition in Connecticut held up well in the main. The President's percentage declined but slightly from 1940, and his principal sources of strength—urban and industrial areas and lower-income, foreign-stock, black, non-Protestant, and working-class voters—remained essentially the same. Republicans again did best in Yankee, Protestant, upper-

195

income, suburban, small-town, and farming areas. (See Tables IV-1, IV-2, and IV-3.) Again the cities were the backbone of the Democratic vote, and big-city pluralities were as crucial to

Table IV-1. ELECTION OF 1944, CONNECTICUT: WARD-LEVEL STATISTICS[1]

	Hartford (N = 15)	New Haven (N = 33)	Bridgeport (N = 16)	Combined (N = 64)
I. Simple correlation coefficients for percentage Roosevelt				
A. Percentage Roosevelt 1944 with percentage Roosevelt				
1940	+ .97	+ .92	+ .94	+ .92
with percentage Roosevelt				
1936	+ .91	+ .75	+ .80	+ .78
B. Percentage Roosevelt with average monthly rent				
1944	− .72	− .55	− .73	− .51
1940	− .84	− .68	− .76	− .66
1936	− .89	− .73	− .71	− .71
C. Percentage Roosevelt with percentage foreign-born				
1944	+ .85	+ .42	+ .50	+ .54
1940	+ .85	+ .59	+ .65	+ .69
1936	+ .83	+ .75	+ .68	+ .77
II. Multiple correlation coefficients for percentage Roosevelt with average monthly rent and percentage foreign-born as independent variables				
1944	+ .89	+ .57	+ .80	+ .61
1940	+ .94	+ .74	+ .89	+ .79
1936	+ .96	+ .86	+ .88	+ .87
III. Simple correlation coefficients for change in percentage Roosevelt 1940–1944 (percentage Roosevelt 1940 minus percentage Roosevelt 1944)				
A. With average monthly rent				− .52
B. With percentage foreign-born				+ .54
C. With percentage Roosevelt 1940				+ .47

[1]See Appendix for an explanation of the statistics used in this table. Tables A-1 through A-6 provide more statistics for each election from 1936 to 1948.

Table IV-2. ELECTION OF 1944, CONNECTICUT: TOWN-LEVEL
STATISTICS[1]

	All towns (N = 169)	Towns in Hartford, New Haven, and Fairfield counties (N = 79)
I. Simple correlation coefficients for percentage Roosevelt		
A. Percentage Roosevelt 1944 with percentage Roosevelt		
1940	+ .96	+ .97
1936	+ .92	+ .94
B. Percentage Roosevelt with average monthly rent		
1944	− .39	− .58
1940	− .43	− .63
1936	− .32	− .55
C. Percentage Roosevelt with percentage foreign-born		
1944	+ .64	+ .71
1940	+ .65	+ .71
1936	+ .61	+ .72
D. Percentage Roosevelt with total population		
1944	+ .38	+ .50
1940	+ .38	+ .49
1936	+ .46	+ .52
E. Percentage Roosevelt with percentage rural-farm		
1944	− .40	− .49
1940	− .34	− .44
1936	− .44	− .46
II. Multiple correlation coefficients for percentage Roosevelt		
A. With percentage foreign-born, average monthly rent, total population, and percentage rural-farm as independent variables		
1944	+ .81	+ .87
1940	+ .80	+ .87
1936	+ .79	+ .85
B. With percentage foreign-born and average monthly rent as independent variables		
1944	+ .68	+ .83
1940	+ .71	+ .84
1936	+ .64	+ .81
III. Simple correlation coefficients for change in percentage Roosevelt, 1940–1944 (percentage Roosevelt 1940 minus percentage Roosevelt 1944)		
A. With average monthly rent	− .18	− .25
B. With percentage foreign-born	+ .07	+ .06
C. With total population	− .01	+ .02
D. With percentage Roosevelt 1940	+ .19	+ .25

[1]See Appendix for an explanation of the statistics used in this table. Tables A-1 through A-6 provide more statistics for each election from 1936 to 1948.

Table IV-3. ELECTION OF 1944, CONNECTICUT AND UNITED STATES POLL DATA[1]

	Percentage Roosevelt, Connecticut	Percentage Roosevelt, United States
I. Connecticut and United States		
A. Religion		
Protestant	24	49 (approx.)
Catholic	68	73
Jewish	90	92
B. Occupation		
Professional	39	42
Farmer	29	48
Proprietor, manager	43	41 ("business")
White collar	57	51
Skilled worker	51	59
Semiskilled worker	64	65
Unskilled worker	61	—
Union worker	63	72
CIO	68	78
AFL	58	69
Non-union worker (for Connecticut includes "no answer")	47	56

[1]Connecticut data from Opinion Research Corporation, "The 1944 Campaign: Connecticut," dated Oct. 12, 1944, copy in Baldwin Papers, Box 6. United States data drawn from Wesley and Beverly Allinsmith, "Religious Affiliation and Politico-Economic Attitude," *Public Opinion Quarterly*, XII (Fall 1948), 387; *Public Opinion Quarterly*, IX (Spring 1945), 84; George Gallup, *The Political Almanac, 1952* (New York: J.C. Forbes & Sons, 1952), 37. (Figure for Protestants in U.S. computed from data in Allinsmith, "Religious Affiliation," Table 3, p. 387, for six major denominations.)

the Democratic victory in Connecticut as they were in the rest of the nation. Hartford, New Haven, and Bridgeport together gave Roosevelt a larger margin than in 1940; and whereas the President had won the aggregate state vote outside those cities in 1940, he did not in 1944. The decisive Democratic urban pluralities in turn owed much to the hard grass-roots work of the CIO-PAC, which in Connecticut as in the nation often outperformed the Democratic organization and which evidently helped Connecticut depart from the national trend of a turn-

II. Connecticut only

    A. Percentage Roosevelt by country of father's birth

U.S. and Possessions	38
England, Scotland, Wales	28
Germany, Austria	44
Denmark, Finland, Norway, Sweden	28
Italy	54
Canada (86% Catholic)	68
Ireland	74
Poland	78
Catholic	72
Jewish	91
Russia (82% Jewish)	84
Other European	68

    B. Strongest groups for Roosevelt and Dewey

Roosevelt		*Dewey*	
Jewish	90%	Protestants	76%
Russian	84	Danes, Finns, Swedes,	
Polish	78	Norwegians	72
Irish	74	English, Scottish, Welsh	72
Catholic	68	Farmers	71
Canadian	68	Germans, Austrians	66
Semiskilled workers	64	Retired	65
Union members	63	Native-born	62
Unskilled workers	61	Professionals	61
		Managers	57

out decline from 1940.[82] In all, the election provided another victory for the now well-tested Roosevelt Coalition. Indeed, there was less change in voting patterns than there had been between 1936 and 1940, a phenomenon which like the division of the vote followed the national results.

Yet the returns did not simply replicate those of 1940. Nationally some 10 percent or more of those voting in both elections voted differently in 1944.[83] Within the overall framework of stability in Connecticut voting patterns there were also important changes, especially in the cities. While the President won roughly the same share of the aggregate big-city vote as in 1940, his percentage increased slightly in Hartford and New Haven, held steady in New Britain, dropped a bit in Bridgeport, and fell sharply in Waterbury. The pattern of the vote within the cities changed, too, as shown by Table IV-1, and for reasons that help to clarify the politics of 1944.

Once the banner city of the Democratic party in Connecticut, Waterbury gave Roosevelt only 54 percent of its vote as compared to 70 percent in 1936 and 61 percent in 1940. In Bridgeport, Roosevelt's share of the major party vote fell to 62 percent from 70 percent in 1936 and 65 percent in 1940. Party factionalism helped account for those substantial declines. In both cities, the organizations had sided with Maloney in the struggle over nominations, and they failed to go all out in the autumn for the Democratic slate. But since Hartford, where Roosevelt did better than he had in 1940, also had "disgruntled and vengeful leadership" and had sharp local factionalism as well, other factors evidently played a role in shaping the Bridgeport and Waterbury returns.[84]

For one thing, both cities had unusual political situations. McLevy's long mayorship in Bridgeport had deprived the Democratic organization there of local power and patronage and made it by far the most anemic of the Democratic urban organizations. In 1944, moreover, Socialist voting centered in Democratic (especially ethnic) areas and hurt Democratic candidates.[85] Waterbury had been the center of the 1938 scandals, which had implicated and tarnished the city's Democratic organization, and during the war years charges of communism in the city's CIO brass unions, raised by Republicans, the local press, and the Catholic Church, may have made Waterbury voters especially responsive to the GOP's Communist issue. Perhaps most important of all, however, was the ethnic composition of the two cities. Neither had large populations of Poles, Jews, or blacks, three groups that in Connecticut as elsewhere held up solidly for Roosevelt in 1944.[86] Bridgeport had an unusually large Hungarian area, which defected substantially from Roosevelt in 1944. Both cities, Waterbury especially, had important Italian concentrations, and Italians there as throughout the East continued their departure from the Roosevelt Coalition.[87]

The importance of ethnicity was demonstrated also in Hartford and New Haven, where the President did slightly better than in 1940. In New Haven, the two most heavily Italian wards, which had given the President 73 and 76 percent of the vote in 1936 and 54 and 56 percent in 1940, fell further to 46 and 52 percent. Less densely Italian areas showed similar, though smaller, continuing declines. Conversely, Roosevelt held roughly steady in the city's Irish wards, gained slightly in Jewish wards (from 69 to 73 percent in ward 3, for example), and increased his share of the vote in the Negro ward from 59 to 67 percent. The Polish population in largely Italian ward 12 again apparently prevented that ward from having Democratic losses parallel to other Italian areas. In New Haven's most Yankee (and most wealthy) ward, Roosevelt gained eight percentage points; and his share of the vote there—41 percent—fell but five points below that of the most Italian (and lowest-rental) ward. Chiefly because of the shift away from Roosevelt in the low-income Italian areas and the shift toward him in the relatively high-income Jewish areas and the high-income Yankee areas, the Roosevelt vote in New Haven was based far less on low-income, immigrant voters than in the two previous presidential elections there or in the other two largest cities in 1944.

In Hartford, the pattern of the vote much more closely resembled the 1936 and 1940 returns. Helped by John Bailey's hard work, the cio-pac, and other nonparty groups, the Democrats evidently suffered little from their factional and organizational problems.[88] Too, Hartford's Italian population was proportionately far smaller than New Haven's or Waterbury's, and, in contrast to those two cities, Hartford's principal Italian political leaders were Democrats. Still, the most heavily Italian area fell to 65 percent Democratic from 85 percent in 1936 and 72 percent in 1940. Hartford had a Jewish population comparable to New Haven's in size and voting alignment;

ward 4, for example, rose from 78 percent to 82 percent for Roosevelt. The fairly sharp Democratic decline from 1936 to 1940 in Irish wards was arrested, while the French-Canadian and black areas held steady at 80 and 75 percent Democratic respectively. As in New Haven, Roosevelt registered a significant gain in the most Yankee (and third wealthiest) ward.

The big-city returns taken together told a common tale. Besides demonstrating anew how local circumstances could affect voting, they also revealed important patterns common not only to the state's cities but also to voting patterns throughout the nation. Resentful of the chain of events affecting them and their homeland since 1940, Italians continued to defect from the Roosevelt Coalition, though at a reduced rate. Republicans did much less well, however, among Polish-Americans, the other major immigrant group among whom ethnic and old-country concerns had seemed to promise substantial GOP inroads —New Britain's Polish area, for example, fell only from 88 to 84 percent Democratic. Similarly, Irish areas seemed little affected by Republican charges of communism and showed scant political change. Jews, liberal and sensitive to perceived anti-Semitic overtones in the GOP campaign, and blacks, still grateful to the President for the help and recognition he had given them, gave the President as much or more of their vote as in past elections.[89] Upper-class, Yankee areas shifted toward Roosevelt, evidently because of a distrust of Dewey and Danaher on foreign policy. The cross-currents of voter switching, especially in New Haven, combined to reduce the association of the Roosevelt vote with low-income, immigrant areas.

The statewide vote, examined by towns, revealed patterns similar to those in the major cities. The Roosevelt Coalition remained notably stable. (See Table IV-2.) Democrats again drew their strength from the larger towns and cities and from lower-income and especially ethnic areas. Towns with substantial Polish, Jewish, and French-Canadian populations generally remained at their staunchly Democratic 1940 levels, while most towns with significant Italian concentrations registered declines, usually smaller than those of 1940, in their Democratic percentages. Republicans again easily carried most of the state's small and suburban towns. Roosevelt did less well than before in agricultural areas, and in some of Litchfield County's Yankee farming towns the President polled barely one-fifth of the vote. In many other small towns and suburbs, however, Roosevelt made small but distinct gains over 1940. That trend was most evident in suburban towns in western Connecticut that had shifted substantially toward Willkie in 1940. Such towns, still for the most part strongly Republican, provided essentially the nonurban equivalent of Roosevelt gains in the Yankee, high-income big-city wards. An influx of war workers probably also helped the Democrats in the big-city suburbs.

Some of the town-level changes indicated that class and occupational status influenced changes in voting patterns. But while V.O. Key found a "class-tinged pattern of party switching" less than but similar to that of 1940, Connecticut election returns, like George Gallup's findings, suggested a different situation.[90] Causing class-line voting differentials to narrow in 1944 after widening in 1940, net upper-income switching was evidently to Roosevelt, not to Dewey, and stemmed from foreign policy, not economic, concerns. More important, voting patterns, especially at the ward level, indicated that ethnicity best explained deviations from 1940. The result of that, too, was a softening of class divisions in the vote.

The election of 1944 has been called, then and since, a "clear-cut mandate for international organization." Most isolationists of both parties lost their places in Washington. Explaining Danaher's defeat at the hands of a virtual unknown, the *Hartford Times* pointed to the Senator's weak position on a world organization to keep the peace, a great liability when "more than anything else the American people want a powerful organization of nations as a means of preventing war. . . ." The President, too, evidently profited in Connecticut from the foreign policy issue, and national polls showed that on the matters of winning the war, maintaining peace, and conducting foreign policy Roosevelt and the Democrats enjoyed a clear edge in the nation's confidence. Foreign policy, in particular the strong internationalist consensus of the war years, played an important role in the election.[91]

Yet voting did not revolve primarily around international issues. An October poll revealed that 36 percent of the nation's people thought jobs would be the most important problem of the next four years, while only 12 percent thought it would be making peace. (Of the other problems listed, none of them chosen by as many as 8 percent of those polled, most involved the domestic economy.) Although polls earlier in the year had suggested that Americans thought Dewey and the GOP could better handle domestic affairs and ensure prosperity, polls in October showed that they had changed their minds.[92] In job-conscious Connecticut, as in other states, that confidence helped Roosevelt. Concern about employment may also have contributed substantially to Baldwin's victory, for while the Governor's personality was an asset, his supporters usually spoke of his record in explaining why they would vote for him.[93] In 1944, the Governor's record, as he was at pains to make clear in the campaign, largely involved plans and preparations for postwar employment.

The importance of domestic issues to the election went beyond jobs. Responses to a variety of national polls inquiring about attitudes toward the presidential candidates and the two parties revealed the dominating importance of domestic public policy concerns. (Communism was scarcely mentioned.) The responses also showed the continuing importance of Roosevelt and the New Deal to voting, whether the respondents voted Democratic or Republican.[94]

The war and foreign policy, then, softened but did not obscure the salience of the sorts of issues, appeals, and attachments of the earlier Roosevelt elections. No wonder that the Democratic party rebounded from the 1942 election, held in a much different atmosphere, or that the core of the Roosevelt Coalition held up so well in Connecticut. Tested a second time in a presidential election since its coalescence in 1936, the coalition had for the most part withstood the pressures and changing concerns of the war years. Political cleavages in the state seemed hardened; and reinforced loyalty to the Democratic party, the party of Roosevelt and the New Deal, surely accounted for much of the stability of the vote.

The politics of 1944, finally, reflected nicely the divisions and the temper of the society. Voting patterns revealed the continuing and fundamental partition of the people along ethnic and religious lines and the continuing salience of ethnic-oriented issues to the foreign-stock population. The returns also revealed the persistence of the society's class lines. In conjunction with campaign rhetoric and public opinion studies they showed further the general public's dominant concerns: prosperity and peace. Peace meant the absence of war; hence the equation of military force and internationalism, the focus on an international organization to keep the peace. Yet even peace was secondary to jobs, the first worry of the people. "Peace is a job"—so one acute observer wrote in summarizing American attitudes.[95] After so many years of depression and then war, the public wanted freedom from want and freedom from fear. There were few calls for melioristic internationalism or far-reaching domestic reform. Realizing that, national party leaders had rejected the candidacies of Wendell Willkie and Henry Wallace. Though in 1944 the voters had to make a judgment about the nation's guidance in the future, the case before them came from the dreadful experiences of the recent past. From that past, too, came their answer. Franklin Roosevelt, symbol of security in depression and war, was chosen to provide security—prosperity and peace—in the days ahead.

V

"HAD ENOUGH?"

The Troubled Transition from War to Peace

The American people should have been content in 1946. Peace had come the year before, and by mid-1946 the nation enjoyed general prosperity as well. But a variety of troubles soured the fruits of victory. The United States had helped defeat the Axis only to perceive in the Soviet Union a new menace to world peace and national security. Domestic problems and vexations—those involving the economy foremost, but many others as well—provided more immediate and tangible sources of unhappiness. Looking for leadership to solve postwar problems and allay postwar worries, Americans found Harry S Truman, not Franklin D. Roosevelt, in the White House, and he seemed a poor substitute indeed. The security and peace of mind so badly wanted seemed nearly as distant as ever. Instead of celebrating peace and prosperity, therefore, the public seethed, sometimes anxiously, sometimes angrily, at Russian behavior, economic problems, Harry Truman, and more besides.

Such troubles seemed to define the transition from war to peace, and they provided the issues for and shaped the outcome of the election of 1946. At once the last election of the Roosevelt era of depression and war and the first of the postwar era of affluence and the cold war, the 1946 election gave Republicans control of the Congress for the first time since the Hoover years. Connecticut made up part of the GOP tide, and Republicans swept the state. In producing what proved to be a deceptively easy and anomalous GOP victory in Connecticut and the nation, the politics of 1946 gave important clues about

206

the nature of postwar society and politics and about the continuity as well as the change in postwar American life.

As it had for so long, the economy commanded much attention during the biennium after Roosevelt's fourth-term reelection. In the winter of 1944–45, the problem of finding workers enough for war jobs again took priority when the German thrust at the Battle of the Bulge temporarily bolstered the military's claims that war production lagged behind needs. Then as the German lines collapsed, primary attention returned by the spring of 1945 to postwar reconversion and reemployment, matters that had been deemphasized in the interim but had not been ignored and had remained sources of real anxiety. Nevertheless, concern and even planning had not necessarily meant action, especially at the macroeconomic level. The economic transition from war to peace would be essentially *ad hoc*, and dislocation and consternation accompanied the progress toward peacetime prosperity.

The first stage of the economic readjustment came after the German surrender in early May 1945. In Connecticut, contract cutbacks and cancellations helped pull the business index down from 66 points above normal in May to + 52 in July. In the same period manufacturing employment fell some 6 percent. Job seekers jammed employment offices, and unemployment compensation claims jumped sharply.[1]

All that was but prelude to V-J Day and its consequences. The jubilant celebrations that erupted on the news of Japan's surrender yielded almost immediately to anxiety about peacetime economic security. Jobs worried most people, of course, but the certain end of regular overtime work, so important to wartime income gains, caused apprehension too. A wave of contract cancellations and plant shutdowns and cutbacks soon gave palpable cause for concern. In its sharpest drop ever, Connecticut's business index plummeted nearly 30 points in August, while the employment index fell to its lowest point since the summer of 1940. Within ten days of the Japanese surrender, 73,000 workers had been laid off in the state; within a month, 90,000 industrial workers had been idled—almost one-fourth the number employed in mid-August. Manufacturing employment for September stood at only some 60 percent of the wartime peak. Unemployment compensation claims sky-rocketed, and those production wage-earners still employed saw their weekly earnings drop by some 5 percent in September. The awful predictions about the postwar seemed on their way to coming true.[2]

Responding to the economic dislocations, Governor Baldwin called a conference of business and labor leaders immediately after V-J Day to discuss reconversion and reemployment. From the meeting came a labor-management council on postwar economic problems, and Baldwin took other limited steps to ease adjustment. In the face of the massive layoffs, such measures did not satisfy labor, which pressed the Governor to call a special session of the General Assembly to enact a program including public works spending, a state minimum wage of 65 cents per hour, and increased unemployment compensation. Requesting as well a statewide wage hike of 50 percent to counteract inflation and reduced working hours, CIO spokesmen were especially strenuous in their demands.

The reaction to such proposals fell out predictably along ideological and political lines. So, too, did responses to the liberal program including a full employment bill that President Truman urged on Congress at war's end. Organized labor and Democrats backed the full employment bill and pressed for quick action by the General Assembly. With the Republican press, Connecticut industry opposed a special session of the legislature, denounced "make work," "doles," and "Santa Claus" profligacy, and pilloried the "prophets of despair." While liberals and labor retained the wartime fears of a postwar bust and called for New Dealish nostrums, most businessmen insisted that unfettered private enterprise would quickly bring full production and high employment and that unemployment was largely "statistical," the result of many women and migrants voluntarily leaving the state's labor force and of other workers shunning unappealing available jobs or going on vacation.[3]

208

Although reconversion proceeded more slowly than they initially forecast, the opponents of government action had the better part of the argument, at least with regard to the potential of the economy. As in the nation, expectations of chronic hard times proved false. The higher incomes and virtually forced savings of the war years together with fifteen years of substantial material deprivation ensured great consumer demand. Recognizing that John Q. Public had replaced Uncle Sam as the nation's foremost consumer, advertisers counseled that a "peace of selling" must replace the "war of production" as the dynamo of prosperity. But since goods had to be made to be sold, production remained crucial to good times. And reconversion went with a speed that surprised many. By early October Connecticut's remarkable progress in reconversion and reemployment persuaded Baldwin that a special session of the legislature was unnecessary.[4]

Still, if the depressed economy feared by labor and liberals did not materialize, neither at first did the booming good times visualized by conservatives and businessmen. The business index rose, but so did the relief index. Employment increased, but not rapidly enough to absorb all the displaced war workers and discharged veterans. From September to December manufacturing employment rose by just 30,000, only about half the total of unemployment compensation applications. Weekly wages for production workers fell by 13 percent in the second half of the year. Then early in 1946 a wave of strikes snarled production throughout the country. Connecticut business activity fell in February below the level of the previous September, and the number of workers in state factories dropped to the lowest point since the end of the war. With roughly 100,000 Connecticut workers unemployed (nearly one-fifth of the number with nonagricultural jobs), the relief index reached a postwar peak in late winter.

Connecticut's economy finally turned the corner in the spring of 1946 and thrived in the remainder of the year. Strikes diminished, production rose, and new jobs opened up. Paced by manufacturing industries, the business index rose 30 points

209

from February to June, to +41. Between June and November it rose only another 5 points, but that marked a high plateau, some 30 points higher than in the previous autumn. As more jobs became available and as the influx of returning veterans slackened, unemployment began to shrivel. By August 1946 manufacturing employment had increased by 25 percent over the September 1945 low point. By mid-November, employment and weekly wages had both reached record peacetime levels, while hourly wage rates climbed to unprecedented highs.[5] Surveying the many signs of prosperity, the state department of labor reported that "the general labor situation in Connecticut reached an almost ideal condition in October. . . ." Here was the sort of economic progress that had led *Time* to call the American summer of 1946 "super-colossal."[6] Connecticut like the nation had entered the unparalleled peacetime prosperity that would characterize postwar America.

Despite that, Connecticut's people—like other Americans— lacked the sense of security and contentment they desired. As Baldwin said in November 1945, the coming of peace seemed to have "replaced one set of troubles with another."[7] Economic advances seemed slow in coming and threatened by strikes, shortages, and soaring prices. A year of "pessimistic prosperity,"[8] 1946 was also a year of uneasy peace. The wartime alliance proved fragile as the United States and the Soviet Union drew further and further apart. Most Americans thought that the fault lay with Russia. Seemingly reneging on wartime agreements, extending control into eastern Europe, quarreling about and then within the United Nations, and possessed of a different ideology, the Soviet Union increasingly came to be perceived as a threat to world peace and to American security. The awesome atomic bomb injected a new element of worry into international affairs, and the Soviet Union and the United States bickered about atomic control.

Because people did not want to abandon their hope for world peace, anti-Russian sentiment seemed to grow slowly and reluctantly for the most part. Thus the *Hartford Courant* in March 1946 criticized the call for an anti-Russian Anglo-American alliance which Churchill made in his famous "iron curtain" speech. Though talking in May 1946 of the "split between East and West" and admitting in June to "the reluctant conclusion that Russia is still bent on ultimate world domination through communism," the *Courant* in September advocated constructive, nonbelligerent statesmanship to allay Russian fears and lessen the threat of war. But by late 1946, the emphasis clearly was on firm and alert policies among the *Courant's* editorial writers as among the American public generally. Gallup polls in September indicated that three-fifths of the public felt less friendly toward Russia than a year before, while a bare 2 percent felt more friendly, and that the Truman administration commanded wide support for its increasingly tough-talking diplomacy. Fifty-seven percent of the public rated as good or excellent the performance of Secretary of State James F. Byrnes; critics said Byrnes was not tough enough.[9] Only slightly more Democrats than Republicans gave Byrnes high ratings, a fact that reflected the consensual and bipartisan nature of the nation's foreign policy. The general agreement on principles and approach evident in 1944 continued into the postwar era and underwrote America's emerging cold war posture.

Not just Soviet Russia but also internal communism seemed to some Americans to threaten the security and stability the nation so badly wanted. As with the related fear of Soviet expansion, the Catholic press and clergy issued especially strident warnings about the danger to America of Communist espionage, subversion, and infiltration of the nation's government and political and economic systems.[10] Other traditionally anti-Communist and antiradical groups helped raise the hue and cry. But while fearful anticommunism fed on old sources, its growth sprang largely from postwar developments. The perceived menace of Russia, sensational revelations of Communist espionage in Canada, and even the again loud, if tiny, American Communist party fueled fears.

Connected as it was with long-standing Republican charges

of communism in the New Deal and in labor, the mounting concern about domestic communism was politically charged. By mid-1946 conservatives and Republicans were worrying more loudly than ever about domestic communism and subversion and about administration laxity in ensuring the loyalty of federal employees. The GOP was ready to try again to exploit anticommunism in the coming election; and given the events and the mood of the early postwar period that tactic seemed to hold more political promise than in 1944.

Communism and the Soviet Union posed special and intense threats to those millions of Americans from European nations that were under or threatened by Soviet domination. The concerns and protests of those ethnic groups revealed the continuing importance of old-country ties and gave added strength to anti-Russian sentiment in the United States and in Connecticut. Although ethnic old-country nationalism, not only with regard to the Soviet Union, affected American society and politics less than after World War I, it had a real social significance and political impact.

That was especially so in the case of Polish-Americans. For them, and soon for many others as well, the Yalta Conference of early 1945 and its aftermath became the great issue. Hoping that the Yalta accords represented a major step toward postwar peace and big-power cooperation, as President Roosevelt declared they did, most Americans at first greeted them warmly. For Polish-Americans, however, deeply concerned about the territorial integrity and the sovereignty of their homeland, the Yalta agreements on Poland came as a shock. In Connecticut as throughout the nation they reacted wrathfully. Polish-American priests in the state excoriated as an "outrageous act of injustice" the awarding of eastern Poland to Russia, and they complained bitterly about the implications of the vague provisions for the Polish government. Laymen and Polish organizations joined the priests and the diocesan newspaper in denouncing the "Yalta Crime."[11]

Unable and usually unwilling to ignore the Polish issue or

the ire of Polish-Americans, politicians also took up the cause of Poland. In Connecticut, Republicans like Representatives Clare Booth Luce and Joseph Talbot, as part of their criticism of the Roosevelt administration for "appeasing" Russia and "softness" on communism, condemned what was happening to Poland. But in a state with so many Polish-American voters, Republicans had no monopoly on defending Poland, though most Democrats naturally criticized Russia, not Roosevelt. Few people more forcefully criticized the Yalta provisions for Poland or tried harder to help Poland than did Democratic Polish-American Congressman-at-large Joseph Ryter.

Although Polish-Americans and their spokesman did not reconcile themselves to the territorial arrangement made at Yalta, they increasingly focused on conditions in Poland and on the establishment of a government there. Deeply disturbed by the harrowing stories of want and repression in postwar Poland, they worried most about the Polish government, for that as they knew would decide the fate of the people. But despite protests and demonstrations, hope withered as Communist control tightened. Polish-Americans were left with memories of their homeland and bitter resentment about its plight.[12]

Italian-Americans were also unhappy about postwar provisions for their homeland, and they, too, came to have special reasons for disliking the Soviet Union and fearing Communist inroads. Though continuing to press for more generous relief and rehabilitation measures for the old country, Italian-Americans agitated most loudly about the peace treaty. They demanded "Giustizia per l'Italia!"—"justice" meaning a mild treaty and recognition of Italy's territorial desires—on the grounds that Italian suffering throughout the war and Italian service and sacrifice on behalf of the Allies had earned Italy special consideration. Connecticut politicians advocated a properly just peace for Italy, and in the spring of 1946 the Sons of Italy received assurance from the State Department that American policy was "certainly not" to reward Italy's contributions to the Allied cause by a "harsh or punitive peace" but was rather "to assist a just and honorable peace settlement."

213

But at the Paris peace negotiations, the Soviet Union dashed hopes for the sort of terms desired by Italy and by Italian-Americans. Most important, Italy's claims to Trieste, the gateway to the Adriatic and an emotional symbol for Italians, were not honored. Even though the peace provisions overall were essentially quite mild, Italian officials denounced the treaty and its "extreme severity." Italian-Americans were also unhappy with the treaty, and they were aroused as well by the growing strength of the Italian Communist party and the role of Soviet agents and propaganda in Italy.[13]

Great Britain, not Russia, drew the anger of Connecticut Jews, who also had reason for dissatisfaction with American efforts on behalf of their folk overseas. Hitler's defeat, joyously received though it was, neither ended the suffering nor resolved the future of European Jews. While Jewish relief activity went ahead, Zionists in Connecticut as throughout the nation pressed still more vigorously for an end to British restrictions on Jewish immigration to Palestine and for the establishment there of a Jewish commonwealth.

Like other ethnic concerns, and more so than any such issue but Poland, the question of Palestine was highly politicized in the early postwar years. To demonstrate support of the cause and to enlist still more, Zionists held mass rallies and sent delegations and petitions to state and federal officers in 1945 and 1946. By late 1945 Truman urged England to admit 100,000 Jewish immigrants to Palestine, and the Senate went further by calling for the establishment of Palestine as a Jewish national home and for the unrestricted entry of Jews to Palestine. In Connecticut, said to have a larger proportional Zionist membership that any other state, both parties endorsed Jewish aims in Palestine. But satisfying though such support was to Jews, it did not much affect the realities of Palestine. In 1946 Palestine was rent by violence, and Great Britain, unwilling to offend the Arabs, adopted Palestine immigration policies that outraged Zionists. Domestic political maneuvering and pressures consequently intensified in 1946 and seemed likely to af-

214

fect the election. Connecticut's Republican state chairman termed the plight of Jewish refugees "a highlight in the callous and brutal record of delay and indecision" of the Truman administration, and Hartford's Democratic town chairman wrote Democratic national chairman Robert Hannegan in late summer that the Palestine situation was "reacting most unfavorably in this strong Democratic area of Connecticut" and might cost the party dearly in the fall elections if Democrats did not abide by their 1944 platform stand on Palestine.[14]

Though the war had raised new problems for the European immigrant groups in Connecticut and the nation and had sometimes exacerbated old ones, it had also in fundamental ways made the newcomers more a part of American society. To be sure, prejudice and discrimination continued, just as did old-country ties among the ethnic groups. Jews found that the easing of wartime tensions did not mean the quick end of anti-Semitic incidents and discrimination. The inflamed reaction of Italians to news that Mississippi's flamboyantly racist Senator Theodore G. Bilbo had addressed an Italian-American as "My dear Dago" (and had advised her to keep her "dirty proboscis" out of Mississippi affairs) reflected the sensitivity of that group to continuing bias. By refusing (until 1948) to authorize special immigration of European refugees, Congress indirectly told foreign-stock Americans that the war had not brought their complete acceptance, as did the town of Greenwich in opposing the location there of the United Nations, partly on the grounds that "all kinds of people" might move in.[15] Still, the experience of war did make a difference. Providing a common enemy and enlisting the support of almost every American, the war had brought the nation's old- and new-stock groups together in sentiment and action and helped reduce the ethnocentric suspicions and barriers separating them.[16]

Nowhere was the corrosive effect of the war on old antagonisms clearer than in the experience of Italian-Americans. Embracing America and Americanism during the war, they in turn won a fuller acceptance into the society. Politics provided a good index of that, particularly in the increasing success of Italians in local politics in the middle and late 1940s.

In Connecticut, New Haven provided the most important instance of that success. In the 1945 city election, William Celentano swept to easy victory to become New Haven's first Republican mayor in a decade and a half and the first Italian mayor ever of a major Connecticut city. For Italians, ethnicity was of crucial importance to the election. Winning by five to one in the most Italian ward, Celentano did even better in Italian areas than he had in his 1939 try for the mayorship. The Italian-American press greeted his victory with ecstasy. Yet Celentano, who carried two-thirds of the city's wards and 55 percent of its vote, did not win simply because Italians voted for him, and the nature of his campaign and the overall composition of his support were perhaps more significant than the simple fact of his victory. Capitalizing on the deterioration of schools and municipal services under the Democrats, Celentano forged an issue-oriented coalition which included Irish, Yankees, municipal employees, and civic groups. Democrats tried hard to exploit anti-Italian sentiment as they had in Celentano's 1939 campaign, but they found the cutting edge of ethnic hostilities blunted.[17] On the news of Celentano's victory, "New Haven citizens from all groups of society turned out en masse . . . in one of the most spontaneous celebrations ever to hail the election of a new mayor. It was a tribute to William C. Celentano, the man who brought persons of all creeds, of all ethnic strains and from both political parties by the thousands, to the City's center."[18] That reaction, like the election returns, revealed the changes wrought in ethnic relations during the war years. The again festive Columbus Day celebrations in 1946 marked the pride and confidence of Italian-Americans in both their Americanism and their Italian background.

Blacks had also profited from the war. Throughout the North more actively voicing their complaints and pressing for change, they had made substantial gains in employment and

216

had helped force recognition of their problems on the public and public officials. Besides the advances made in the quantity and quality of industrial jobs, Connecticut blacks had in 1946 nearly twice as many business, professional, and public service jobs as in 1940. Unions in the state had become less restrictive, while newspapers reported Negro problems with more perception and sympathy. Perhaps most important, blacks apparently were laid off after V-J day in rough proportion to other groups. Wartime gains seemed ratified.

Still, Connecticut Negroes, again like blacks elsewhere, had come only part way on the road to acceptance and equal treatment. Set apart by color and prevented by segregation from fully joining other Americans in the war effort, they still constituted a distinctly separate and subordinate group. Their economic gains, however real and welcome, left them far behind other groups, particularly in white-collar employment, where they still encountered substantial opposition and made minimal advances. Housing problems—terrible conditions and virtual segregation—had grown worse during the war. Despite laws to the contrary, blacks met discrimination and often exclusion in places of public accommodation. Business, nursing, and vocational schools admitted few blacks or barred them entirely.[19]

But the pressure for change and the recognition of the need for improved racial relations did not end with the war. Connecticut blacks continued to protest slights and injustice and to organize and to work for better jobs, better housing, better treatment. Labor unions, civic and religious groups, public agencies, and elected officials joined those efforts in growing number. Still concerned largely with education and with lessening tension, the state Inter-racial Commission implemented a variety of programs to combat prejudice and end discriminatory practices.

Reflecting the greater attention given black problems and paralleling developments in other Northern states, a number of antidiscrimination bills came before the 1945 General Assembly. Especially important were several measures modeled

217

on the recent New York fair employment practices act, and one such bill easily passed the Democratic Senate before dying in the Republican House. In part, the fair employment bill failed because the notion of legislation with punitive provisions aroused opposition, especially among employers. But the bill also failed for reasons of politics. Democrats made it part of their legislative agenda, and once ensnarled in the partisan politics of Connecticut's divided General Assembly, the bill stood little chance. Action on it in both houses followed nearly straight party lines. Still, the measure had almost succeeded, and despite their opposition to the Democrats' bill, Republicans did seem interested in fair employment legislation, as did the influential Inter-racial Commission.[20] Black problems remained essentially unresolved in 1946, but for blacks in Connecticut as elsewhere the war years had been a time of important advances and significant new departures, a crucial germinal period for the postwar civil rights movement.

In addition to the special problems of Connecticut's ethnic and racial groups and the anxieties about communism at home and abroad, an assortment of domestic worries and nuisances plagued the society in general, roiled the transition from war to peace, and frustrated the enjoyment of what was, after all, peace and prosperity. Labor relations were one of those problems. It sometimes seemed, in fact, that world peace had bred home-front economic war. Stemming primarily from union demands for large wage hikes to compensate for the take-home pay lost by shortened work weeks, strikes cost the nation an estimated 120 million man-days of work in the year after V-J Day. Though that total represented less than 2 percent of the available working time, it was four times higher than the number of man-days lost to strikes in 1937, when labor had so angered much of the nation. The postwar strikes came, moreover, in the midst of reconversion, and they often occurred in such key basic industries as steel, automobiles, electricals, coal, and railroads. In the spring of 1946, indeed, coal and railroad disputes seemed likely to paralyze the nation. Ordering government seizure of coal mines and railroads, Truman halted a rail strike only by going to Congress with a stern set of recommendations which included drafting strikers. Such measures and proposals outraged labor—the labor-draft idea in fact aroused widespread criticism, including that of Senator Robert Taft—while Republicans and businessmen found the President's overall labor policies too soft. Labor relations were just one area where Truman found himself in a no-win situation which sent his reputation plummeting in 1946.[21]

Connecticut had its own labor problems, which compounded and brought home the growing resentment against labor. The number of man-hours lost to strikes soared from not quite 8,000 in July 1945 to 2.4 million in November and to 6.3 million in February 1946. Thereafter, Connecticut labor relations improved steadily. In May, only 1.8 million man-hours were lost to strikes, in June only 500,000, and in October just 150,000. But the year since V-J Day had been one of troubling labor strife. Inconveniencing, irritating, and worrying many Connecticut citizens, the sometimes ugly strikes outraged others, especially businessmen, who joined other critics of labor in urging legislation to restrict union activity. The National Association of Manufacturers took out full-page advertisements in the state's newspapers saying that "good times have been held up by an agony of strikes" and entreating people to write their congressmen for action if they wanted "industrial peace and prosperity." Union foes sometimes claimed that Communists, seeking to weaken America, had a hand in the labor unrest.[22] Though most people shared neither the worst fears nor the sternest aims of the businessmen, the strikes often did seem excessive and irresponsible threats to domestic peace and prosperity and inevitably worked against the Democrats and Harry Truman.

A severe housing shortage provided another source of frustration, worry, and anger. In Connecticut, the postwar housing shortage that authorities had belatedly foreseen exceeded expectations when the state's estimated quarter-million veterans began returning home. Never exceeding 1 percent in 1945, the rental vacancy rate fell to 0.5 percent by mid-1946. By that time, Connecticut's cities reported huge backlogs for public housing, swamped private realty agencies, overcrowding, and increased evictions. Thousands of "desperate cases" and "stories of tears, bribes, hardships, delayed marriages and the entire scope of human emotions" were routine in the scramble for housing. And things got worse, not better. Temporary housing programs, too modest to begin with, were reduced and slowed. Lacking material, partly because of continued material controls, private construction remained stagnant, while the failure of Congress to pass the Wagner-Ellender-Taft housing bill doomed badly needed expansion of public housing projects. By the autumn of 1946 the urban poor still lived in their long-inadequate housing while others searched for housing of any sort. Doubled-up and divided families were distressingly common. There was no cause to believe that matters might soon improve, much cause for the rampant discontent and worry.[23]

The housing situation particularly aroused veterans, whose demands precipitated much of what action was taken. Wanting to live in the security and comfort they had dreamed of, and often felt they had fought for, the returning servicemen frequently failed to find any accommodations at all. Because veterans and their families formed a large, vocal, and, it seemed likely, politically pivotal segment of the population, politicians paid close attention to the GIs and their desires. By early in the election year of 1946, both parties had begun to claim credit for the state's many efforts on behalf of its veterans and to advocate a special bonus for them. Though action on the bonus was deferred, a special session of the General Assembly did act on housing. The most important measure authorized the state to pay half the costs, up to 5 million dollars, incurred by localities for temporary veterans' housing. Since the act would apply to only a few thousand housing units at most, the authorized expenditure was an absurdly high sum which was really a "political gesture" aimed at the veterans.[24] It may have satisfied the legislators' felt political needs, but it did little about the housing crisis, even for the veterans.

220

Despite their other troubles, nothing so vexed Americans just after the war as various controls and shortages involving consumer goods. As it had in 1942, the Office of Price Administration served as a lightning rod for the public's discontent. The end of the war did bring relief from many of the wartime shortages and restrictions, which had become increasingly unpopular in the last months of the conflict. When rationing ended on canned goods and gasoline just after V-J Day, excited housewives responded with "one grand shopping splurge," while happy motorists clogged the roads as "'Fill 'er up' came back into the American language." The end of individual meat rationing late in November 1945 touched off another shopping spree. Apparently mellowed by peace and plenty, Hartford housewives decided that rationing had not really been so bad after all. Primarily, they said, it had provided a source of gripes and had made them feel part of the war effort. But they were glad it was over.[25]

Antipathy toward the opa did not suddenly vanish, however. If many controls had been discarded, others remained. Above all, price control—the heart of opa—continued. Backed by Republicans and conservatives, business began immediately after V-J Day a nationwide campaign, part of the general postwar conservative-business offensive against federal controls and New Dealism, to abandon the opa. opa price ceilings, said business spokesmen in Connecticut and elsewhere, impeded reconversion, reemployment, and production. Worse still, planning and central direction of the economy were antithetical to the American free enterprise system. End controls, they insisted, and American industry would achieve full production and full employment, while the market system would ensure price stability. Nor were just the manufacturers unhappy and vocal. Connecticut landlords complained about continuing rent control, construction firms and lumber dealers about controls on building materials, farmers about subsidies and price ceilings. Perhaps most important, the public also chafed under opa and the shortages attributed to it. Shoppers picked the counters bare during the first postwar Christmas season and clamored for more of the niceties restricted during the war, and then at Easter complained that they could not find the higher-priced merchandise they wanted. Food shortages, of meat especially, caused the greatest stir. Seeking to win support for its campaign against the OPA, the National Association of Manufacturers asked in advertisements, "Would you like some BUTTER or a ROAST of BEEF"? Those who did, and who wanted clothes, appliances, and other goods besides, should write their congressmen about the removal of price controls.[26]

The battle over OPA raged throughout the nation in 1946. In Connecticut business groups, Republicans, and much of the press kept up their attacks on the agency, while labor, Democratic leaders, and a few citizens' groups tried to mobilize support for it. Similar forces contended in Washington, where Connecticut's Chester Bowles, OPA Administrator and then head of the Office of Economic Stabilization, led the battle to maintain price ceilings. In late June 1946 Congress passed a weak one-year extension of OPA. Truman vetoed the bill, Bowles resigned, and OPA's opponents crowed about the agency's demise. But many people soon missed the OPA. Prices jumped more in the month of July than in any month on record, and some of the hikes threatened real hardships. In Connecticut, tenants flooded the offices of OPA and of state and local government with complaints about rent increases of 30, 40, 50 percent and more. Baldwin immediately invoked his war powers to prevent eviction for failure to pay rents above OPA levels, and work began for a special session of the General Assembly to enact rent control legislation. The inflationary surge also invigorated the organized campaign on behalf of OPA and brought it new support. Late in July Congress passed another weak OPA bill, and Truman, though still wanting a stronger measure, this time reluctantly signed it.[27]

The OPA returned with changes. The agency now had a special decontrol board, and many price ceilings were above June levels. Those for meat and other items were lifted entirely. Indeed, to the other grievances against OPA could now be added its failure, largely the fault of Congress, even to control infla-

222

tion. Retail prices for essentials rose 10 percent from June to September. Because of the sharp price advances in the last half of 1946, an 18 percent rise in the cost of living during the year offset a 13 percent rise in Connecticut factory wages.

Meat remained the salient and symbolic issue. Supplies increased, but so did prices—by 30 to 85 percent above old ceilings —and the OPA reimposed ceilings. With that, meat again vanished from the markets. Although some people were unsure at first whether high prices or short supplies were worse, the public soon decided between the two evils. The combination of Depression deprivation, wartime restrictions, and postwar prosperity made red meat on their tables more important to most people than a little more greenstuff in their wallets. Looking at a bare meat counter, a New Haven woman muttered, "Isn't it awful?"[20]

Many things seemed awful in the early postwar period, most of them with obvious political implications. Republicans had since 1945 criticized the Truman administration at every chance, and their opportunities seemed to grow geometrically in 1946. Yet while the polls showed a deterioration of Truman's popularity and of Democratic strength, the precise political consequences of the postwar problems, even of the OPA situation, seemed unclear as late as the summer of 1946. For the better part of the biennium national politics, and Connecticut politics too, were in a state of flux and no little uncertainty.

A major source of that was the death of Franklin Roosevelt in April 1945. Besides sharing the shock and sorrow common to most people, Democrats felt a special loss and consternation. The man whose programs and popularity had helped reshape American politics was gone. So, too, were his generous coattails and the political magnetism that had helped keep together his divided party and disparate coalition. Whether the Democrats could unify the party, maintain the coalition, and thus sustain their power was an open question. In Connecticut, that question was all the more pressing, for the popular Frank Maloney, apparently assured of reelection to his Senate seat in 1946, had died suddenly of a heart attack in January.

Nevertheless, Connecticut Democrats were optimistic in the last months of the war. Truman won praise early in his presidency, and developments in Connecticut augured well for the future. Robert Hurley's 1944 defeat had finished him as a potential candidate and active leader, and with the passage from Connecticut politics of Hurley and Maloney, leaders of the party's feuding factions since 1940, chances seemed good for Democratic unity under the leadership of newly elected Senator Brien McMahon, who had fallen heir to Maloney's patronage and to many of Maloney's followers dependent on that patronage. Then after an unusually rancorous and partisan, and for him particularly frustrating, session of the General Assembly, Governor Baldwin announced in June 1945 that he had had enough of politics and would take an executive position with the Connecticut Mutual Life Insurance Company when his term of office expired. The assurance that the party would not have to contend again with Baldwin and the likelihood of Republican factional bloodletting over the 1946 nominations further brightened Democratic prospects.[29]

But whatever optimism the Democrats possessed in the spring and summer of 1945 proved ephemeral. In the municipal elections that fall, they carried only one of the four big cities—Waterbury—and that narrowly. Not only did they lose New Haven for the first time since 1929, but they lost Hartford for the second consecutive election when voters there crushingly rebuffed Long Tom Spellacy in what proved to be his last serious candidacy. The big-city debacles fed already growing doubts about the party's chances in 1946. Reconversion and demobilization delays, strikes, unemployment, shortages, inflation, housing woes, and foreign policy difficulties all counted against the Democrats. So also did President Truman, who seemed to symbolize the nation's troubles. Suffering from comparison with Roosevelt, Truman came to be seen as indecisive, even incompetent, and he became the butt of the nation's jokes as 1946 wore on. His approval rating in the Gallup Poll, an astronomical 87 percent soon after he took office, plunged downward until it reached just 32 percent in October 1946.[30]

Republicans soon began organizing their 1946 campaign around the country's discontent. In February, GOP Lincoln Day speakers in Connecticut lashed out at the "bungling, inept efforts" of the Truman administration and of the "confused" man who had "failed to grow into the stature of a President." Two months later the Republican national committee issued a biting review of Truman's first year as president. The GOP's new national chairman, B. Carroll Reece, revealed something more of the party's intended line of attack when in his first major address he claimed that the nation faced terrible peril because a "group of alien-minded radicals" had seized control of the Democratic party. GOP candidates must be elected in the autumn, he said, to ensure "the triumph of Republicanism over Communism."[31]

Connecticut was a key state and, because of that, Raymond Baldwin a key figure in Republican calculations. Needing to elect twenty-seven additional congressmen to capture the House, the GOP coveted the four Connecticut seats that had fallen to Democrats in 1944. National and state leaders believed that Baldwin could carry several congressional candidates into office, and together they worked to lure him back into politics and onto the ticket as the party's nominee for Maloney's old Senate seat, held by an avowedly temporary appointee. Although Baldwin had this time firmly resolved to leave politics in order to devote more time to his family and repeatedly made his intentions plain, the pressure on him to run, heightened by prominent state businessmen and by the public, kept building in the spring and summer of 1946. It became irresistible when the president of Connecticut Mutual, also eager for Baldwin to try for the Senate and help the Republican ticket, told him that his job with the company was no longer open. That turned the trick, and in mid-August Baldwin declared for the nomination.[32]

Although Baldwin made his declaration with grace and apparent enthusiasm, he resented having been dragooned into running again by such heavy-handed means. His anger, and his desire to ensure that he would have some job come 1947, steeled him to insist on having his way on the other GOP nominations. If he had been forced to run again, he felt, then he would be the boss and he would take every precaution to ensure a victory. The most important decision to be made involved the gubernatorial nominee. Fifth-District Congressman Joseph Talbot had campaigned actively for the nomination, but Baldwin and organization leaders opposed him. For one thing, since J. Kenneth Bradley supported Talbot, Talbot's nomination might return control of the state organization to Bradley and Fairfield County. More important, at least to Baldwin, Talbot had earned the enmity of organized labor, and Baldwin did not want his election chances hazarded by a gubernatorial candidate with that liability. Instead of Talbot, Baldwin favored James McConaughy, former president of Wesleyan University, lieutenant governor in Baldwin's first term, and head of United China Relief. State chairman Mitchell announced his support of McConaughy just before the September convention, and Talbot, protesting all the way, finally withdrew at the last minute.

The convention, under Baldwin's thumb, then proceeded as smoothly as Republican gatherings usually did. Bradley even placed Baldwin's name in nomination. Headed by McConaughy, the state ticket was a model of recognition politics and balance and was testimony to Baldwin's control and his desire for a potent slate. To appeal to labor and to placate any Irish-Catholics unhappy with Talbot's rejection, James Shannon, counsel for the Connecticut Federation of Labor, was given the lieutenant governor nomination. Adroitly combining recognition of veterans with ethnic politics, the party picked a Polish-American Navy veteran for congressman-at-large and an Italian-American Army veteran for state treasurer. When their artful work was done, Republicans had a ticket which recognized veterans (both Army and Navy), labor, women, Italians, Poles, Irish, Catholics, Yankees, and party regulars. Seven of Connecticut's eight counties won representation in the bargain.[33]

So far as substance went, too, the GOP cast a broad net. While various of its planks appealed to business and conservatives, the platform also recounted Baldwin's progressive achievements and pledged to continue them. McConaughy declared himself a liberal and a friend of labor. The party advocated statutory proscription of discrimination by employers and by unions. Veterans got the promise of a bonus and other assistance. Above all, the GOP emphasized the nation's postwar problems and the threat of communism. Like the platform and keynoter Harold Stassen, Baldwin and McConaughy lambasted the Truman administration. Reaffirming the party's "faith in the American way of life," the platform also said:

> The American people must keep alert. Communism is a real threat. In the United States it seeks to destroy our way of life. It is boring from within, and is playing a prominent part in our national affairs. The Republican Party is the arch enemy of Communism.

That passage "brought down the house" when the platform was read aloud, and Baldwin and McConaughy also stressed the Communist menace. The GOP adjourned with great confidence in its candidates, issues, and prospects.[34]

Democrats spent a more unsettling summer than did Republicans. Not only did they worry about their apparently declining strength and Truman's obviously declining popularity, but they encountered great trouble in deciding upon a ticket to put up in the autumn. The slate-making difficulties revolved around national price control chief Chester Bowles, a Yale graduate and a legal resident of Essex, Connecticut, who had served as Connecticut's OPA administrator before moving on to Washington. By late spring long-standing rumors that Bowles, a big, ruddy, forty-five-year-old liberal, wanted to seek office in Connecticut had multiplied, to the displeasure of Senator McMahon and other party leaders. Bowles's identification with the increasingly unpopular OPA partly explained their opposition to his possible candidacy, but so as usual did considerations of power and place. Bowles apparently wanted the gubernatorial nomination and was understood to have national ambi-

227

tions. Remembering that he had not favored the organization as they had desired when he was state OPA administrator, party professionals feared that Bowles might use the fat patronage due the next governor to take control of party machinery and use it in his own behalf. For his part, McMahon, who was winning a solid name and national reputation for himself as chairman of the Senate committee on atomic energy, had no desire to share leadership of the state Democratic party with an ambitious, liberal governor. Party leaders nonetheless seemed ready by June to offer Bowles the senatorial nomination. He could do much less damage to the state organization as senator, and a Senate candidacy would relieve pressure from Bowles's liberal and labor supporters as well as from some administration spokesmen. Too, some felt that were prices to shoot up, Bowles might campaign effectively as the champion of a good cause.

With Bowles's late-June resignation from the Truman administration there began a more intense, typically confusing, but relatively bloodless period of Democratic maneuvering. Bowles now obviously wanted the gubernatorial nomination. So did Lieutenant Governor Wilbert Snow, and he had strong support from important organization leaders. McMahon, seen as the key, was in a quandary. Liberals pulled one way, party regulars the other. Partly dependent on both for his leadership, McMahon wanted to offend neither. Nor had he come to look more favorably on a gubernatorial nomination for Bowles. Beyond that, Bowles's success as a candidate would obviously depend largely on how people felt about the OPA, and in midsummer 1946 the political fallout of that nettlesome situation remained uncertain. McMahon resorted to a public opinion poll to gauge the strength of the possible gubernatorial candidates of both parties.[35]

Local conventions and caucuses late in August brought the first head-to-head test of strength between Bowles and Snow. Reflecting the fairly clear but inconclusive geographical division of support, Snow did well in the towns while Bowles showed substantial strength in the cities. The gatherings were generally quiet affairs, except in Hartford, where the city convention climaxed a complicated and furious struggle for local control. Following his defeat in the 1945 mayoral election, Thomas Spellacy had set out to claw his way back to the top. He had to contend with his onetime protégé, John Bailey, who was now in full revolt against Spellacy. Bailey had opposed his old mentor on the Democrats' 1944 state nominees and had backed the successful candidates, and he had since become one of the party's chief legislative strategists at the General Assembly. Joining in loose alliance with Rocco Pallotti of the Italian East Side, Bailey aimed in 1946 to replace the old Hartford leaders. State politics became involved because Bailey supported Snow while Spellacy tried to ride to victory in Hartford on the strength of Bowles's large following among city Democrats. The convention turned into an uproarious shambles, where power in Hartford passed from the men who had dominated the city's Democratic politics for a quarter-century. None of them was even chosen for the state convention, and Long Tom Spellacy, now sixty-six years old, would miss the gathering for the first time in forty years. John Bailey, aged forty-one, controlled Hartford.[36]

State Democrats still awaited McMahon's decision on the gubernatorial candidates. The poll, which indicated that no Democrat would win, gave the better-known Bowles a slight edge over Snow. Pressured on all sides, McMahon finally announced his position, such as it was, in early September. Though hinting broadly that he preferred that Bowles run for the Senate, McMahon said that he wanted a "free and open" convention. Behind the scenes, the Senator played a baffling game, evidently encouraging both Snow and Bowles. Meanwhile, Bowles, largely because of his apparent urban strength and the money he could bring to the campaign, had begun to win support from some important organization leaders, including the state chairman, and John Bailey adroitly maneuvered the Snow forces.

At the state convention, Snow led on the first ballot, and Bowles graciously moved to make Snow's nomination unanimous. Bowles's candidacy failed for a number of reasons. He had waited too long to begin a concerted campaign, had ignored some important Democrats, John Bailey not least, had not dickered with others who took important uncommitted blocs to the convention, and had erred in aligning with Spellacy. For his part, Snow profited from the shrewd generalship of John Bailey, from his own contacts and popularity, and also from his clever denunciation of any effort to railroad the convention, which gave McMahon (who voted for Bowles) good reason to permit a "free and open" process, which in turn enabled Bailey to reassure nervous Democrats that supporting Snow did not mean opposing the organization.

Still, more than tactics accounted for Bowles's defeat. By mid-September the OPA was near the peak of its unpopularity, and no man was more identified with the agency than Chester Bowles. Quite beyond OPA, moreover, Bowles had a reputation for aggressive liberalism that seemed too much for many delegates in 1946. Snow by contrast seemed a moderate, and he had a Connecticut Yankee image that Democrats remembering Wilbur Cross's successes in the 1930s thought a real asset. Snow could be expected to run well in the towns and among independents while winning the support of liberals who had no place else to turn.

A poet and an English professor at Wesleyan University, Wilbert Snow had vaulted suddenly and improbably to the top of Connecticut politics just two years before. For more than two decades he had participated in town affairs and local Democratic politics in Middletown, but his only try for office had come in 1930 when he ran unsuccessfully for state senator. Then in 1944, at age sixty, he had been plucked from obscurity and handed the nomination for lieutenant governor as part of the year's complicated factional byplay. When Robert Hurley lost to Baldwin for governor, Bill Snow found himself formally the state's foremost Democrat by virtue of riding into office on Roosevelt's coattails. He won friends in the Democratic hierarchy by championing Democratic legislation at the General Assembly and by turning out for countless party affairs in 1945 and 1946. Snow in fact was not quite the conservative Yankee of his image. Though not an outspoken and readily identifiable New Dealer like Chester Bowles, Snow was instinctively liberal, particularly on such social issues as public housing, labor, welfare, and civil rights; and though his father's line stretched back some three centuries in New England, Snow's mother was the daughter of Irish emigrants to Canada. (Through his mother, Snow was distantly related to a young man in neighboring Massachusetts who was starting out in politics in 1946— John F. Kennedy.) But Snow, a likable, lanky, craggy-faced man born in Penobscot Bay, Maine, and still an amateur, even something of an innocent, in politics, came across as an avuncular down-East Yankee scholar reminiscent of Wilbur Cross. Even more than to his personality or to his image, however, Snow owed his political rise to the maneuverings of politicos who used him, out of his element in political intrigue, to further their own ambitions. The factional struggle of 1944 and the particular needs of Middletown's Democratic boss, John Tynan, had brought him the 1944 nomination for lieutenant governor, and in 1946 he landed the gubernatorial nomination in important part because of John Bailey's aspirations and talents and Bailey's need for a "horse" he could ride to the top of the party.

Snow was not the only Democrat to profit from the maneuvering that gave him the nomination. McMahon escaped nicely from a potentially harmful situation. The Senator got his original wish—that Bowles not land the gubernatorial nomination —without angering either side or putting his prestige on the line. And while McMahon maintained his position, John Bailey, whom Snow chose as state chairman, advanced his yet further. Under Bailey's chairmanship, which eventually stretched over some three decades, the period of changing and weak organizational leadership ended and a new era in Connecticut Democratic politics began. In terms of the future of Connecticut politics, indeed, no development of 1946 was more important than John Bailey's arrival at the top.[37]

Once the gubernatorial nomination was settled, party leaders reverted to form and handpicked the rest of the ticket. Snow's victory meant renomination for the incumbents, and two of the three remaining spots went to veterans, for Mc-Mahon like Baldwin insisted on recognizing the GIs. The Democratic state ticket had nearly the balance of the GOP's with veterans, Italians, Poles, Irish, and Yankees all represented. As in 1944, Democrats failed to nominate a woman candidate, but this time no explosion followed the omission. For the Senate nomination, the party chose Joseph Tone of New Haven, whose unenviable task it was to deflate the "Baldwin myth" by being a "combination bulldog, buzz saw, leech, grand inquisitor and ferocious debunker." Finally, the Democrats had also to nominate a candidate to fill the unexpired portion of Maloney's term running from election day until January. (Republicans had nominated Baldwin.) Eager to remind people of the past and to appeal to town and independent voters, Democrats selected eighty-four-year-old Wilbur Cross for the short-term nomination.

In other ways, too, the Democracy tried to make the past speak to the present. Assuring the delegates that the magic of Roosevelt's name had not died, the keynote speaker, Rhode Island Governor John Pastore, condemned the Republican 1920s and lauded Roosevelt and the New Deal. The platform was a long and sometimes eloquent document, which endorsed the principles of the Atlantic Charter and of Roosevelt's "economic bill of rights" but which missed the mood of 1946. Like the entire convention, the platform revealed the Democratic party's understandable desire to avoid the gloomy political realities of 1946 and to bring Roosevelt and his allure to life again. It stemmed from the same despair that led New York's Democratic nominee for governor to FDR's graveside during the campaign and that prompted the Democratic national committee to prefer old Roosevelt recordings to live Truman speeches.[38] But Roosevelt could not be brought back or the problems of 1946 wished away. The campaign and election demonstrated that.

On the hustings, Connecticut Republicans like their counterparts throughout the nation hammered away at the troubles at home identified with the Truman administration. Foreign affairs seemed at first a far less promising area, for overseas problems were less immediate and the nation generally approved Truman's foreign policy.[30] The GOP, moreover, still suffering to some extent from an isolationist image, had largely endorsed a firm, bipartisan, internationalist foreign policy.

Republicans nonetheless found opportunity for partisan attack in the area of foreign affairs. As part of their efforts to win the ethnic vote, they appealed to the resentment of immigrant groups about problems abroad. Trying to nail down predicted shifts in the Polish vote, for example, Republicans flayed the administration for having "shamefully betrayed" Poland and for "selling out" that nation to Communist domination. Similar messages went to other east European ethnic groups. Italian-Americans were reminded of their homeland's postwar difficulties and unhappiness with the peace treaty, Jews about the unresolved problems of Palestine and Jewish refugees.[40]

In mid-September, Secretary of Commerce Henry A. Wallace provided ammunition for a broader Republican attack when he criticized as too harsh American policy toward the Soviet Union and urged that the United States modify and moderate its approach. Coming when anti-Russian sentiment was growing and when Truman and Secretary of State Byrnes were toughening their stance, the speech caused a sensation. Though Truman fired Wallace from the Cabinet within a week, the episode gave Republicans material to use throughout the campaign. It provided, the GOP claimed, more evidence yet that Truman's presidency was inextricably bogged down in ineptitude and confusion, and it enabled Republicans to claim that it was they who were the staunch supporters of a firm, bipartisan foreign policy. The Wallace speech also gave Republicans opportunity to pin the radical tag on elements of the Democratic party. Wallace, gubernatorial nominee McConaughy said, represented the "pinkish fringe" of the party, and he and other Connecticut Republicans continually tried to identify Democrats with Wallace and with appeasement of Russia and softness toward communism.[41]

233

Communism, indeed, provided a central GOP issue in Connecticut and throughout the nation. From their state convention until election day, Connecticut Republicans stridently raised the cry of communism. Especially after Radio Moscow called for the election of candidates endorsed by the CIO-Political Action Committee, most Republicans associated the Communist menace at home and abroad with Democrats and suggested that many Democrats were the sort of "intellectual tinkerers" and "pink radicals" who by their votes and their voices gave aid to Communist subversion and aggrandizement. McConaughy claimed that "the Communists are firmly entrenched in the Democratic Party and . . . they exert a tremendous influence in Democratic ranks. So firmly are they entrenched that Democrats, even if they desired, cannot dislodge them." The plain warning, from him and other Republicans, was that a vote for a Democrat was a vote for communism, if not necessarily for a Communist. Only the GOP, Republicans said, could combat the Red Peril, present in government and labor as well as in the Democratic party. Some of the Republican press made similar charges and claims, as did Clare Booth Luce (who after converting to Catholicism had decided not to run again for office) in two typically vitriolic and vivid red-baiting radio speeches at the end of the campaign.[42] As they had two years before, Republicans directed the domestic communism issue in substantial part toward the Catholic ethnic groups; but with fears of communism mounting among almost every group, the issue seemed to promise general gains.

Still, for all the stress on communism, the GOP's fundamental campaign message was, as one congressional candidate put it, that "the existing situation in this great nation is simply a mess." Shortages, inflation, controls, taxes, housing, strikes, confusion, dissension, and communism, too—all those ills and more, Republicans said, stemmed not simply from the ineptitude of the Truman administration but from too many years of Democratic rule. It was time for a change.[43]

As they pressed those issues and took up the themes of the postwar conservative counteroffensive, Republicans repeated

234

arguments they had made in preceding election years. Without attacking New Deal programs that by 1946 seemed basic parts of national life, they sharply differentiated between Republican and Democratic philosophics. On fiscal policy, for example, they accused Democrats of taxing and spending the nation to death. At the heart of the Republicans' argument was the distinction they drew between the Democrats' senseless, even un-American and red-tinged, bureaucratic central planning and regimentation—of which OPA was the chief symbol in 1946—and the Republicans' faith in the American free enterprise system. Condemning controls and shortages, they said that only by replacing a regulated with a free economy could there be a return to abundance, true prosperity, and the American Way. Americanism—anticommunism, a less active central government, individualism, and unfettered free enterprise—remained fundamental to the Republican appeal in Connecticut and the nation and had a more insistently conservative coloration than in recent elections. As one observer said, such issues were "in the Republican blood," and in 1946 Republicans were surer than ever that those issues would carry them to victory.[44]

Democrats also stressed their old issues and images. They campaigned as the party of labor, liberalism, and the "little people" against Republican "selfish interests," "reaction," and "princes of privilege." Frequently invoking Roosevelt's name, they scarcely mentioned Truman. They claimed that because of the long period of Democratic rule the American people had never been so well off and argued that such problems as there were stemmed from the war and would soon be corrected. Proposing the sort of limited expansion of the New Deal that would characterize the Fair Deal and postwar liberalism, Democrats said that they could make things still better. To protect the advances made since 1933, the people must ignore deceptive Republican blandishments and return Roosevelt's party to power. Indeed, Democrats warned that a GOP victory would mean the loss of prosperity itself. One congressman claimed that a Republican Congress would mean a return to the 1920s: "inflationary prosperity" followed by a "terrible bust." Democrats also warned against Republican isolationism. "LET'S NOT REPEAT 1920," said one of their advertisements. "Remember the Republican Bungling"—"Teapot Dome*Depression*Isolation."[45]

Democrats used comparable tactics in replying to Republican charges of communism and in trying to win the ethnic vote. United States Attorney General Tom Clark argued in a radio address that "what breeds Communism in this or any country is reaction." Similarly, Connecticut Democrats said that indifference to the common people and programs that deprived people of jobs and purchasing power were what really led to communism. Democratic candidates at Polish and Italian rallies stressed New Deal programs that might be lost should Republicans win. Congressman-at-large Ryter carried a parallel argument on foreign affairs to Polish-Americans. Should Republicans control the Congress, he asserted, America could expect greater Russian demands because the GOP would repeat its isolationist errors of the 1920s.[46]

Yet even as they drummed up the old issues, Democrats knew they campaigned at a great disadvantage. It was not the 1930s, Roosevelt was not alive, and nearly every current circumstance favored the GOP. Out of desperation, Bailey and Snow concocted a curious strategy to salvage the governorship: ignore McConaughy and try to blame as many problems as possible on Baldwin. Filling the role chosen for him at the convention, Tone led an abusive, outrageous assault on the Governor. Snow meanwhile focused on state affairs and problems.[47]

In his most audacious move, Snow tried early in October to saddle Baldwin with responsibility for the state's infuriating meat shortage. Though some politicians and political analysts thought Snow's thrust shrewd and effective—and it did temporarily nonplus Baldwin—it raised to even greater political prominence a problem identified with Truman, the OPA, and the Democrats. Truman knew how people felt about the meat shortage, and in mid-October he finally bowed to intense public and political pressure and ended the price ceilings on meat. Serving to vindicate Baldwin and to reinforce Truman's reputation for confusion and vacillation, the President's action did bring meat back to the markets. People complained about high prices—another debit for the administration and another problem Snow tried to blame on Baldwin—but shoppers generally bought what they could. As election day neared, other decontrol edicts came in profusion.[48]

Snow also lashed out at Baldwin for neglecting veterans. The resulting exchange, full of promises for housing and a bonus, only intensified a campaign-long scramble for the veterans' vote. One ex-GI wrote Baldwin that veterans would "vote for the side who is promising the most," and most Connecticut politicians acted as though they would.[49] Besides the promises, political leaders heaped recognition on the veterans. Not only did World War II servicemen win spots on both state tickets, but they also received nomination to Congress from the GOP in three of the five congressional districts and from the Democrats in both districts not held by a Democratic incumbent. Those candidates who were veterans missed few chances to mention the fact.

Snow also pressed Baldwin hard on the issue of fair employment legislation. The upshot was that major candidates of both parties affirmed platform commitments to fair employment;[50] and even if Snow raised the issue simply for partisan purposes, the episode had a fundamental importance. As blacks had switched from the party of Lincoln to the party of Roosevelt and had become more numerous in Connecticut, and as Connecticut politics had become competitive, politicians had much more actively courted the Negro vote. By 1946, following the events of the war years, fair employment had become both an important campaign issue and a goal explicitly endorsed by both parties.

Despite some new emphases and issues, the 1946 Connecticut campaign largely repeated tactics and appeals from previous years. Foreign affairs had become a political staple by 1946, even if within the narrow confines of the wartime internationalist consensus and of anticommunism, but domestic issues once more predominated, and both parties carried their familiar images to the public. Much as in 1942, prosperity dulled the Democrats' appeal while the manifold accompanying problems sharpened the GOP's. Republicans projected a sterner, even a more conservative, image than in 1942, and they gave a new salience to charges of communism; but they did not frontally attack popular New Deal programs, and they vigorously countered Democratic charges that they were reactionaries. As before, too, group politics were as important as general issue politics. By recognition, rallies, and issues of immediate concern, candidates appealed to a variety of groups defined in a variety of ways. Ethnic groups won much attention, as did labor, but so also did a new political bloc—the GIs of World War II. (In another pattern symptomatic of the times, the number of women nominated for Congress fell from three to one, for the state senate from seven to three, and for the lower house from 100 to 71,[51] while candidates appealed to women simply as housewives; and women seemed satisfied with their treatment.)

In the main, the Connecticut campaign was of a piece with those in other states, and so was the preelection outlook. Nationally, Republicans seemed likely to capture the Congress and sure to pick up added strength almost everywhere outside the South. In Connecticut, a GOP sweep of landslide proportions did not seem out of the question. After sixteen years of depression and war, of hardship and insecurity, Americans wanted to enjoy peace and prosperity. Instead they found themselves beset by high taxes, inflation, labor strife, insufficient housing, the OPA, not as much food, clothing, and consumer goods as they wanted, by Communist expansion and perhaps subversion. The last fourteen years had been Democratic years, and Democrat Harry Truman sat in the White House. "Had Enough?" asked the GOP's brilliant campaign slogan. "Vote Republican." Or in Italian: "Ne Avete Avuto Abbastanza? Votate Repubblicano."[52]

The people did vote Republican. Nationally, the GOP swept to a victory that gave the party control of the Congress for the first time since 1930. Connecticut Republicans, winning an even larger share of the vote than did their counterparts in the nation as a whole and in most of the Northern industrial states, won each state and congressional office and overwhelming control of the General Assembly. Baldwin captured 58 percent of the vote with a 105,000-vote plurality, a margin slightly greater than Roosevelt's in his 1936 landslide. Other GOP candidates fared nearly as well as Baldwin. Not since the mid-1920s had Connecticut Republicans won such huge pluralities, and, significantly, not since then had Democrats done so badly in the cities. Joining the fall of Democratic big-city bastions in other states to the GOP, New Haven, Bridgeport, Waterbury, and New Britain all went Republican in a federal election for the first time since the far-off days of Calvin Coolidge. And the big-city results, important though they were, only mirrored the statewide trend. While the Democratic share of the vote fell by eleven percentage points from 1944 in the five big cities, it fell by ten points, to some 42 percent, in the state as a whole.[53]

The Democratic decline was as general in incidence among voting groups as it was widespread geographically. Voting patterns as a result were close to those of preceding elections, though at a much reduced Democratic level. (See Table V-1.) Still, some patterns of differential change did emerge. As ever, local factors helped breed varying results. In Hartford, for example, a solid Democratic victory owed much to the still-potent Democratic organization there and to the hard work of new leaders John Bailey and Rocco Pallotti, who had their prestige at stake.[54] Differing patterns in the urban Italian vote also reflected differing local situations. In New Haven, the most Italian ward gave the Democrats barely one-third of the vote (as compared with three-fourths in 1936). In Bridgeport, perhaps because of Italian-American war hero Henry Mucci's candidacy for Congress, the Democratic vote in Italian areas stayed at 1944 levels. In Hartford, where Pallotti worked to buttress his position, the most Italian area showed a striking Democratic increase of 15 points to 80 percent.

Most urban constituencies, however, showed more uniformity

Table V-1. Election of 1946, Connecticut: Ward-level and Town-level Statistics[1]

| | a. Ward level | | | | | b. Town level |
	Hart- ford (N = 15)	New Haven (N = 33)	Bridge- port (N = 16)	Com- bined (N = 64)	All towns (N = 169)	Towns in Hartford, New Haven, and Fairfield counties (N = 79)

I. Simple correlation coefficients for percentage
Democratic[2]

A. Percentage Democratic 1946 with:
Percentage Democratic Congressman

| 1944 | +.93 | +.94 | +.85 | +.90 | +.91 | +.94 |

Percentage Roosevelt

| 1944 | +.93 | +.92 | +.85 | +.90 | +.91 | +.94 |

B. Percentage Democratic
with average monthly rent

| 1946 | −.75 | −.60 | −.68 | −.46 | −.52 | −.62 |
| 1944 | −.72 | −.55 | −.73 | −.51 | −.39 | −.58 |

C. Percentage Democratic
with percentage foreign-born

| 1946 | +.89 | +.44 | +.51 | +.51 | +.58 | +.64 |
| 1944 | +.85 | +.42 | +.50 | +.54 | +.64 | +.71 |

D. Percentage Democratic
with total population

| 1946 | — | — | — | — | +.29 | +.41 |
| 1944 | — | — | — | — | +.39 | +.50 |

E. Percentage Democratic
with rural-farm

| 1946 | — | — | — | — | −.25 | −.40 |
| 1944 | — | — | — | — | −.40 | −.49 |

[1]See Appendix for explanation of statistics used here. See Tables A-1 through A-6
for more statistics for each election 1936 to 1948.

[2]In section I of this table, percentage Democratic means percentage Roosevelt for
1944 statistics, percentage Democratic congressman-at-large for 1946 town and combined ward statistics, and percentage district congressman for 1946 individual city
statistics.

—and substantial Democratic losses. Only in Irish areas did
the Democrats manage to retain most of their previous strength.

a. Ward level		b. Town level	
Hartford, New Haven, *Bridgeport* *combined wards* (N = 64)		*All towns* (N = 169)	*Towns in Hartford,* *New Haven, and* *Fairfield counties* (N = 79)

II. Simple correlation coefficients for change in percentage Democratic, 1944–1946 (percentage Democratic congressman-at-large 1944 minus percentage Democratic congressman-at-large 1946)

	a. Ward level	b. All towns	b. Fairfield counties
A. With average monthly rent	+ .01	+ .31	+ .26
B. With percentage foreign-born	– .15	+ .12	+ .18
C. With total population	—	+ .24	+ .23
D. With percentage Democratic 1944	– .13	+ .19	+ .06
E. With turnout 1946 divided by turnout 1944[3]	– .22	– .52	– .59

[3]Turnout by wards measured by total vote for governor 1944 and 1946; turnout by towns measured by total number counted by registrar as voting in 1944 and 1946. The negative coefficients in this row indicate an equal and positive correlation between Democratic decline and turnout decline.

Jewish wards fell away sharply, particularly in New Haven, where the Democratic vote in the most Jewish ward dropped to 56 percent from Roosevelt's 73 percent of 1944. Polish areas also had striking GOP gains, and in New Britain's Polish wards the Democratic vote fell from 84 to 66 percent. Black areas, too, shifted toward the GOP. In New Haven the predominantly Negro ward gave the Democrats only 47 percent, down 20 points from 1944, while the Democratic vote in Hartford's black area fell from 75 to 62 percent. But while the Republican advances in Jewish, Polish, and black areas crippled Democratic

241

chances, the Democratic declines in such areas did not differ much from those in other wards. Consequently the correlates of the urban vote did not depart greatly from those of 1944.

Similar patterns of stability and change could be found at the town level. The town-level vote generally conformed fairly closely to that of the 1944 election—indeed to the patterns of elections throughout the New Deal period—but some weak patterns of change did emerge. Democratic losses were marginally greater in normally Democratic areas and in the larger towns and cities. Italian areas tended to fall off from the Democrats at about an average rate. So also did Polish, Jewish, and French-Canadian areas, though that was significant because such towns had previously resisted the trend away from the Democratic party. In some Polish towns the Democratic share of the vote declined sharply. But despite the variations in Democratic decline, the main pattern in the returns was that of Republican gains almost everywhere.

As in 1942, turnout was low and seemed to some observers to provide at least part of the reason for the poor Democratic showing.[55] But the correlations between turnout decline and Democratic deline (though higher than for 1942) indicate that turnout made very little difference at the ward level and not much at the town level in Connecticut.[56] It does seem likely that many normally Democratic voters manifested their feelings simply by staying home—in New Britain, for example, where the Poles were so disgruntled, there was a particularly large turnout decline—but as in 1942, nonvoting of that variety reflected cross-pressures, not apathy, and the pressures would not necessarily have been resolved in favor of the Democrats had the abstainers voted. At any rate, few analysts thought turnout crucial to the election—and with good reason.

The Democratic losses in state and nation stemmed from simple and obvious reasons: the resentments and irritations of the electorate. In explanation of the national GOP advances, political analysts, polls, and candidates agreed that the troubled domestic situation lay behind the Republican gains. Connecticut observers subscribed to the consensus.[57] The Wallace affair

242

added to the general sense of malaise about the Truman administration. Besides the common sources of public unhappiness, other factors helped bleed away Democratic votes. Liberals were angered by Truman's falling out with liberal Cabinet members, labor by his handling of the rail and coal disputes. In Connecticut, the rejection of Bowles may further have disenchanted those groups, though Bowles campaigned actively for the Democratic ticket. Democratic city machines, not alone in Connecticut, had weakened still further, and there had been no CIO-PAC effort equivalent to that of 1944. Special ethnic concerns reduced the Democratic vote still further, most obviously in Polish and Jewish areas, while the Communist issue may have deflected some normally Democratic Catholic votes.[58] But although specific groups and areas often had special reasons for defecting from the Democrats, they also shared the larger, general ones. The voters of 1946 cast a protest vote against a number of things, chiefly the domestic mess and the problems which seemed to threaten peace, prosperity, and contentment. They had indeed had enough of those troubles, and enough, for a time, of the Democrats.

Despite the crushing defeat, however, the Democratic party emerged from its debacle with better prospects than had the GOP ten years before. The Democrats had not been defeated in a presidential election, and in 1940 and 1944—with Roosevelt heading the ticket, to be sure—had rebounded from midterm setbacks. Further, while the returns often brought to mind the 1920s, that decade remained a memory only. Each party's fundamental appeals and images sprang from the 1930s, and so did the voters' basic perceptions of the parties. Nor did the Republican majorities indicate quite the reaffirmation of conservatism that some perceived. The GOP campaign was in 1946 more conservative than in recent elections and the electorate not as responsive to New Deal liberalism. But as in 1942, the Democratic decline reflected a protest vote against specific ills, not a call to restore the pre-New Deal political economy. The voters may have wanted normalcy of a sort, but not of the Harding-Coolidge variety. Despite the enormous Republican pluralities, moreover, the pattern of the vote did not depart greatly from those of recent elections. The voting cleavages established in the 1928–1936 reshuffling of Connecticut politics had not been overturned by the war and the troubled postwar transition. The election of 1946 meant not that Connecticut was again a Republican state—or the United States a Republican nation—but rather that the political competitiveness reestablished a decade and a half before remained, like the voting patterns established then, a fact of political life. Democrats had yet to face the 1948 election without Franklin D. Roosevelt, but read closely (with hindsight's benefit), the politics of 1946 suggested that the developments and issues of the war and early postwar periods had altered rather than transformed public concerns and political issues and had eroded rather than unraveled the Roosevelt Coalition.

THE AFTERMATH AND LEGACY OF THE WAR YEARS

The dimensions of their 1946 defeat jarred Connecticut Democrats. Meeting at a gloomy postmortem conference shortly after the election, party leaders decided that they had neither met adequately the issue of communism nor campaigned positively enough on the Democratic record. What had especially been lacking, they thought, was a sufficiently progressive stance, and they believed too that the party organization badly needed overhaul and revitalization. The essentials of that critique could be found applied to the national Democratic party a year later in presidential adviser Clark Clifford's famous memorandum to Truman on "The Politics of 1948."[1] Based largely on Clifford's shrewd analysis, of course, Truman's 1948 conduct of the presidency and of the presidential campaign ultimately helped rescue the White House from what seemed sure GOP control. Connecticut Democrats also scored surprising successes in 1948.

In Connecticut and in the nation, however, Democrats found the road to their happy 1948 surprise rocky, winding, and frequently disheartening. Providing Connecticut Democrats with their first opportunity to rebuild strength toward 1948, the 1947 municipal elections brought dismal showings in the big cities—Republicans even captured Waterbury for the first time in a quarter-century—and the Democrats ended the year in "near despair." Then through much of 1948 Democrats bore the added burden of sharp party factionalism which mirrored the party's divisions nationally among Truman supporters, liberal Democrats of the type who had in 1947 founded the Americans for Democratic Action, and, further to the left, the adherents of Henry Wallace. Chester Bowles was again at the center of party conflict in Connecticut. One of the founders of the ADA, Bowles eagerly sought the gubernatorial nomination again and called as well for new, liberal programs in the state and nation. Much of his criticism of current policies was aimed at the GOP, but not all of it, for like others in the ADA, Bowles thought the Truman administration too conservative, too cautious, and politically weak besides. But while an outspoken liberal opposed to renominating Truman, he kept a wary distance from the small but fervent Wallace group in Connecticut. Bowles's main opposition for the gubernatorial nomination came from Irish-Catholic Thomas Dodd, a loudly anti-Communist Truman man who was nearer personally and ideologically than Bowles to party regulars and had the support of most of them.[2]

Resolution of the Connecticut factionalism came in the summer of 1948 after the national party had made its decisions. A dump-Truman movement, headed by liberals and also by party professionals who feared that Truman would lose in November and carry local Democrats down with him, collapsed by the time of the national convention. The Wallace forces (and because of the civil rights plank, the Dixiecrats) bolted the party, but most Democrats rallied behind the President after the insistently if only moderately liberal convention. In Connecticut, observers had thought that renomination for Truman would doom Bowles's bid for the governorship, but John Bailey, dominant in the state party by 1948, had other ideas. Concerned about the state ticket, Bailey, too, had been among Truman's opponents. That same concern led him to choose Bowles over Dodd. He wanted to prevent liberal defections to Wallace's third party, he sensed that Bowles's campaign had already aroused interest and widespread support, and he knew that Bowles could bring needed campaign funds to Democratic coffers. Although Bailey's decision for Bowles distressed many party regulars, the chairman had his way. The rest of the carefully picked slate was heavily ethnic and Catholic, in large part because Republicans would for the first time have an Irish Catholic atop their ticket.[3]

The 1948 Connecticut campaign followed the contours of the national campaign. Public and private polls pointed to a landslide rout of Truman and the Democrats. Like the President, Bowles campaigned strenuously as the friend of the common man and of labor. He stressed high prices, the housing shortage, social and labor legislation, and GOP responsibility for shortcomings in those and other areas. With other Democrats he worked hard to keep the votes of the ethnic and working-class voters so important to past Democratic successes. Like Republican presidential nominee Thomas E. Dewey and the national GOP, Connecticut Republicans were "supremely confident" of victory. They campaigned lethargically for the most part, except toward the end when some apparent Bowles momentum led them to launch an abusive attack on him and to try to link him with Wallace and with communism. But despite the vigorous Democratic campaign and the enthusiastic welcome given Truman when he visited Connecticut, a huge Republican victory seemed inevitable.[4]

The Connecticut results, like those in the nation, dumfounded the experts, the pollsters, and most politicians.[5] Truman lost the state, but just barely, and Democrats narrowly captured the governorship and all but one of the other state offices contested, won three of the six congressional seats, and regained control of the state senate. In so close an election, any one of a number of things might have decided the outcome of individual races;[6] but the overall results showed that the Democratic party had rebounded from the election of 1946. The 1948 returns revealed further the continuing strength of the coalition that had come together behind Roosevelt, for Democrats did well in the cities, and the pattern of the vote nearly everywhere closely resembled those of presidential elections since 1936. In Hartford, New Haven, and Bridgeport, Truman's vote correlated at +.98, +.92, and +.90 respectively with Roosevelt's 1936 vote, while at the town level the correla-

247

tion was +.93 in the three metropolitan counties with four-fifths of the state's people and +.88 for the state as a whole.[7]

There were, to be sure, changes in the vote in 1948 from previous elections. Many Jewish voters, for example, defected to Wallace. Among Italians, Democrats did better than in any election since 1936; New Haven's Italian wards gave Truman some three-fifths of their vote, while in Hartford the President captured a lopsided 80 percent of the vote in the most heavily Italian precinct. Similarly, Truman's support in the black areas of New Haven and Hartford rivaled Roosevelt's best showings. The shape of the ethnic vote in Connecticut resembled patterns elsewhere, with Democrats declining in Jewish areas but otherwise holding or increasing their strength. Especially dramatic was the flow of the Italian and German votes back toward the Democrats with the war over and Roosevelt gone.

As significant in Connecticut as the Democratic resurgence among ethnic voters, indeed perhaps more so, was the sharper division than before of the vote along class lines. In 1948 the class cleavage was actually more marked and more important to the results than in the Roosevelt elections.[8] As elsewhere, lower-income voters feared that the GOP might undo much of the New Deal, and in casting an essentially conservative vote to preserve and protect the New Deal they heightened the class divisions in voting patterns. Reflecting another national circumstance, the work of organized labor was crucial in throwing working-class votes, especially those of the new blue-collar middle class so indebted to Roosevelt, to the Democrats. Helped by the "do-nothing" yet, to many, menacingly reactionary 1947–48 Republican Congress and by the maladroit GOP campaign, Democrats had regrouped their forces, revitalized 1930s-style domestic issues, refurbished in a new context their image as the party of the little people, and reworked the prewar politics of reform for the postwar era of security. So doing, they achieved a remarkable political comeback.

At bottom, the election of 1948 revealed that the Roosevelt Coalition had in the main become the Democratic Coalition. No longer dependent on Franklin Roosevelt (though Democrats

248

still effectively exploited his name and his image), that coalition, forged in the 1930s and hardened in the war years, had provided the basis for Truman's victory. The coalition, moreover, would continue to be a dominant fact of national politics. It would not, to be sure, remain perfectly stable—as it had not in the Roosevelt years—nor would it again be so powerful as it had been in 1936. Indeed, the coalition had declined steadily in strength from its 1936 high-water mark to Truman's narrow plurality of 1948; and Democrats would carry only four of the eight presidential contests after 1944 and a majority of the presidential vote only in 1964 and 1976. (The erosion of Democratic strength in the South—1944 was the last year of the old Solid Democratic South—would be of especially large future significance.) But the basic urban-industrial-ethnic state Roosevelt Coalition, resting on ethnic, black, and working-class voters in metropolitan areas, would show a remarkable persistence and great continuing strength in future years. Despite the continual cries that the old Roosevelt Coalition was crumbling and the continuing evidence that political alignments were changing, Democrats remained the majority party and the Roosevelt-Democratic Coalition remained an important factor in political reckoning and in voting patterns three decades and more after Roosevelt had died.

What was true for the nation was true as well for Connecticut. The 1948 election showed the continued coherence and strength of the state's Roosevelt Coalition—and it showed as well that the coalition was neither immutable nor invincible. The coalition of 1948 was relatively smaller and based less on ethnic voters, more on working-class voters, than the coalition of 1936. Not until Roman Catholic John F. Kennedy ran for the presidency in 1960 (when the early pro-Kennedy returns from Connecticut signaled Kennedy's victory nationally[9]) did Connecticut again vote for the Democratic national standard-bearer. But if Connecticut was not a sure Democratic state after Roosevelt's death, neither had it been one before; and an overview of Connecticut politics in the three decades after World War II shows that the state remained fundamentally

249

Democratic and that it did so because of the enduring strength of the Roosevelt Coalition. In providing the first test of that coalition in Connecticut and in the nation, then, the era of World War II had also provided the first evidence of its durability. It was then that the Democrats consolidated their new political strength, then that the political divisions hacked out between the world wars were hardened, and then that the Roosevelt Coalition became the Democratic Coalition. For politics, the era of World War II was of great importance.

World War II had a large and lasting impact on American life. Indeed, it has come to be identified as one of the watersheds of American history—a pivotal period which clearly separates one era from another. And it is hard to dispute the importance of the war years for the course of American history. The United States assumed a new and much larger role in world affairs. The federal government, the executive branch in particular, acquired new powers and augmented old ones. In the political economy, not only did the federal government assume greater authority, but big business became bigger and regained prestige lost in the Depression decade, big farmers became more powerful, and big labor won a more integral role. The military became a larger part of national life and entered more clearly and closely into the relationship with industry and with the federal bureaucracy that would characterize postwar history. Prosperity was restored—indeed, more than restored, for postwar prosperity exceeded anything ever before seen, even predicted, and with the war came some income redistribution, much chance for upward economic mobility. Connected with that, and with the government's larger responsibilities, was the real beginning of the Keynesian revolution in American public policy. Nor did just the government and the economy undergo major change. The war speeded a population redistribution away from rural areas and toward industrial centers, the suburbs, and the newer cities of the South and West. It contributed to the changing role and status of women in the postwar nation. It brought a fuller integration of ethnic groups into the mainstream of American life. It helped renew the migration of rural Southern blacks, begin an era of change and progress for black Americans, and trigger the postwar civil rights movement. With the war came a "baby boom" which had multiple ramifications for postwar society. Technology, greatly advanced by war-related research, increased its manifold effects on American life. By bringing victory and new power abroad and prosperity at home, the war restored the nation's self-confidence and bred substantial self-satisfaction. Still other effects of the war might be enumerated, but the point should be clear enough. The United States was different in 1945 from what it had been before the war, and different because of the war; and the impact of and the changes stemming from the war would continue to ramify in future years. Certainly they would in politics. Not immediately and not completely, but clearly and importantly nonetheless, postwar politics took on features different from those of the Roosevelt years. Concern about foreign affairs, about enjoying the good life, and about social inequalities and inequities, for example, all of them apparent in the war years, would mount thereafter and foster a politics of the cold war, consumer culture, and civil rights that altered the context and content of the nation's politics.

Still, the impact of World War II on American life and politics should not be exaggerated. Much changed or began to change, yet much remained the same or substantially so. Blacks, and women too, remained on the margins of society, and the old notions of an American melting pot and of cultural liberalism remained elusive of attainment. Poverty and class divisions remained facts of American life. Domestic and foreign policies, the former most obviously but the latter as well, were in basic ways continuous from the prewar period. Moreover, many trends evident in World War II were well under way before then. The greater power of the government and of the presidency, the larger importance of big business, big farming, and big labor, the social integration of American life, the increased uniformity of the culture, the effects of technological advance—all these and more besides owed much to the war but much also to long-term trends simply speeded by the war. Beyond that, and in the short run perhaps even more important, attitudinal change did not match economic, institutional, and technological change. And finally, of course, the war did not transform American politics, which in the middle and late 1940s (and beyond) revolved largely around the same concerns, issues, party images, and voting patterns as in the 1930s.

The continuity in politics sprang from the continuities in other areas of American life, especially the persistence of politically salient attitudes, aims, attachments, and polarities. The attitudinal continuity had several sources. For one thing, the "cultural lag" of attitudes and values behind physical change that has been such an important part of modern American history was evident in the period of World War II. It was obvious among servicemen, who dreamed of returning to home, Mom, sweetheart, apple pie, and the way things had been—or the way they nostalgically believed things had been; but it marked as well the attitudes of the millions more who remained behind and experienced the flux of the wartime home front.[10] Except where they welcomed change that would help them as individuals or as members of a special group, most Americans evinced a desire for the status quo and a reluctance to depart from old patterns, old values, old standards. During the war that helped breed the opposition to such things as public housing, economic restrictions and regulations, new social patterns, indeed any substantial challenge to or change in the collection of values and symbols and practices that represented the American way.

But more than cultural lag contributed to the attitudinal conservatism and aversion to change among home-front Americans. Unlike its major allies and adversaries, the United States was not a nation fully mobilized physically and emotionally for war. With no real threat to the continental United States, with time, energy, emotion, productive capacity, and money left over from the war effort, Americans had leeway for pursuing creature comforts and personal satisfaction and for resisting inroads on accustomed ways. Perhaps, too, the attitudinal conservatism of Americans lay partly in the lack of any large understanding of the nature of the war and of any larger war aims than victory. Although it has often been said that World War II was and was perceived to be a war of ideology—democracy versus fascism—little of that filtered down to public opinion in any form more meaningful than sloganeering and lip service. Indeed, Americans typically showed some confusion about the causes and nature of the war and little desire to use it as a springboard for the further democratization of American society. Accordingly, the only real aim for most Americans was to whip the Axis and be done with it[11]—an understandable and hardly mean goal which nonetheless carried with it implications of reestablishing the status quo ante bellum, less, of course, Axis aggression and the Depression.

And that desire for a modified status quo points to still another source of continuity in attitudes and aspirations. Americans of 1945 were, by and large, the Americans of 1939; and for them, the experience of war had supplemented rather than supplanted the prewar experiences and the attitudes and values, hopes and fears based upon them. What prewar Americans had most wanted was to escape the Depression and avoid a war. They had longed for peace and prosperity; they had coveted security. Dominating American aspirations during the war, those aims were heightened and changed into expectations by the experience of war. During the war and postwar years alike, the attention given peace, prosperity, and security overshadowed the pursuit of other national goals. What most Americans of the time wanted in their present, as their politics revealed, was a better past—a past without deprivation and war, but a past which otherwise was much the same. A major consequence of that, apparent by the late war years and evident in the general political culture as well as in voting patterns and issues, was to considerable extent a politics not only of continuity but also of the status quo—a politics in which the longing for the several aspects of security made much of what had been new in the 1930s, in particular the New Deal and the Roosevelt Coalition, accepted and central parts of national life by the 1940s. Thus while Truman's New Dealism seemed radical and dangerous still to some Americans in 1948, Truman's reelection victory and its bases of support bespoke a practical (not Taftite) conservatism and reflected important strands of continuity between the prewar and postwar eras.

In important ways, then, World War II was less a watershed in national life than has often been suggested. Though the war brought great changes, there remained major and fundamental continuities between prewar and postwar America, especially in attitudes and aspirations; and the combination of change and continuity is crucial to understanding wartime and postwar American society. It is especially important for understanding the era's politics, which at once reflected and provided a major example of that mix of change and continuity.

Certainly that is so for Connecticut, a state, moreover, that because of its representativeness and its wartime history helps illuminate the story of American society and politics, particularly (but not only) in kindred Northern industrial states, during the era of World War II. In Connecticut, continuity was basic to the period's politics—to issues, to party images, to voting patterns. Related to that, indeed back of it, Connecticut's people manifested concerns and attitudes grounded in the prewar era. But the war years were also a time of developments that affected and altered the social bases of politics, produced new concerns and new issues, caused some changes in voting patterns, and therefore made the politics of the period more complex than a politics of continuity.

Each election from 1940 to 1946 reflected, on the hustings and in the voting booths, effects of the war on Connecticut's people and politics. Economic good times, for example, diminished the immediate importance and political salience of the New Deal and gave new meaning to old Republican charges of bureaucracy, inefficiency, spendthriftiness. In 1942 and 1946, when prosperity was combined with the absence of a presidential election, with irritating government controls, and with a variety of troubles and tensions, Connecticut voted the Democrats out of office. In those 1940s elections, the contours of the postwar politics of inflation and the consumer culture can be perceived. New ethnic concerns also affected politics, especially among Italian-Americans, who began in 1940 a significant defection from Roosevelt's party. Many of the group worries—among Italians, Jews, and blacks in particular—partly or wholly involved domestic conditions, but many stemmed from events abroad. For the society as a whole, foreign affairs and foreign policy also became increasingly important. That, too, affected politics, provided yet another element of change from the depression decade, and gave another large hint about the shape of postwar politics. If the Roosevelt Coalition remained essentially stable, then, especially in presidential election years, it was in part a shifting coalition which proved vulnerable to erosion, sometimes substantial and sometimes lasting, when politically salient concerns and issues changed.

The war did not have only a short-range impact on Connecticut society and politics. The state was in 1950 more suburban than ten years before, and it had relatively more skilled, white-collar, and professional workers and fewer common laborers. Such geographical and occupational changes, like the healthy economy they reflected, provided the GOP with new sources of potential strength that continued to grow after the war. Social changes of the war years would also have continuing importance. For Italian-Americans, developments of the period hastened their assimilation, bolstered their economic position, helped to increase their political assertiveness and influence, and, in New Haven especially, made them the most unreliably Democratic of the major immigrant groups. Events of the war and early postwar period also had important social and political implications for other groups, but perhaps most significant for the future was the impact of the war on Connecticut Negroes. An increased migration of blacks to the state began, and during the war Negroes manifested a new determination to rectify their position in the society. That assertiveness, and a fear of racial conflict, catalyzed an already growing sentiment among public officials and civic leaders in favor of investigation and amelioration of racial problems. With politics tightly competitive and blacks more numerous, politicians began to pay more attention to the black vote and ultimately to black grievances. Though it proved no panacea, a state fair employment act finally became law in 1947, and Connecticut subsequently began action to alleviate black housing ills.[12]

Reflecting new circumstances, the substance of political campaigns also underwent change of continuing importance during World War II—change that served further to modify the political climate in which the Democrats had risen to power. Foreign policy took on new significance, even if most debate was within the narrow consensus that emerged in the war and early postwar years. Domestic issues were altered, though more in context than in content, as the politics of prosperity and inflation and the status quo succeeded the politics of depression and reform. And late in the period there rose to political prominence the issue of communism. Though apparently of little impact as a voting determinant in Connecticut in 1944 or 1946—indeed it evidently had little influence on national elections even at the height of the McCarthy era[13]— charges of domestic communism were perceived by politicians to have political importance and significantly affected postwar politics and policies.

Yet despite the changes in Connecticut society and politics during and stemming from the war, continuity and connectedness seem equally basic to the period, perhaps more so. Connecticut remained divided along ethnic and racial lines, and those divisions had continuing political ramifications. The post-1940 population was wealthier, had better jobs, and was more suburban, but urban and working-class attitudes, concerns, and voting power remained basic to Connecticut life and politics.

More generally, fundamental hopes and fears stemming from the prewar period continued through the war years. Rooted in the experiences of the 1930s—of the Great Depression and the coming of World War II—and augmented by the experience of war, a desire for security dominated public attitudes, influenced political responses of parties, candidates, and voters alike, and shaped public policy. Connecticut's ambivalent response to the war boom, the worried preparations for the postwar, and the direction of foreign policy all reflected the yearning for security. So, too, did presidential politics, especially in 1944 when Connecticut's people exhibited not only their faith in Roosevelt but also their desire for prosperity and peace. As a further legacy of the Depression decade, people wanted more than anything else assurance of jobs and a sound economy. Related to the concern about security was a longing for contentment, stability, and a sense of well-being after the trials of the interwar and war years. That sentiment, reflected by irritation with controls and shortages, by anxiety about radicalism and subversion, by the antipathy toward rapid social change that marked wartime Connecticut, found political expression most decisively in 1942 and 1946. The desire for prosperity, peace, and a placid, pleasant life would remain at the heart of public attitudes and politics in the postwar era.

Political debate also showed an essential continuity from the 1930s. Reflecting the people's continuing focus on conditions at home and the abiding majority faith in Franklin D. Roosevelt, Connecticut Democrats campaigned primarily as the party of the common man, of prosperity, of labor, and of Roosevelt and his New Deal. Republicans, though in Connecticut often more liberal than elsewhere, portrayed themselves as the party of healthy free enterprise, limited central government, fiscal prudence, caution, and, above all, Americanism. Those party images, derivative from the previous decade, persisted into the postwar era and formed the public's basic perception of the two parties.[14] Even GOP charges of communism were not wholly new and played on long-standing American fears. Since the coming of the New Deal, Republicans had called Roosevelt's policies un-American; and if in 1940 they had warned chiefly about dictatorship, some had rumbled about communism since the 1930s. In 1944 and then especially in the postwar years when to many Americans communism seemed a threat

257

to the stability and security they wanted, the political use of anticommunism came easily to the party of "Americanism" and traditional American ways.

The continuities in the social bases of politics, in public attitudes and concerns, in party images and appeals, and in the salience of domestic economic issues combined in the era of the Second World War to produce what was for politics the most important continuity of all: the durability of the Roosevelt Coalition. Especially because of new economic circumstances and ethnic concerns, the coalition, shifting from election to election, suffered erosion and defections, and attracted new adherents, too; but the fundamental political divisions established by 1936 persisted. Tested in the war years, the Roosevelt Coalition endured, and by war's end had truly become the Democratic Coalition. That coalition, despite changes in it and in the undergirding political culture, would remain central to politics, in Connecticut and in the nation, in the years to follow.

APPENDIX

A NOTE ON METHOD

$\mathbf{M}$y approach to and methods of studying Connecticut politics in the era of World War II have been influenced both by recent historical examinations of American politics and by relevant political science literature. Among the studies that provided essential background on American voting behavior, I profited especially from Angus Campbell et al., *The American Voter* (New York, 1960); Robert Lane, *Political Life* (Glencoe, Ill., 1959); Angus Campbell et al., *Elections and the Political Order* (New York, 1966); Walter Dean Burnham, *Critical Elections and the Mainsprings of American Politics* (New York, 1970); William McPhee and William Glaser, *Public Opinion and Congressional Elections* (n.p., 1962); and V.O. Key, Jr., *The Responsible Electorate* (Cambridge, Mass., 1966). For the statistical analysis of voting returns, I relied mainly on Charles M. Dollar and Richard J. Jensen, *Historian's Guide to Statistics* (New York, 1971); Edward R. Tufte, *Data Analysis for Politics and Policy* (Englewood Cliffs, N.J., 1974); and V.O. Key, Jr., *A Primer of Statistics for Political Scientists* (New York, 1954).

ANALYSIS OF VOTING RETURNS

I examined Connecticut elections from 1936 through 1948 in large part through computerized regression analysis of voting returns. Though the computer programs generated a variety of information, I have presented in the tables to the text and in the appendixes only part of that information and only some of the relationships measured. In discussing election returns, I

259

have tried as far as possible to avoid technical language and have focused on those matters most important to the pattern of the vote in each election and to changes in the vote between elections.

Several measurements obtained through regression analysis are used throughout in the text and tables. The *simple correlation coefficient* (in this study, the Pearson product-moment correlation) is a measure of the linear relationship between an independent variable and a dependent variable; it indicates the degree of association between the two variables, or how closely the dependent variable and the independent variable change together in magnitude. The coefficient can range from 0, which indicates no linear relationship, to $+1.00$ (a perfect positive linear relationship) or to -1.00 (a perfect negative linear relationship). The *multiple correlation coefficient* indicates the strength of the relationship between a dependent variable and two or more independent variables taken together. Correlation coefficients, then, are an index of how closely the dependent variable varies with the independent variable(s). The *regression coefficient* (the slope of the fitted regression line), by contrast, indicates how much an independent variable affects a dependent variable; it indicates the average rate of change in the dependent variable given a unit change in the independent variable. Correlation coefficients and regression coefficients thus work together in measuring the relationship of the independent and dependent variables: the correlation coefficient indicates how closely they change together in magnitude; and if the correlation coefficient is high, then the regression coefficient enables a close estimate of the actual value of the dependent variable given the value of the independent variable. Though I have not usually given the regression coefficients in the tables or text, I have made much use of them in examining and analyzing election returns. Yet another measure, and one I have included in tables, is the *standardized beta coefficient* (or standardized beta weight). Derived from the partial regression coefficients obtained in multivariable regression analysis, this measure provides an index of the relative effect on a dependent variable of each of the independent variables and is used for comparing the impact on the dependent variable of the several independent variables.

Two important features of the coefficients explained above must be noted. First, the correlations are aggregate and areal—or "ecological"—correlations, not individual correlations. That is, a high positive correlation between, say, percentage foreign-born and percentage Democratic shows a high association between increasing foreign-born percentages and increasing Democratic percentages ward by ward or town by town, but it does not necessarily reflect an association between foreign-born voters and Democratic voters. Nonetheless, the correlations in this study do seem to reflect individual and group voting patterns, and, with appropriate caution, I have so interpreted them. The regression coefficients support this inference, as does such other evidence as analyses by contemporary politicians and political reporters, identification of relatively homogeneous voting units, and the 1944 Connecticut poll (see Chapter IV). Too, my analysis of individual and group voting in Connecticut fits with national polls and local studies of voting in the period.

A second important aspect of the correlation and regression coefficients is that they show patterns of association but not necessarily of cause and effect. That is, even if a high correlation between percentage foreign-born and percentage Democratic does reflect a propensity for foreign-born voters to vote Democratic, it does not necessarily mean that they voted Democratic *because* they were foreign-born. Statistics reveal patterns, but they do not explain those patterns and may reveal misleading patterns. Multivariable analysis and scatter diagrams (explained below) help in this regard, but the crucial matters of determining whether and why a causal relationship lay behind a statistical relationship depend on rigorous historical inquiry and judgment.

A central task involving the statistics described above was to measure the relationship between the Democratic vote (as dependent variable) and various socioeconomic characteristics of wards and towns. I used percentage foreign-born and average monthly rent for ward-level analysis in Hartford, New Haven, and Bridgeport, and I used percentage foreign-born, average monthly rent, total population, and percentage rural-farm for town-level analysis. These characteristics were selected because they represent variables that historians and political scientists have demonstrated to be central to voting in the Roosevelt-Truman era; and analysis of residual observations (explained below) in scatter diagrams confirmed the importance of these characteristics, as did the correlation and regression coefficients obtained for them. Simple correlation coefficients and regression coefficients were obtained for each of the characteristics above (the independent variables) with percentage Democratic (the dependent variable); and multiple correlation coefficients, partial regression coefficients, and standardized beta coefficients were obtained for every combination or two or more independent variables with percent Democratic. Socioeconomic data for wards and towns came from the federal census and from Nathan L. Whetten and Henry W. Riecken, *The Foreign-Born Population of Connecticut, 1940* (Storrs, Conn., 1943). Voting returns and registration totals at the town, county, congressional district, and state levels came from the appropriate editions of the *Connecticut State Register and Manual*, while ward-level data came from city newspapers. Unless otherwise indicated, percentages of the vote and statistics based on them are for the major-party vote.

In the socioeconomic analysis of voting returns, I have for each election obtained statistics for the independent variables with percentage Democratic for several of the offices contested —for governor, congressmen, and comptroller every election, and for president and U.S. senator when those offices were on the ballot. I have also correlated the percentage Democratic for various pairs of those offices in each election. The latter measurements, not presented in the tables, were made to help assess the amount and effect of split-ticket voting and to ensure that the pattern of the vote for the office(s) my discussions focus on followed the pattern for other offices. Because virtually identical patterns did exist—the correlations between different offices in an election year typically exceeded +.99—I usually employed multiple regression analysis for only one race per election: the presidential vote in 1936, 1940, 1944, and 1948, and the congressman-at-large vote in 1942 and 1946.

I also conducted two-variable regression analysis for several other combinations of variables. A major portion of my examination of voting involved interelection regression analysis of the Democratic vote—the relationships, for example, of the Democratic presidential vote of 1936, 1940, 1944, and 1948. Besides studying these relationships by means of correlation coefficients, regression coefficients, and scatter diagrams, I did the same for the relationships between socioeconomic variables and Democratic percentage changes from election to election, between turnout change and Democratic change, and between socioeconomic variables and turnout change. To search out patterns of turnout and partisan change I also plotted raw vote totals (total vote and total Democratic vote) for various pairs of elections by means of scatter diagrams.

Scatter diagrams were indispensable, and in a variety of ways. For one thing, they reveal whether a nonlinear relationship existed between variables. Beyond that, they identify deviating wards and towns (more technically: residual observations) which lay well off the fitted regression line and which depressed correlations. By investigating those deviating wards or towns, one can seek to find what depressed the correlation and can search out other factors to be investigated. Scatter diagrams were especially useful in searching for patterns of change between elections. To make maximum use of the scatter diagrams, of course, it is essential to identify as many characteristics and special political circumstances of wards and towns as possible in order to search for explanatory patterns. Not all deviating wards and towns could be adequately explained from the data I collected, but the great majority could.

Besides examining election returns by means of regression analysis, I used other methods as well. I constructed maps with a variety of social and economic data in order to study election returns geographically. I collected and scrutinized various election data for the state, congressional districts, counties, and big cities; some of these data are shown in Tables A-1 and A-2. Throughout, I examined the vote in selected wards and towns (by ethnicity and by income, for example). And I studied as well national polls, contemporary studies by political scientists, and historical accounts of voting in the period both to frame my inquiry into Connecticut politics and to provide perspective for my findings.

For the period 1936–48, I used almost entirely my own data as explained above. For the period before 1936, I initially made a quick pattern-seeking survey, relying on secondary material, aggregate vote totals, selected towns and wards, and rank-order (Spearman's rho) and tetrachoric correlations. I then was able to use Andrew Levinson's Yale University senior honors essay, "Connecticut Politics, 1896–1936." Based on some of the same methods I employed for the later period, Levinson's statistics and findings were very helpful for confirming, amplifying, and sometimes amending my own.

CAMPAIGNS

Examinations of voting behavior in the 1940s and 1950s by political scientists indicate that the effect of campaigns and issues on voting has usually been overrated and that party loyalty and social and economic group membership principally determined voting behavior. Campaigns apparently tended to reinforce or activate preexistent party loyalties rather than to educate or convert voters. Yet that does not mean that campaigns did not influence voting, and even less does it mean that campaigns somehow existed wholly apart from voting. Even the most vigorous proponents of the views outlined above concede some importance to campaigns (and still more to the events transpiring between elections), and V.O. Key has argued in addition that the rigidity of partisan division has been overestimated and that there was a significant correlation between voters' policy preferences and party choices. Still, elections cannot be interpreted simply in terms of issues or even candidates. Probably the chief role of campaigns was to establish issue salience —to fix the relative priority of issues rather than to change minds on those issues.

I have not assumed that there was any easy or inevitable relation between election returns and the rhetoric and tactics of campaigns, but I have assumed that campaigns merit examination. If they were not precisely voting determinants, they were part of the political process, and examination of them can help toward understanding voting patterns, partisan divisions, and public concerns, whether general or of specific groups. By studying campaigns in conjunction with intensive historical research on the one hand and close analysis of voting patterns on the other, one can often learn much about the temper of the society and much about why an election turned out as it did—or at least, and very importantly, why there were shifts in the vote from preceding elections. Too, victorious candidates often supposed that they did have a direct issue-based mandate, and to that extent campaigns were important to performance by officeholders.

To examine the campaigns year-by-year and over a period of time, I have studied party platforms and newspaper (at least one in each congressional district) accounts of what the candidates said and did. For the platforms, I conducted elementary content analysis, chiefly by categorizing party positions by subject and computing the proportion of space allotted to each. I could thus make various comparisons between and among each party's national and state platforms, and I could chart changing concerns and emphases. I also tried to gauge, impressionistically, the tone and appeal of the platforms, a more difficult but at least equally important task. More important than the platforms, of course, were the candidates themselves, and I carefully went through newspapers (and other sources when available) to determine the strategy, substance, and tactics of the candidates' campaigns. In the text, I have paid most attention to the races for president, governor, and

U.S. senator, for congressional campaigns normally followed the general pattern set by the more important contests. In discussing campaigns, I have been interested largely in establishing the salient issues and the "party dichotomy" that emerged and the images projected by candidates and parties. To the extent that campaign rhetoric influenced or was related to voting, it was mainly in such areas as those.

Besides discussing the general issue content and the style and tone of campaigns, I have also tried to show how politicians sought the votes of specific groups, usually defined by ethnicity or by class and occupational status. People voted for reasons and because of experiences common to the society in general, but they also voted for more specific reasons affecting them as individuals or as members of groups. Politicians knew that, and in seeking votes they seized on the events of the present and recent past and on concerns, fears, desires, and attitudes not just of the public generally but also of those specific groups. Indeed, my research has buttressed my initial persuasion that campaigns can help to illuminate both voting patterns and the underlying social bases of politics.

Appendix

Table A-1. CONNECTICUT STATE-LEVEL VOTING DATA, 1924–1948

	Democratic percentage of major party vote for:				Total registration	Total vote
Year	President	Governor	Senator	District congress-men		
1924	30.9	32.5		32.9	483,700	403,162
1926		35.7	36.0	35.7	477,805	304,679
1928	45.9	46.0	45.8	45.7	612,837	556,380
1930		50.6		49.0	602,633	435,381
1932	49.4	51.0	50.4	49.6	675,879	601,304
1934		50.8	51.7	51.3	692,093	556,388
1936	57.8	57.4		56.9	773,525	693,514
1938		49.7[1]	48.3	47.8	789,029	636,544
1940	53.6	51.0	53.8	53.1	871,819	788,710
1942		47.6		47.9	839,945	582,911
1944	52.7	48.4	52.4	51.1	967,886	840,474
1946		42.6	42.0	42.9	957,646	691,876
1948	49.2	50.1		50.0	1,033,901	890,909

[1]1938 Republican gubernatorial total includes 3,046 votes won on Union party ticket.

Table A-2. CONNECTICUT CONGRESSIONAL DISTRICT AND BIG-CITY
VOTING DATA, 1936–1948

	1936	1940	1942	1944	1946	1948
I. Democratic percentage of major party vote for district congressman						
A. 1st Congressional District	60.7	54.4	48.6	54.0	46.9	55.3
B. 2nd Congressional District	52.4	52.6	48.6	51.2	44.7	51.6
C. 3rd Congressional District	57.5	53.7	48.3	51.5	41.1	50.3
D. 4th Congressional District	54.4	50.2	47.2	49.5	38.2	44.0
E. 5th Congressional District	58.8	55.2	46.0	47.7	43.4	48.1
II. Democratic percentage of major party vote in five big cities[1]						
A. Bridgeport	70.3	65.3	60.9	61.8	46.5	55.6
B. Hartford	70.5	65.0	60.4	66.8	59.8	65.9
C. New Britain	70.4	65.7	54.6	65.7	49.3	60.8
D. New Haven	65.9	60.5	57.1	61.4	48.8	58.1
E. Waterbury	70.3	60.6	55.0	53.9	47.4	54.5
F. Aggregate	69.2	63.2	58.1	62.3	51.3	59.3
III. Influence of five big cities[1]						
A. Democratic percentage of:						
1. Statewide vote	57.8	53.6	47.7	52.7	42.4	49.2
2. Aggregate big-city vote	69.2	63.2	58.1	62.3	51.3	59.3
3. Aggregate vote outside five big cities	51.5	48.4	42.7	47.6	38.1	44.2
B. Aggregate big-city percentage of:						
1. Statewide vote	35.9	35.3	32.3	34.6	32.2	33.0
2. Democratic statewide vote	42.9	41.6	39.3	40.9	39.0	39.7
3. Republican statewide vote	26.2	28.0	25.9	27.6	27.3	26.4

[1]For elections of 1936, 1940, 1944, and 1948, percentages are for vote for President; for elections of 1942 and 1946, percentages are for vote for congressman-at-large.

Table A-3. INTERCORRELATION OF DEMOCRATIC PERCENTAGE OF VOTE FOR PRESIDENT, CONNECTICUT, 1936–1948

	1940	1944	1948
I. Town-level correlations			
A. All towns statewide			
1936	+ .94	+ .92	+ .88
1940	—	+ .96	+ .91
1944		—	+ .92
B. Towns in Hartford, New Haven, and Fairfield counties			
1936	+ .96	+ .94	+ .93
1940	—	+ .97	+ .95
1944		—	+ .97
II. Ward-level correlations			
A. Hartford			
1936	+ .97	+ .91	+ .98
1940	—	+ .97	+ .97
1944		—	+ .94
B. New Haven			
1936	+ .91	+ .75	+ .92
1940	—	+ .92	+ .93
1944		—	+ .81
C. Bridgeport			
1936	+ .93	+ .80	+ .90
1940	—	+ .94	+ .95
1944		—	+ .94
D. Combined wards of Hartford, New Haven, and Bridgeport			
1936	+ .93	+ .78	+ .87
1940	—	+ .92	+ .88
1944		—	+ .86

Table A-4. INTERCORRELATION OF DEMOCRATIC PERCENTAGE OF VOTE
FOR CONGRESSMAN, CONNECTICUT, 1936–1946

	1940	1942	1944	1946
I. Town-level correlations				
A. All towns statewide[1]				
1936	+ .94	+ .88	+ .93	+ .84
1940	—	+ .93	+ .97	+ .89
1942		—	+ .94	+ .88
1944			—	+ .91
B. Towns in Hartford, New Haven, and Fairfield counties[1]				
1936	+ .96	+ .92	+ .95	+ .89
1940	—	+ .94	+ .97	+ .91
1942		—	+ .95	+ .90
1944			—	+ .94
II. Ward-level correlations				
A. Hartford[2]				
1936	+ .97	+ .94	+ .90	+ .95
1940	—	+ .99	+ .97	+ .95
1942		—	+ .98	+ .95
1944			—	+ .93
B. New Haven[2]				
1936	+ .93	+ .85	+ .80	+ .81
1940	—	+ .96	+ .94	+ .93
1942		—	+ .92	+ .94
1944			—	+ .94
C. Bridgeport[2]				
1936	+ .94	+ .92	+ .81	+ .91
1940	—	+ .86	+ .94	+ .88
1942		—	+ .82	+ .89
1944			—	+ .85
D. Combined wards of Hartford, New Haven, and Bridgeport[1]				
1936	+ .94	+ .89	+ .81	+ .79
1940	—	+ .95	+ .91	+ .83
1942		—	+ .89	+ .84
1944			—	+ .90

[1]Vote for congressman-at-large used.
[2]Vote for district congressman used.

270

Appendix

Table A-5. Simple Correlation Coefficients (R) and Standardized Beta Coefficients (B) for Socioeconomic Variables and Percentage Democratic, Connecticut, 1936–1948[1]

	Percentage Democratic and:							
	Percentage foreign-born		Average monthly rent		Total population		Percentage rural-farm	
	R	B	R	B	R	B	R	B
I. Town level								
A. All towns								
1936	+.61	+.44	−.32	−.30	+.46	+.18	−.44	−.38
1940	+.65	+.47	−.43	−.40	+.38	+.11	−.34	−.33
1942	+.58	+.41	−.35	−.33	+.38	+.12	−.37	−.35
1944	+.64	+.47	−.39	−.36	+.38	+.10	−.40	−.40
1946	+.58	+.41	−.52	−.47	+.29	+.08	−.25	−.29
1948	+.62	+.41	−.46	−.42	+.36	+.10	−.40	−.39
B. Towns in Hartford, New Haven, and Fairfield counties								
1936	+.72	+.43	−.55	−.41	+.52	+.18	−.46	−.19
1940	+.71	+.42	−.63	−.50	+.49	+.16	−.44	−.18
1942	+.72	+.45	−.46	−.33	+.52	+.17	−.50	−.22
1944	+.71	+.41	−.58	−.46	+.50	+.16	−.49	−.24
1946	+.64	+.37	−.62	−.51	+.41	+.10	−.40	−.19
1948	+.68	+.36	−.64	−.52	+.46	+.12	−.49	−.28
II. Ward level								
A. Hartford								
1936	+.83	+.46	−.89	−.61	(not applicable for wards)			
1940	+.85	+.54	−.84	−.51				
1942	+.89	+.65	−.75	−.38				
1944	+.85	+.66	−.72	−.31				
1946	+.89	+.66	−.75	−.38				
1948	+.82	+.45	−.88	−.60				
B. New Haven								
1936	+.75	+.51	−.73	−.48				
1940	+.59	+.33	−.68	−.52				
1942	+.49	+.22	−.67	−.54				
1944	+.42	+.10	−.55	−.45				
1946	+.44	+.18	−.60	−.51				
1948	+.53	+.16	−.83	−.75				
C. Bridgeport								
1936	+.68	+.54	−.71	−.57				
1940	+.65	+.48	−.76	−.62				
1942	+.47	+.35	−.68	−.56				
1944	+.50	+.34	−.73	−.64				
1946	+.51	+.39	−.68	−.60				
1948	+.57	+.41	−.74	−.63				
D. Combined city wards								
1936	+.77	+.56	−.71	−.45				
1940	+.69	+.48	−.66	−.43				
1942	+.61	+.41	−.63	−.43				
1944	+.54	+.38	−.51	−.33				
1946	+.51	+.38	−.46	−.29				
1948	+.56	+.31	−.68	−.53				

[1]For 1936, 1940, 1944, and 1948, Democratic vote for President is used; for 1942 and 1946, Democratic vote for congressman-at-large is used for towns and for combined city wards, and Democratic vote for district congressman is used for wards of individual cities.

271

Table A-6. MULTIPLE CORRELATION COEFFICIENTS FOR PERCENTAGE DEMOCRATIC AND SOCIOECONOMIC VARIABLES, CONNECTICUT, 1936–1948[1]

	1936	1940	1942	1944	1946	1948
I. Town level, with average monthly rent, percentage foreign-born, total population, and percentage rural-farm as independent variables						
A. All towns	+.79	+.80	+.73	+.81	+.76	+.79
B. Towns in Hartford, New Haven, and Fairfield counties	+.85	+.87	+.82	+.87	+.82	+.88
II. Town level, with average monthly rent and percentage foreign-born as independent variables						
A. All towns	+.64	+.71	+.62	+.68	+.69	+.67
B. Towns in Hartford, New Haven, and Fairfield counties	+.81	+.84	+.78	+.83	+.79	+.83
III. Ward level, with average monthly rent and percentage foreign-born as independent variables						
A. Hartford	+.96	+.94	+.94	+.89	+.95	+.95
B. New Haven	+.86	+.74	+.68	+.57	+.63	+.84
C. Bridgeport	+.88	+.89	+.74	+.80	+.79	+.84
D. Combined city wards	+.87	+.79	+.72	+.61	+.57	+.73

[1]For 1936, 1940, 1944, and 1948, Democratic vote for President is used; for 1942 and 1946, Democratic vote for congressman-at-large is used.

NOTES

ABBREVIATIONS USED

Baldwin Papers   Raymond E. Baldwin Inactive File [per-
                                    sonal papers], Connecticut State Library

Connecticut Labor *Bulletin*   Connecticut Department of Labor,
                                    Monthly Bulletin (This publication went
                                    under slightly different titles and authors,
                                    but was consecutively numbered and al-
                                    ways easily identifiable.)

CSJ   *Connecticut State Journal*

HC   *Hartford Courant*

NHR   *New Haven Register*

RecGovOff   Records of the [Connecticut] Governor's
                                    Office, Connecticut State Library

CHAPTER ONE

1. Rowland L. Mitchell, Jr., "Social Legislation in Connecticut, 1919–1939" (Ph.D. diss., Yale Univ., 1954), 1–16; I.G. Davis and C.I. Hendrickson, *A Description of Connecticut Agriculture,* Storrs Agricultural Experiment Station (Conn.) Bulletin 127, March 1925, *passim*; Connecticut Chamber of Commerce, *Facts About Connecticut* (Hartford, 1929), 149–76; *Connecticut Industry,* June 1937 through Oct. 1938, *passim.*

2. Seymour E. Harris, *The Economics of New England* (Cambridge, Mass.: Harvard Univ. Press, 1952), *passim*; Mitchell, "Connecticut, 1919–1939," pp. 42–56; Harold J. Bingham, *History of Connecticut,* Vol. II with addendum (New York: Lewis Historical Publishing Co., 1962), 803–804.

3. Connecticut Development Commission, *Population—Demographic Analysis of Connecticut, 1790–2000,* Connecticut Interregional Planning Program, Technical Report 131 (Hartford, 1962), *passim*; Connecticut Post-War Planning Board, *Post-War Connecticut, Interim Report* (Hartford, 1944), A-1, A-11, Table 7.

4. Robert G. Burnight and Nathan L. Whetten, *Studies in the Population of Connecticut, I: Population Growth, 1900–1950,* Storrs Ag. Exp. Sta. Bull.

288, July 1952, p. 32, Table 8, p. 34, Table 9, p. 48, Table 3; Nathan L. Whetten and E.C. Devereux, Jr., *Studies of Suburbanization in Connecticut, 1: Windsor*, Storrs Ag. Exp. Sta. Bull. 212, Oct. 1936; Nathan L. Whetten and R.F. Field, *Studies of Suburbanization in Connecticut, 2: Norwich*, Storrs Ag. Exp. Sta. Bull. 226, May 1938; Nathan L. Whetten, *Studies of Suburbanization in Connecticut, 3: Wilton*, Storrs Ag. Exp. Sta. Bull. 230, Feb. 1939.

5. Robert G. Burnight, *100 Years of Interstate Migration—1850–1950: Studies in the Population of Connecticut, No. 3*, Storrs Ag. Exp. Sta. Bull. 330, June 1957, p. 6; Nathan L. Whetten and Henry W. Riecken, Jr., *The Foreign-Born Population of Connecticut, 1940*, Storrs Ag. Exp. Sta. Bull. 246, Sept. 1943, p. 7, p. 12, fig. 4.

6. Samuel Koenig, *Immigrant Settlements in Connecticut: Their Growth and Characteristics*, Works Progress Administration, Federal Writers' Project for the State of Connecticut (Hartford, 1938), 17, Table II; Mitchell, "Connecticut, 1919–1939," p. 17.

7. The following discussions of Connecticut ethnic groups are drawn principally from these sources: Koenig, *Immigrant Settlements in Connecticut;* Whetten and Riecken, *Foreign-Born Population of Connecticut, 1940;* Samuel Koenig, "Ethnic Groups in Connecticut Industry," *Social Forces*, XX (Oct. 1941), 96–105; Samuel Koenig, "Ethnic Factors in the Economic Life of Urban Connecticut," *American Sociological Review*, VIII (April 1943), 193–97; David Rodnick, "Group Frustrations in Connecticut," *American Journal of Sociology*, XLVII (Sept. 1941), 157–66; Irvin L. Child, *Italian or American? The Second Generation in Conflict* (New Haven: Yale Univ. Press, 1943); Jerome K. Myers, Jr., "The Differential Time Factor in Assimilation: A Study of Aspects and Processes of Assimilation among the Italians of New Haven" (Ph.D. diss., Yale Univ., 1949); Nathan L. Whetten and Arnold W. Green, *Ethnic Group Relations in a Rural Area of Connecticut*, Storrs Ag. Exp. Sta. Bull. 244, Jan. 1943.

8. Robert Austin Warner, *New Haven Negroes: A Social History* (New Haven: Yale Univ. Press, 1940), *passim;* R.A. Barrett to Raymond E. Baldwin, Sept. 25, 1939, RecGovOff, Baldwin, 1939–1941, Box 6; Child, *Italian or American?*, 35–38; Rodnick, "Group Frustrations," 157–58.

9. David M. Chalmers, *Hooded Americanism: The First Century of the Ku Klux Klan, 1865–1965* (Garden City, N.Y.: Doubleday, 1965), 266–68; Kenneth T. Jackson, *The Ku Klux Klan in the City, 1915–1930* (New York: Oxford Univ. Press, 1967), 177–84.

10. See Appendix for sources of election data used in this study.

11. Samuel T. McSeveney, *The Politics of Depression: Political Behavior in the Northeast, 1893–1896* (New York: Oxford Univ. Press, 1972), *passim,* esp. 190–96; Andrew J. Levinson, "Connecticut Politics, 1896–1936: Building a Democratic Majority" (Senior essay, Yale Univ., 1972), *passim;* Mitchell, "Connecticut, 1919–1939," pp. 36–42, 56–121; John D. Buenker, "The Politics of Resistance: The Rural-Based Yankee Republican Machines of Connecticut and Rhode Island," *New England Quarterly*, XLVII (June 1974), *passim.*

12. Buenker, "Politics of Resistance," 229–30; McSeveney, *Politics of De-*

pression, passim; Joseph I. Lieberman, *The Power Broker: A Biography of John M. Bailey* (Boston: Houghton Mifflin, 1966), 23–26; Lane W. Lancaster, "The Background of a State 'Boss' System," *American Journal of Sociology*, XXXV (March 1930), 785.

13. Jerome K. Myers, "Assimilation in the Political Community," *Sociology and Social Research*, XXXV (Jan.–Feb. 1951), 175–82; Robert A. Dahl, *Who Governs? Democracy and Power in an American City* (New Haven: Yale Univ. Press, 1961), 32–51; Raymond E. Wolfinger, "The Development and Persistence of Ethnic Voting," *American Political Science Review*, LIX (Dec. 1965), 896–908; Whetten and Green, *Ethnic Group Relations*, 54–55; Levinson, "Connecticut Politics, 1896–1936," p. 31; Buenker, "Politics of Resistance," 229–32, 236.

14. Warner, *New Haven Negroes*, 289–90.

15. Lane W. Lancaster, "The Democratic Party in Connecticut," *National Municipal Review*, XVII (Aug. 1928), 452–54; Lieberman, *Power Broker*, 31–32; Mitchell, "Connecticut, 1919–1939," pp. 84–85, 121–28; *HC*, Nov. 18, 1942, Mar. 8, 1955, Sept. 11, 1956, Dec. 6, 10, 1957, Aug. 25, 1964; *NHR*, Nov. 17, 1942; author's interview with Jack Zaiman, July 26, 1977.

16. J. Joseph Huthmacher, *Massachusetts People and Politics, 1919–1933* (Cambridge: Harvard Univ. Press, 1959), 117–49.

17. Lancaster, "Democratic Party," 454–55.

18. David Burner, *The Politics of Provincialism: The Democratic Party in Transition, 1918–1932* (New York: Knopf, 1968), 179–216.

19. *HC*, Oct. 26, 30, Nov. 6, 1928; *New Britain Herald*, Nov. 2, 7, 8, 1928; *Hartford Catholic Transcript*, Oct. 18, 25, Nov. 1, 1928.

20. Levinson, "Connecticut Politics, 1896–1936," p. 35 and Table VII following.

21. Samuel Lubell, *The Future of American Politics* (3rd ed. rev., New York: Harper & Row, 1965), 48–55. The place of the 1928 election in American political history has become much controverted. The debate revolves around the longstanding view that the election was a "critical election"—one which caused a "sharp and durable realignment" in voting patterns by raising Democratic strength in urban-ethnic areas to levels much greater than in previous elections and thus preparing the way for the subsequent Roosevelt Coalition of the 1930s. Recently a number of important studies have maintained that the importance of the 1928 election has been greatly exaggerated, particularly by incautious popularizers of the critical-election thesis. Though not all of a piece, these studies taken together challenge the critical-election thesis from two perspectives. In the first place, some say, the urban-ethnic support won by Smith was no startlingly new thing, and, particularly when the unusual elections of 1920 and 1924 are excluded, Smith's 1928 strength can be seen in terms of a long-term secular trend to the Democrats. In the case of Connecticut, essentially this argument has been made for Hartford voting patterns down to 1928. (See David J. Alvarez and Edmond J. True, "Critical Elections & Partisan Realignment: An Urban Test-Case," *Polity*, V [Summer 1973], 563–76.) The designation of 1928 as a critical election has also been challenged from the other perspective, that of the post-1928 future.

Here the basic argument is that even if the 1928 election did produce "sharp" changes in voting patterns, it did not necessarily produce "durable" ones— that the added urban-ethnic strength Smith brought to the Democratic party might well have been ephemeral had not the Great Depression and the New Deal reinforced urban-ethnic allegiance to the Democrats. Some analyses from this perspective suggest instead of a single "critical election" a "critical period" of electoral realignment dating from 1928 (or 1924) and culminating in the Roosevelt Coalition of 1936. (For a guide to the historiography of the 1928 election, one taking the revisionist side, see Bernard Sternsher, "The Emergence of the New Deal Party System: A Problem in Historical Analysis of Voter Behavior," *Journal of Interdisciplinary History*, VI [Summer 1975], 127–49; for an important recent study which "denies that the presidential election of 1928 was either a critical election or an important component of a realigning era of electoral change" and which in addition criticizes "critical election theory," see Allan J. Lichtman, "Critical Election Theory and the Reality of American Presidential Politics, 1916–40," *American Historical Review*, LXXXI [April 1976], 317–51.) Based on my data and those of others, my conclusion as regards Connecticut is that while 1928 was an important election which produced significant changes in Democratic urban and ethnic strength from preceding presidential elections and which helped lay foundations for the Roosevelt Coalition, it is better to think in terms of a realigning period which began most obviously in 1928 and culminated in 1936 and which was the product of the cumulative and reinforcing effects on turnout and on voting patterns of ethnocultural tensions, the Great Depression, and the New Deal.

22. Bingham, *Connecticut*, II, 820–21, 846–47; *Connecticut Industry*, Aug. 1930, pp. 30–32; Connecticut Unemployment Commission, *Measures to Alleviate Unemployment in Connecticut* (Orange, Conn., 1932), 35–57.

23. Levinson, "Connecticut Politics, 1896–1936," p. 39; Mitchell, "Connecticut, 1919–1939," pp. 329–40; Wilbur L. Cross, *Connecticut Yankee* (New Haven: Yale Univ. Press, 1943), *passim*, esp. 228–38.

24. *Connecticut Industry*, Oct. 1932, p. 14; U.S. Treasury Department, Bureau of Internal Revenue, *Statistics of Income, 1932* (Government Printing Office, 1934), 86.

25. *HC*, Sept. 9, 1932.

26. For presidential vote correlations, see Levinson, "Connecticut Politics, 1896–1936," Table VI following p. 35. The Democratic gubernatorial votes of 1928 and 1932 correlated at +.90 (figure provided by Levinson).

27. Bingham, *Connecticut*, II, 862–63; *HC*, Sept. 13, 1934; *New Britain Herald*, Nov. 5, 7, 1934; *CSJ*, Nov. 1934, p. 11.

28. Bingham, *Connecticut*, II, 843–47; National Emergency Council, Statistical Division, "Connecticut: State and National Reports, 1933–1938" (mimeo., Washington, D.C., 1938); *Connecticut Industry*, Jan. 1937, p. 25, Feb. 1937, pp. 23–24; *Hartford Times*, Nov. 7, 1936; U.S. Treasury Department, *Statistics of Income, 1936* (GPO, 1938), Pt. I, 110, Pt. II, 60.

29. *HC*, Sept. 10, 11, 1936.

30. John M. Bailey to James A. Farley, Sept. 15, 1936, Franklin D. Roosevelt Library, Records of the Democratic National Committee [Official File

300], Correspondence to the Chairman, 1936; W.J. Farley to James A. Farley, undated [1936], *ibid.*; James A. Farley to W.J. Farley, Sept. 18, 1936, *ibid.*; undated, unsigned memorandum [1936], *ibid.*; *NHR*, Nov. 3, 1936; Warner, *New Haven Negroes*, 293.

31. *HC*, Oct. 23, 1936.

32. Political analysts thought they did (see, e.g., *HC*, Dec. 13, 1936), and that belief is supported by the nearly perfect (over +.99) correlations between the votes of Democratic candidates.

33. See Table A-2 for aggregate big-city voting totals for 1936–48. In winning nearly three-fifths of the Connecticut vote, Roosevelt carried only 64 of the state's 169 towns. (Connecticut was divided into 169 political units called "towns," which ranged in size and character from small farming communities of a few hundred people to large urban-industrial centers like Hartford. In this study, the word "town" sometimes refers to the specific political-geographical unit—as it does in tables on voting—sometimes to the smaller towns as contrasted to the cities; the meaning should be clear from the context).

34. Levinson, "Connecticut Politics, 1896–1936," Table VII following p. 35. Levinson's data have Smith's vote correlating at +.56 and Roosevelt's at +.65 with the foreign-born population.

35. *NHR*, Nov. 4, 1936.

36. Historians and political scientists usually stress the working-class and lower class foundations of the Roosevelt Coalition and of 1936 voting patterns; some recent studies, however, argue that ethnicity was more important than class. See esp. John M. Allswang, *A House for All Peoples: Ethnic Politics in Chicago, 1890–1936* (Lexington: Univ. Press of Kentucky, 1971), and John L. Shover, "Ethnicity and Religion in Philadelphia Politics, 1924–40," *American Quarterly*, XXV (Dec. 1973), 499–515. A contemporary study of New Haven's social structure, which nicely revealed the city's interrelated economic and ethnic divisions and their ramifications, including the political ones, found ethnicity more important than class to New Haven voting in the 1930s. See John W. McConnell, *The Evolution of Social Classes* (Washington, D.C.: American Council on Public Affairs, 1942), 152–66 and *passim*.

37. In terms of total division of the major-party vote—not just the foundations of the Roosevelt vote—ethnicity seems clearly more important than class. Some people of immigrant background (Scandinavians, e.g.) voted Republican largely for reasons of ethnicity, while surely few poor people voted Republican or wealthy people Democratic because of class status. (White-collar and middle-income Jews voted heavily Democratic, for ethnic reasons.) Furthermore, blacks would seem to have voted Democratic at least partly for reasons that might be termed "ethnic." Ethnicity, then, was more important as a factor in the overall division of the vote than the correlates of the Roosevelt vote would indicate. Still, so far as the Roosevelt Coalition is concerned, ethnicity and class independently affected voting patterns and were the basic and roughly equivalent foundations of the coalition.

38. On the importance of Catholic recognition by Roosevelt, see George Q. Flynn, *American Catholics & the Roosevelt Presidency, 1932–1936* (Lexington: Univ. of Kentucky Press, 1968), 231–39, and Lubell, *Future of American Politics*, 86–87.

39. McConnell, *Social Classes*, 106–107, 131, 156; Whetten and Green, *Ethnic Group Relations*, 44, 58; Connecticut Emergency Relief Commission, *Connecticut Social Trends*, Nov. 1935, p. 5.

40. On the importance of first-time voters in the building of the Roosevelt Coalition, see Norman H. Nie, Sidney Verba, and John R. Petrocik, *The Changing American Voter* (Cambridge: Harvard Univ. Press, 1976), 74–95; for statistics on Connecticut voting patterns down to 1936, see Levinson, "Connecticut Politics, 1896–1936," esp. Tables VI and VII following p. 35.

41. *HC*, Nov. 4, 1936 (editorial); *Hartford Times*, Nov. 4, 1936; *CSJ*, Dec. 1936, pp. 6, 58.

42. Walter Duane Lockard, "The Role of Party in the Connecticut General Assembly, 1931–1951" (Ph.D. diss., Yale Univ., 1952), 170–73; *HC*, Dec. 8, 1931, Mar. 2, May 22, 1932, Dec. 2, 1940, Jan. 17, 1945, Feb. 6, 1959; *Meriden Record*, Jan. 17, 1945; *Hartford Times*, May 16, 1936; author's interview with Jack Zaiman, July 26, 1977.

43. For analyses along these lines, see *CSJ*, Dec. 1936, pp. 6, 58, and "His Excellency's Loyal Opposition," *Fortune*, Feb. 1937, pp. 67ff.

44. William E. Leuchtenburg, *Franklin D. Roosevelt and the New Deal, 1932–1940* (New York: Harper & Row, 1963), 231–74.

45. Cross, *Connecticut Yankee*, 351–406; *Connecticut Industry*, Feb. 1938, p. 26, Aug. 1938, p. 25; Office of the [Connecticut] Commissioner of Welfare, *Public Welfare Statistics*, Aug. 1938; Bingham, *Connecticut*, II, 881–84. Ironically, Cross's fourth term also brought his greatest success— achievement of most of the governmental reorganization program that he had sought since 1931.

46. *New York Times*, July 24, Aug. 5, 31, Sept. 8, 9, 14, 15, 1938; *HC*, June 12, Aug. 14, Sept. 14, 15, 1938; *NHR*, Sept. 15, 18, 1938; various correspondence in Official File 300, FDR Library.

47. *HC*, Dec. 26, 1937, Mar. 20, 1938, June 26, 27, July 7, 1969; "The Republican Party: Up from the Grave," *Fortune*, Aug. 1939, pp. 101–102; Mitchell, "Connecticut, 1919–1939," pp. 473–75; Univ. of Connecticut Oral History Project, Raymond E. Baldwin, Vol. II, 482–520; Raymond E. Baldwin, *Let's Go Into Politics* (New York: Macmillan, 1952), 81–87; author's interview with Jack Zaiman, July 26, 1977.

48. *HC*, Sept. 15, 17, 1938; *CSJ*, Nov. 1938, p. 6, Dec. 1938, p. 1.

49. *HC*, Nov. 7, 1938; Univ. of Connecticut Oral History Project, Baldwin, II, 574–77.

50. The 1938 Democratic senatorial vote and the 1936 Roosevelt vote correlated on the order of +.8 to +.9.

51. *HC*, June 11, 1938; Mitchell, "Connecticut, 1919–1939," pp. 479–84; Univ. of Connecticut Oral History Project, Baldwin, II, 719–36; *NHR*, Jan. 4, 1940.

52. On Baldwin and his career, see Curtiss S. Johnson, *Raymond E. Baldwin: Connecticut Statesman* (Chester, Conn.: Pequot Press, 1972), and Baldwin volumes in Univ. of Connecticut Oral History Project.

53. *HC*, Dec. 4, 1938, July 2, Sept. 3, 1939; *CSJ*, Jan. 1940, p. 6; Herbert S. Parmet and Marie B. Hecht, *Never Again: A President Runs for a Third Term* (New York: Macmillan, 1968), 51–53, 69.

54. *HC*, Oct. 22, Nov. 12, 1939; Wolfinger, "Ethnic Voting," 901–903; *CSJ*, Oct. 1939, pp. 10, 33, Dec. 1939, pp. 6, 34.

55. *CSJ*, Dec. 1938, p. 12, Jan. 1940, p. 34.

CHAPTER TWO

1. *NHR*, May 26, June 30, 1940; *HC*, Dec. 31, 1939, Jan. 5, 1941; *Connecticut Industry*, Jan. 1940, p. 25.

2. *NHR*, Jan. 4, 31, 1940; *HC*, Feb. 29, 1940; *CSJ*, March 1940, p. 12.

3. *NHR*, Feb. 5, 18, Apr. 14, 1940; Herman P. Kopplemann to Roosevelt, Dec. 28, 1939, FDR Library, President's Personal File 1647.

4. *NHR*, Jan. 9, 10, Apr. 28, 29, May 5, 1940; *Waterbury Republican*, June 9, 1940; *CSJ*, April 1940, p. 12, June 1940, pp. 7, 29; *HC*, Apr. 21, May 5, 1940, May 5, 1968; author's interview with Jack Zaiman, July 26, 1977.

5. *HC*, May 2, 1940; *NHR*, May 5, 9, 1940; *Bridgeport Post*, Dec. 3, 29, 1940; author's interview with Raymond E. Baldwin, Jan. 28, 1975.

6. Parmet and Hecht, *Never Again*, 51, 53, 68–74, 93–94; *HC*, May 5, 8, 16, 19, 1940; *NHR*, May 8, 19, 1940; various correspondence in Baldwin Papers, Box 24.

7. *HC*, Jan. 5, 1941; *Connecticut Industry*, Dec. 1940, pp. 5–6, 38, Jan. 1941, p. 27; *NHR*, Oct. 27, Dec. 20, 1940; Connecticut Labor *Bulletin*, Feb. 1941, p. 5; [Connecticut] Commissioner of Welfare, *Public Welfare Statistics*, Nov. 1940; U.S. Treasury Department, *Statistics of Income: 1940* (GPO, 1943), Pt. I, 162–63.

8. *IIC*, Sept. 23, Dec. 31, 1940, Jan. 5, 24, 1941; Connecticut Development Commission, *Connecticut Progress*, Aug. 1940, pp. 1, 3.

9. *NHR*, Aug. 30, Sept. 23, 1940; *HC*, July 25, Sept. 10, Oct. 25, 1940, Jan. 5, 1941; *Bridgeport Post*, Sept. 15, 1940; *New Britain Herald*, Sept. 20, 1940; *Christian Science Monitor*, Oct. 5, 1940 (magazine).

10. "The Fortune Survey, XXIV," *Fortune*, Nov. 1939, p. 172; Gerhart Saenger, "The Effect of the War on Our Minority Groups," *American Sociological Review*, VIII (Feb. 1943), 16–18; Constantine Panunzio, "Italian Americans, Fascism, and the War," *Yale Review*, XXXI (Summer 1942), 774–79; *Fortune*, Nov. 1940, pp. 85ff; Child, *Italian or American?*, 47, 171–95; Michael John Parenti, "Ethnic and Political Attitudes: A Depth Study of Italian Americans" (Ph.D. diss., Yale Univ., 1962), 56–72; Joseph S. Roucek, "Italo-Americans and World War II," *Sociology and Social Research*, XXIX (July–Aug. 1945), 465–68; David M. Kennedy, "Italian-Americans, 1935–1942: A Study in Assimilation" (Research paper, Yale Univ., 1965), 7–8; *HC*, June 11, 1940; *NHR*, June 12, 13, 17, 1940; *Waterbury Republican*, June 12, 1940; *New Haven Journal-Courier*, June 20, 1940.

11. *Waterbury Republican*, June 12, 13, 1940; James Shanley to Franklin D. Roosevelt, July 9, 1940, FDR Library, President's Personal File 6735; *NHR*, June 11, 13, 17, 20, Sept. 26, 1940.

12. *Time*, June 3, 1940, pp. 12–14, June 10, 1940, pp. 19–22; Geoffrey Perrett, *Days of Sadness, Years of Triumph: The American People, 1939–*

1945 (Baltimore: Penguin, 1974), 87–90, 98–99; *NHR*, June 12, 18, July 24, 25, 1940.

13. *La Sentinella* (Bridgeport), Aug. 30, Sept. 13, 1940; *Il Corriere del Connecticut*, June 14, 1940; *NHR*, Oct. 6, 12, 1940; *Norwich Record*, Oct. 13, 1940.

14. *NHR*, May 19, June 17, 1940. For American public opinion regarding the war in 1940, see articles and polls in *Public Opinion Quarterly*, 1940.

15. James MacGregor Burns, *Roosevelt: The Lion and the Fox* (New York: Harcourt, Brace, 1956), 407–30; Parmet and Hecht, *Never Again, passim*; *NHR*, May 19, 1940.

16. *New York Times*, July 18, 1940.

17. *NHR*, July 15, 16, 19, 22, 1940; Parmet and Hecht, *Never Again*, 202–203.

18. *HC*, July 8–10, Aug. 21–25, 1940; John J. Burns to Steve Early, Aug. 20, 1940, FDR Library, Official File 300; Lieberman, *Power Broker*, 63; *NHR*, May 5, Sept. 1, 1940.

19. *HC*, May 3, Aug. 4, 1940; *NHR*, Aug. 18, 20, 1940; *La Sentinella* (Bridgeport), July 12, Aug. 2, 9, 16, 23, 1940.

20. *NHR*, Aug. 20–26, Sept. 1, 1940; *HC*, Aug. 24–25, Sept. 1, 1940.

21. *NHR*, June 22, 23, 1940; Charles J. Errico, Jr., "Foreign Affairs and the Presidential Election of 1940" (Ph.D. diss., Univ. of Maryland, 1973), 32–105; George L. Gallup, *The Gallup Poll: Public Opinion, 1935–1971*, Vol. I: *1935–1948* (New York: Random House, 1972), 222–31.

22. *NHR*, June 24–28, 1940; *HC*, June 24–28, 1940; Parmet and Hecht, *Never Again*, 123–67; *Christian Science Monitor*, Oct. 19, 1940 (magazine).

23. *NHR*, Sept. 8, 18, 1940; *HC*, Sept. 19, 1940.

24. Warren Moscow, *Roosevelt and Willkie* (Englewood Cliffs, N.J.: Prentice-Hall, 1968), 132–63; Burns, *Lion and the Fox*, 434–37, 442–51.

25. *NHR*, Sept. 29, Oct. 30, 1940; *Hartford Times*, Sept. 21, Oct. 15, 18, 23, 25, 1940. Here, as throughout this study, analysis of and generalizations about Connecticut campaigns and candidates are based on close day-by-day reading of major newspapers in the state, including at least one in each congressional district. To avoid multiplying references, only direct quotations, representative statements or political advertisements, and summary newspaper analyses are cited.

26. *Hartford Times*, Sept. 18, 1940.

27. Parmet and Hecht, *Never Again*, 230–35; *HC*, Sept. 16, Nov. 4, 5, 1940; *NHR*, Oct. 24, 31, Nov. 4, 5, 1940; *Waterbury Republican*, Oct. 27, Nov. 1, 1940; *Bridgeport Post*, Sept. 29, 1940.

28. Errico, "Election of 1940," pp. 319ff; *Bridgeport Post*, Oct. 29, 1940.

29. Errico, "Election of 1940," pp. 349–72; Burns, *Lion and the Fox*, 445–49.

30. *HC*, Sept. 1, 22, Oct. 9, 16, 1940; *Hartford Times*, Oct. 22, 1940; *Bridgeport Post*, Oct. 27, 30, 1940; *Waterbury Republican*, Oct. 12, 31, 1940; *Norwich Record*, Sept. 29, 1940.

31. *Hartford Times*, Sept. 5, Oct. 11, 1940; *NHR*, Oct. 26, 1940; *HC*, Nov. 2, 5, 1940; *Bridgeport Post*, Oct. 23, Nov. 2, 1940; *Waterbury Republican*, Sept. 29, Oct. 18, Nov. 5, 1940.

32. *NHR*, Oct. 9, 10, 1940; *Waterbury Republican*, Oct. 10, 13, 1940; *Hartford Times*, Oct. 12, 1940; Oliver V. Ober to Baldwin, Oct. 10, 1940, and Fred M. Thompson to Baldwin, undated, Baldwin Papers, Box 5; Univ. of Connecticut Oral History Project, Baldwin, III, 897, 899–906.

33. *NHR*, Sept. 6, 1940; *Bridgeport Post*, Sept. 27, 1940; *New Britain Herald*, Oct. 8, 1940; *HC*, Oct. 26–28, Nov. 2, 1940.

34. Theodore Milton Black, *Democratic Party Publicity in the 1940 Campaign* (New York: Plymouth Publishing Co., 1941), 107–32; Moscow, *Roosevelt and Willkie*, 160–63; *NHR*, Sept. 16, Oct. 14, 1940.

35. Jesse W. Wakeman to Baldwin, Oct. 29, 1940, and undated, unsigned memorandum [1940], Baldwin Papers, Box 5; George W. Crawford to Baldwin, Sept. 9, 1940, and Baldwin to Crawford, Sept. 12, 1940, Baldwin Papers, Box 12; *Waterbury Republican*, Oct. 20, Nov. 2, 1940; *HC*, Oct. 5, 13, 30, Nov. 2, 1940.

36. *New Britain Herald*, Oct. 31, Nov. 5, 1940; *HC*, Oct. 8, 1940.

37. *Norwich Bulletin*, Oct. 3, 1940; Frederick W. Palomba to Baldwin, Nov. 2, 1940, Baldwin Papers, Box 5; *Waterbury Republican*, Oct. 20, 1940.

38. *Waterbury Republican*, Oct. 12, 1940; *La Sentinella* (Bridgeport), Oct. 11, 1940; *Bridgeport Telegram*, Nov. 5, 1940.

39. *Waterbury Republican*, Nov. 2, 1940; *Norwich Bulletin*, Nov. 5, 1940.

40. Errico, "Election of 1940," pp. 214–16; Parmet and Hecht, *Never Again*, 245–46; *Time*, Oct. 21, 1940, p. 16; *HC*, Oct. 13, 1940; *Waterbury Republican*, Oct. 20, 1940.

41. *New Haven Journal-Courier*, Nov. 4, 1940.

42. *Il Corriere del Connecticut*, Nov. 1, 1940.

43. These conclusions are corroborated by the classic study of the 1940 election in Erie County, Ohio, by Paul F. Lazarsfeld, Bernard Berelson, and Hazel Gaudet, *The People's Choice* (3rd ed., New York: Columbia Univ. Press, 1968), 116–17.

44. For information on 1940 voting patterns, on which the discussion below draws, see Samuel Lubell, "Post-Mortem: Who Elected Roosevelt?" *Saturday Evening Post*, Jan. 25, 1941, pp. 9ff; *Public Opinion Quarterly*, V (March 1941), 147; Louis Bean, Frederick Mosteller, and Frederick Williams, "Nationalities and 1944," *Public Opinion Quarterly*, VIII (Fall 1944), 371–75; Lazarsfeld et al., *People's Choice*, 16–27; Samuel J. Eldersveld, "The Influence of Metropolitan Party Pluralities in Presidential Elections Since 1920: A Study of Twelve Key Cities," *American Political Science Review*, LXIII (Dec. 1949), 1195–98; Kevin B. Phillips, *The Emerging Republican Majority* (New Rochelle, N.Y.: Arlington House, 1969), *passim*.

45. For additional data on the election of 1940 and subsequent ones in Connecticut, see Tables A-1 to A-6.

46. V.O. Key, Jr., *The Responsible Electorate: Rationality in Presidential Voting, 1936–1960* (Cambridge: Harvard Univ. Press, 1966), 19, 35–38.

47. *Public Opinion Quarterly*, V (March 1941), 147. See also Lubell, "Post-Mortem," 9, 96, and Key, *Responsible Electorate*, 35–39.

48. Phillips, *Emerging Republican Majority*, 176, chart 47.

49. Key, *Responsible Electorate*, 19. The state-by-state correlation be-

tween Roosevelt's 1936 and 1940 votes was +.93; see Gerald M. Pomper, *Elections in America: Control and Influence in Democratic Politics* (New York: Dodd, Mead, 1970), 269, Table 5.5.

50. Lazarsfeld et al., *People's Choice*, viii–xi, argue that party loyalty was the crucial and paramount voting determinant in Erie County in 1940. Subsequent political science research and literature also found party loyalty to be of great importance to American voting behavior. Key, *Responsible Electorate*, provides an important counterargument which stresses the importance of issues and rationality in voting; and in conjunction with the other studies Key's thesis has influenced my approach to the election of 1940 specifically and to voting in the era generally.

51. Key, *Responsible Electorate*, 42–52; Lazarsfeld et al., *People's Choice*, 116–17; Hadley Cantril, ed., *Public Opinion, 1935–1946* (Princeton, N.J.: Princeton Univ. Press, 1951), 619–20; *Hartford Times*, Oct. 11, 1940.

52. Parmet and Hecht, *Never Again*, 277.

53. Moscow, *Roosevelt and Willkie*, 17; Burns, *Lion and the Fox*, 455; Bernard A. Kosicki to Baldwin, Sept. 21, 1940, Baldwin Papers, Box 5; *Bridgeport Post*, Nov. 10, Dec. 15, 1940; *NHR*, Nov. 7, 1940.

CHAPTER THREE

1. *NHR*, Dec. 22, 1940; *HC*, Dec. 25, 1940.

2. *HC*, Jan. 11, 1942; *Connecticut Industry*, Feb. 1942, p. 30, Sept. 1942, p. 28; [Connecticut] Commissioner of Welfare, *Public Welfare Statistics*, Feb. 1942.

3. *Connecticut Industry*, Dec. 1941, p. 13; *NHR*, June 13, July 31, Aug. 5, 21, 1941; *HC*, Jan. 11, 1942.

4. Connecticut Labor *Bulletin*, March through Aug. 1941, *passim*; *NHR*, July 27, 1941; *HC*, Jan. 11, 1942; James Sedalia Peters, II, "A Study of the Psychological and Social Problems of Negro Migrants in Hartford and Its Vicinity" (M.A. thesis, Hartford School of Religious Education, 1942), 78–81.

5. *Connecticut Industry*, Dec. 1941, pp. 2–16, Jan. 1942, p. 29; *HC*, Oct. 6, 1941.

6. Blair Bolles, "The Great Defense Migration," *Harper's Magazine*, Oct. 1941, p. 462; Richard R. Lingeman, *Don't You Know There's a War On?* (New York: Paperback Library, 1971), 22–24; John S. McNamara, "A Boom Town Faces Its Future," *American Mercury*, May 1941, pp. 578–84; "In Bridgeport's War Factories," *Fortune*, Sept. 1941, pp. 86–92; "The Fortune Survey," *ibid.*, Dec. 1941, pp. 119–20; *Bridgeport Post*, Dec. 8, 29, 1940.

7. Hal Borland, "Boom Town, 1941 Style," *New York Times Magazine*, Nov. 2, 1941, pp. 12–13, 26–27; Bolles, "Defense Migration," 460–62, 464–66; *HC*, Feb. 23, 1941, Oct. 25, 1942; *NHR*, May 21, 1941; Connecticut Labor *Bulletin*, May 1941, p. 12; "Bridgeport's War Factories," *passim*; [Connecticut] Commissioner of Welfare, *Report*, July 1939–June 1941, pp. 11–12.

8. *NHR*, Feb. 5, 1942; Bolles, "Defense Migration," *passim*; "Bridgeport's

War Factories," *passim*; *Nation*, Sept. 27, 1941, pp. 278–79; Borland, "Boom Town," p. 27; *HC*, Apr. 26, May 1, 1942.

9. *HC*, Apr. 16, May 30, July 24, Sept. 12, Dec. 2, 3, 23, 1941; *NHR*, July 6, 23, Sept. 21, 25, 1941; RecGovOff, Hurley, 1941–43, Box 4, "Rent Control," *passim*.

10. For patterns elsewhere, see Robert J. Havighurst and H. Gerthon Morgan, *The Social History of a War-Boom Community* (New York: Greenwood, 1968), xiii–xiv, 102–109, 254–55; Louis Wirth, "The Urban Community," in *American Society in Wartime*, ed. by William F. Ogburn (New York: DaCapo Press, 1973), 69–72; Max Parvin Cavnes, *The Hoosier Community at War* (Bloomington: Indiana Univ. Press, 1961), 15–107; Agnes E. Meyer, *Journey Through Chaos* (New York: Harcourt, 1944), 155–57, 286–302.

11. U.S. Department of Commerce, Bureau of the Census, *Sixteenth Census of the United States, 1940: Population*, Vol III: *The Labor Force*, pt. II, *Connecticut*, Table 13; Connecticut Inter-racial Commission, *Report*, 1945, pp. 11–12; RecGovOff, Baldwin, 1939–41, Box 6, "Employment Problems of Negro—Commission to Study," *passim*; Hurley to Paul McNutt, Feb. 21, 1941, RecGovOff, Hurley, 1941–43, Box 6, "Negro Employment Problem"; *HC*, Apr. 26, 1941.

12. Peters, "Negro Migrants," 52–54; *HC*, June 25, 26, 29, Aug. 11, 1941; Connecticut Labor *Bulletin*, July 1941, p. 2, Oct. 1941, p. 8.

13. Connecticut Inter-racial Commission, *Report*, 1945, p. 18; Stephen J. Sfekas, "Family and Agency: Wartime Family Changes in New Haven, Connecticut, 1941–1945" (Research paper, Yale Univ., 1969), 7, 10–12; Peters, "Negro Migrants," ii, 55–65, 71–72. See also Meyer, *Journey*, 323–32; Cavnes, *Hoosier Community*, 137–44; Mary Watters, *Illinois in the Second World War*, Vol. II (Springfield: State of Illinois, 1952), 310–15.

14. *HC*, Oct. 3, 5, Nov. 15, 1940, Feb. 24, Mar. 24, 28, June 29, Nov. 9, 29, 1941; Peters, "Negro Migrants," 84–86.

15. Articles and editorials in *La Sentinella* (Bridgeport) and *Il Corriere del Connecticut* throughout 1941; *NHR*, Apr. 29, May 19, June 17, 24, July 11, 13, 1941; *HC*, Apr. 12, May 1, 19, Nov. 25, 1941; Jeanette Sayre Smith, "Broadcasting for Marginal Americans," *Public Opinion Quarterly*, VI (Winter 1942), 589.

16. Dahl, *Who Governs?*, 110–11; *NHR*, Aug. 31, Nov. 4, 1941; *CSJ*, Dec. 1941, p. 36.

17. *CSJ*, July 1941, pp. 7, 29–34, Aug. 1941, pp. 6, 32–33, Sept. 1941, pp. 7, 12, 32–33; *HC*, July 13, 20, Aug. 20, 1941; *NHR*, Aug. 10, Nov. 30, 1941.

18. *Bridgeport Post*, Dec. 3, 1940; *HC*, Dec. 3, 8, 1940, Nov. 18, 26, 1941; *NHR*, June 24, Nov. 30, Dec. 7, 8, 1941; Donald Bruce Johnson, *The Republican Party and Wendell Willkie* (Urbana: Univ. of Illinois Press, 1960), 170–200; author's interview with Raymond E. Baldwin, Jan. 28, 1975.

19. *HC*, Dec. 8, 1941; *NHR*, Dec. 8–31, 1941, Feb. 24, Mar. 3, 4, 1942.

20. *NHR*, Dec. 8, 28, 1941.

21. Johnson, *Willkie*, 200–204; Robert E. Ficken, "The Democratic Party

and Domestic Politics During World War II" (Ph.D. diss., Univ. of Washington, 1973), 14–26; *CSJ*, Jan. 1942, pp. 8–9, 34–37, Feb. 1942, pp. 8, 33–36.

22. *HC*, Jan. 18, 25, Feb. 13, 15, 1942; *NHR*, Jan. 25, Feb. 1, 15, 1942; Raymond E. Baldwin to R.D. Byrnes, Oct. 8, 1941, Baldwin Papers, Box 4; *CSJ*, Feb. 1942, pp. 9, 29–31.

23. *HC*, Jan. 24, 1943; *Connecticut Industry*, Feb. 1943, pp. 23, 25; Harvey L. Hooke to Robert Hurley, Aug. 31, 1942, with enclosure, RecGovOff, Hurley, 1941–43, Box 2, "Defense—War Industry Commission"; Connecticut Post-War Planning Board, *Interim Report*, 15; [Connecticut] Commissioner of Welfare, *Public Welfare Statistics*, Nov. 1942, p. 11, Feb. 1943, pp. 5, 10, 12.

24. Connecticut Labor *Bulletin*, June 1942, *passim*, Oct. 1942, pp. 6, 8, Nov. 1942, p. 7, Dec. 1942, p. 5, Jan. 1943, pp. 6, 8, 12; *NHR*, Aug. 25, 1942; *HC*, Apr. 19, Nov. 6, 11, 18, 1942, Feb. 4, 1943; *Connecticut Industry*, May 1942, *passim*, Nov. 1942, pp. 5, 7–9, Dec. 1942, pp. 18–19.

25. Hartford Housing Authority, *Third Annual Report* (1942); Bridgeport Housing Authority, *Fourth Annual Report* (1942); RecGovOff, Hurley, 1941–43, Box 3, "Defense—Housing—Emergency Committee," *passim*; *HC*, Mar. 3, Apr. 2, 26, May 17, 30, June 25, July 8, Aug. 6, Oct. 26, 1942; *NHR*, June 1, 21, July 18, 1942.

26. Charles S. Johnson, *To Stem This Tide: A Survey of Racial Tension Areas in the United States* (Philadelphia: Pilgrim Press, 1943), 25–26; *HC*, May 16, 23, June 29, July 2, 14, 1942.

27. Connecticut Labor *Bulletin*, June 1942, pp. 7, 12, Aug. 1942, p. 8; "Hearing on Job Discrimination . . . April 25, 1942," in RecGovOff, Hurley, 1941–43, Box 3, "Defense—Job Discrimination Committee."

28. *HC*, Feb. 23, Mar. 23, Apr. 14, 21, June 29, 1942; *New Haven Journal-Courier*, Oct. 5, 1942. On the issue of World War II and black activism in America, see the insightful though differing analyses in Richard M. Dalfiume, "The 'Forgotten Years' of the Negro Revolution," *Journal of American History*, LV (June 1968), 90–106, and Lee Finkle, "The Conservative Aims of Militant Rhetoric: Black Protest During World War II," *Journal of American History*, LX (Dec. 1973), 692–713.

29. *Il Corriere del Connecticut*, Dec. 12, 19, 1941; *La Sentinella* (Bridgeport), Dec. 12, 1941, May 8, July 3, 1942; *HC*, Dec. 12, 1941, Jan. 30, 1942; *Waterbury Republican*, Dec. 18, 29, 1941; *NHR*, Feb. 1, 1942; *CSJ*, Feb. 1942, pp. 14, 24–25, March 1942, pp. 14, 24–25, March 1943, pp. 31–32; Kennedy, "Italian-Americans, 1935–1942."

30. *NHR*, Dec. 9, 1941, Feb. 15, 27, Mar. 3, 10, Apr. 18, 22, May 13, 20, June 2, Oct. 30, 1942; *La Sentinella* (Bridgeport), July 10, 1942; *HC*, Jan. 15, July 12, 19, 1942; *CSJ*, March 1943, p. 31.

31. *HC*, Mar. 8, 1942; *La Sentinella* (Bridgeport), Aug. 14, 1942; *Il Corriere del Connecticut*, Oct. 9, 1942; *Waterbury Republican*, Oct. 9, 11, 1942; *New London Day*, Oct. 8, 9, 22, 1942; *NHR*, Oct. 8, 11, 13, 15, 1942.

32. Lingeman, *There's a War On*, 284–329.

33. *Ibid.*, 285–96; *HC*, June 27, 1943; *Connecticut Industry*, Feb. 1942,

p. 3; *NHR*, May 17, 1942; Walter C. McKain, Jr., and Nathan L. Whetten, *Occupational and Industrial Diversity in Rural Connecticut*, Storrs Ag. Exp. Sta. Bull. 263, Nov. 1949, pp. 7, 9, 12, 46.

34. *HC*, Jan. 16, 1942.

35. A.A. Hoehling, *Home Front, USA* (New York: Crowell, 1966), 63–79; *Connecticut Circle*, Aug. 1942, p. 8, Sept. 1942, p. 12; *NHR*, July 23, Sept. 24, 27, 30, Oct. 26, 1942; *HC*, Oct. 27, 1942; *New Britain Herald*, Oct. 14, 1942.

36. Henry H. Adams, *1942: The Year That Doomed the Axis* (New York: David McKay, 1967).

37. *HC*, Mar. 1, 29, Apr. 5, 19, June 7, 1942.

38. Johnson, *Baldwin*, 114ff; *CSJ*, March 1942, p. 8, May 1942, pp. 8, 38–39, June 1942, pp. 9, 38–39, Dec. 1942, pp. 6, 32–33; Stephen Shadegg, *Clare Boothe Luce* (New York: Simon & Schuster, 1970), 107–63; *NHR*, Sept. 3, 4, 8, 1942; *HC*, May 31, June 21, Sept. 4–8, 12, 14, 15, 1942.

39. *NHR*, Sept. 6, 11, 13, 1942; *HC*, Sept. 11–13, 1942; *CSJ*, Aug. 1942, *passim*.

40. *NHR*, Sept. 16, 17, 20, 1942; *HC*, Sept. 16, 17, 20, 1942; *CSJ*, Aug. 1942, pp. 10, 32–33, Sept. 1942, pp. 12, 30–31.

41. *HC*, Sept. 17, Oct. 9, 12, 27, 29, 31, 1942.

42. *HC*, Sept. 12, Oct. 1, 2, 9, 23, 29, 30, Nov. 2, 1942.

43. *HC*, Oct. 23, 1942, in part.

44. *Bridgeport Post*, Oct. 3, 1942; *HC*, Oct. 11, 18, 29, 31, 1942; *Waterbury Republican*, Sept. 15, Oct. 17, 20, 21, 30, Nov. 4, 1942; *NHR*, Oct. 9, 1942; *Norwich Bulletin*, Oct. 20, 27, Nov. 3, 1942; Johnson, *Willkie*, 217–18.

45. Johnson, *Willkie*, 218; Ficken, "Democratic Party," 65–68; *HC*, Sept. 15, 27, Oct. 12, 23, 30, Nov. 2, 1942; *NHR*, Oct. 18, 25, 30, 1942; *Norwich Bulletin*, Oct. 20, 27, 29, 1942; *Waterbury American*, Sept. 27, Oct. 3, 26, 1942; *Bridgeport Post*, Oct. 16, 25, 27, Nov. 1, 1942.

46. *Waterbury Republican*, Oct. 4, 1942.

47. *NHR*, Sept. 20, 27, Oct. 18, 1942; *HC*, Oct. 25, 1942; *New Britain Herald*, Oct. 30, 31, Nov. 3, 1942; *Bridgeport Post*, Nov. 8, 1942.

48. *NHR*, Oct. 4, 18, 1942; *Hartford Times*, Sept. 26, 1942; *HC*, Oct. 7, 10, 20, Nov. 1, 3, 1942.

49. *HC*, Oct. 13, 1942; Kennedy, "Italian-Americans, 1935–1942," esp. 12–14.

50. *New Haven Journal-Courier*, Oct. 14, 1942; *HC*, Oct. 22, 23, 1942; *NHR*, Oct. 13, 22, 1942; *New London Day*, Nov. 2, 1942.

51. *Il Corriere del Connecticut*, Oct. 16, 23, 1942; *New London Day*, Oct. 15, 22, 1942; *HC*, Oct. 13, 1942; *NHR*, Oct. 13, 15, 1942.

52. *HC*, Oct. 3, 16, 20, 25, 29, 1942.

53. *Waterbury Republican*, Sept. 17, 1942; *HC*, Sept. 9–12, 29, Oct. 22, 28, 30, 1942; *NHR*, Oct. 16, 23, 1942.

54. *NHR*, Aug. 23, Oct. 4, 28, 1942; *HC*, Aug. 16, Oct. 4, Nov. 2, 1942.

55. *HC*, Nov. 1, 2, 1942; *NHR*, Nov. 1, 1942; *CSJ*, Oct. 1942, pp. 12–13; *New York Times*, Nov. 1, 3, 1942; Ficken, "Democratic Party," 75–76.

56. *NHR*, Nov. 4, 1942.

57. *New York Times*, Nov. 5, 12, 1942; American Institute of Public Opinion, *The Gallup Political Almanac for 1946* (Manchester, N.H.: Clarke Press, 1946), 228; Hadley Cantril and John Harding, "The 1942 Elections: A Case Study in Political Psychology," *Public Opinion Quarterly*, VII (Summer 1943), 222–41; John Harding, "The 1942 Congressional Elections," *American Political Science Review*, XXXVIII (Feb. 1944), 41–57; Louis H. Bean, *How to Predict Elections* (New York: Knopf, 1948), esp. 22–49. Historical accounts have also stressed low turnout; for recent studies see Richard Polenberg, *War and Society: The United States, 1941–1945* (Philadelphia: Lippincott, 1972), 189–90, and James MacGregor Burns, *Roosevelt: The Soldier of Freedom* (New York: Harcourt, 1970), 281.

58. *NHR*, Oct. 4, Nov. 3–5, 1942; *HC*, Nov. 8, 15, 29, 1942; *CSJ*, Dec. 1942, *passim*.

59. Even if the correlations had been strong, moreover, the reduced turnout would have accounted for only about half of the 5-point Democratic decline and might have been decisive in only a few contests. At both the town and the ward levels, regression coefficients show that each decrease of 10 percent in the number voting reduced the Democratic share of the vote by 1 percent—and, generally, voter turnout fell by about 25 percent, the Democratic percentage by 5 points.

60. *NHR*, Apr. 3, 1941, Oct. 4, 1942; *Waterbury Republican*, Oct. 11, 1942.

61. Several studies of the effects of turnout on election results lend general support to this conclusion. See Philip E. Converse, "The Concept of a Normal Vote," in *Elections and the Political Order*, Angus Campbell et al. (New York: Wiley, 1966), esp. 28–30; William A. Glaser, "Fluctuations in Turnout," in *Public Opinion and Congressional Elections*, ed. William N. McPhee and William A. Glaser (n.p.: Free Press of Glencoe, 1962), 46–50; O.C. Press, "The Prediction of Midterm Elections," *Western Political Quarterly*, IX (Sept. 1956), 691–98.

62. Key, *Responsible Electorate*, *passim*; David E. RePass, "Issue Salience and Party Choice," *American Political Science Review*, LXV (June 1971), 389–90; McPhee and Glaser, *Congressional Elections*, 48–50; Campbell et al., *Political Order*, 7–62.

63. See *U.S. News*, Nov. 13, 1942, pp. 24–25, and 1942 Campaign "Post Mortem" Correspondence, Records of the Democratic National Committee, FDR Library. *U.S. News* surveyed candidates for Congress on the election outcome, and the 266 replies, including those of three Connecticut Republicans and two Connecticut Democrats, were tabulated. In the "Post Mortem" correspondence, Democratic candidates for Congress, including all six from Connecticut, advanced their explanations of the Democratic losses; the replies are summarized and analyzed in enclosures to memoranda from Edwin W. Pauley to Roosevelt, Dec. 14, 1942, FDR Library, President's Personal File 1820.

64. *Hartford Times*, Oct. 24, 1942.

65. *New York Times*, Nov. 5, 1942; *U.S. News*, Nov. 13, 1942, pp. 24–25; 1942 "Post Mortem" correspondence, FDR Library.

CHAPTER FOUR

1. *HC*, Dec. 31, 1942, Jan. 31, Feb. 20, 21, 23, Mar. 28, June 1, July 16, Sept. 1, 19, 1943; *NHR*, Mar. 28, July 28, Aug. 11, 1943; *CSJ*, Oct. 1943, p. 13.
2. *HC*, Oct. 21, 1943, Feb. 6, 1944; *CSJ*, May 1944, pp. 7ff; W. Lloyd Warner, *Democracy in Jonesville* (New York: Harper & Row, 1964), 287–88.
3. Roland Young, *Congressional Politics in the Second World War* (New York: Columbia Univ. Press, 1956), 23ff; *CSJ*, Aug. 1943, pp. 14–15, 22–24, 27.
4. Perrett, *Years of Triumph*, 287–89.
5. *HC*, Jan. 3, 7, 1943; *Connecticut Circle*, Feb. 1943, p. 13.
6. *NHR*, May 21 (editorial), 23, 1943; *HC*, May 30, June 6, Sept. 9, 1943; Johnson, *Baldwin*, 122–33; Henry B. Mosle to Baldwin, Sept. 28, 1944, Baldwin Papers, Box 6; material on the State War Council, RecGovOff, Baldwin, 1943–46, Boxes 35–38.
7. Connecticut State Housing Authority, *First Annual Report* (1944), *passim*; *NHR*, Oct. 20, 1944; Connecticut Post-War Planning Board, *Interim Report*, A3, A8-A21. See also reports of the Bridgeport, Hartford, and New Haven housing authorities for 1943 and 1944.
8. Connecticut Labor *Bulletin*, Jan. 1943 through Dec. 1944; *Connecticut Industry*, May 1945, p. 38; *HC*, Jan. 13, Dec. 31, 1944.
9. *CSJ*, Sept. 1943, pp. 7, 50–54, Dec. 1943, pp. 6, 46–48; Connecticut Labor *Bulletin*, Jan. 1944, pp. 4–7; *Connecticut Industry*, March 1943, p. 3, April 1944, pp. 3, 38, June 1944, pp. 13–14, 21; Baldwin to Paul McNutt, Donald Nelson, and others, July 17, 1944, Baldwin Papers, Box 6; *HC*, Feb. 5, 6, 1943, June 2, Aug. 16, 17, 31, Oct. 6, 19, Nov. 2, 3, 1944.
10. Jerome S. Bruner, *Mandate From The People* (New York: Duell, Sloan and Pearce, 1944), 170–87.
11. Connecticut Post-War Planning Board, *Interim Report*, *passim*; Connecticut Labor *Bulletin*, June 1943, p. 5.
12. *Connecticut Industry*, Sept. 1943, p. 31; *NHR*, Sept. 26, 1943.
13. *Connecticut Industry*, June 1943 through March 1945; Connecticut Labor *Bulletin*, March 1944, pp. 7, 10, April 1944, p. 3; [Connecticut] Commissioner of Welfare, *Public Welfare Statistics*, Feb. 1945; *NHR*, May 7, 1944.
14. Connecticut Post-War Planning Board, *Interim Report*, *passim*; Connecticut Reemployment Commission, *First Annual Report* (1944); *HC*, Jan. 23, 1944. The myriad planning efforts led *CSJ* to devote a continuing special section to them beginning in April 1944.
15. Connecticut Inter-racial Commission, 1945 *Report*, 11–13.
16. Richard A.G. Foster to Baldwin, Dec. 22, 1942, RecGovOff, Baldwin, 1943–46, Box 18, "Inter-Racial Commission"; *HC*, Feb. 12, 26, May 23, Aug. 4, 27, 1943.
17. *Connecticut State Register and Manual 1943 and 1944*, 94.
18. Connecticut Inter-racial Commission, 1945 *Report*, 6–7.
19. For national patterns, see Johnson, *To Stem This Tide*; Polenberg,

287

War and Society, 99–130; Carey McWilliams, "What We Did About Racial Minorities," in *While You Were Gone*, ed. Jack Goodman (New York: Simon & Schuster, 1946), 89–111; Selden Menefee, *Assignment: U.S.A.* (New York: Reynal & Hitchcock, 1943), 147–93.

20. Connecticut Inter-racial Commission, 1944 *Report*, 11–19, 25–26; Johnson, *To Stem This Tide*, 19–21, 46, 108; *HC*, Mar. 28, 30, Apr. 14, 17, 18, 27, 1943.

21. McWilliams, "Racial Minorities," 96–97, *HC*, July 1, Aug. 2, 7, Sept. 15, Oct. 23, Dec. 6, 1943, Jan. 8, Feb. 11, Mar. 6, 1944; Connecticut Inter-racial Commission, 1944 *Report*, 11, 20–26.

22. *HC*, Aug. 15, 22, 23, 1944, Jan. 16-18, 21, 24, 25, 1945; *CSJ*, Oct. 1944, p. 5; Connecticut Inter-racial Commission, 1944 *Report*, 26–29.

23. *CSJ*, Nov. 1943, pp. 9, 33–34; *NHR*, Sept. 5, 10, 1943.

24. *NHR*, July 26, Sept. 8, 16, 1943; *HC*, July 26, 1943, April 12, May 24, 1944; *La Sentinella* (Bridgeport), Sept. 10, 1943, May 26, June 9, 1944; *Il Corriere del Connecticut*, May 5, 1944.

25. Polenberg, *War and Society*, 138; Menefee, *Assignment*, 13–15, 22–23, 136–37; Connecticut Inter-racial Commission, 1944 *Report*, 13, 19, 25; *HC*, Jan. 28, Nov. 1, 2, 1943, Feb. 5, 1944; *CSJ*, Feb. 1944, p. 10.

26. *NHR*, June 3, 1944; *HC*, Sept. 26, Oct. 30, 1944.

27. *NHR*, Feb. 6, 9, 1944; Correspondence in RecGovOff, Baldwin, 1943–46, Box 2, "American Palestine Committee."

28. Robert A. Divine, *Foreign Policy and U.S. Presidential Elections, 1940–1948* (New York: New Viewpoints, 1974), 105–108; *NHR*, June 2, 1944.

29. Divine, *Elections, 1940–1948*, pp. 108–12; Peter H. Irons, "America's Cold War Crusade: Domestic Politics and Foreign Policy, 1942–1948" (Ph.D. diss., Boston Univ., 1972), 245ff.

30. *NHR*, May 6, 1943.

31. *HC*, May 4, 8, 1944; *Hartford Catholic Transcript, passim* 1944.

32. Irons, "Cold War Crusade," 286ff; *HC*, Sept. 11, 1944; Divine, *Elections, 1940–1948*, pp. 110–12.

33. See Robert A. Divine, *Second Chance: The Triumph of Internationalism in America During World War II* (New York: Atheneum, 1971).

34. *Ibid.*, 4, 183, and *passim*; Bruner, *Mandate*, 20–35, 55; Joseph H. Ball, "How We Planned for the Postwar World," in *While You Were Gone*, ed. Goodman, 552.

35. Divine, *Second Chance*, 183.

36. Johnson, *Willkie*, 165–260; *CSJ*, Sept. 1942, pp. 13, 28; Divine, *Second Chance*, 103–107, 129–33.

37. *CSJ*, Nov. 1943, p. 34, Feb. 1944, p. 16; *NHR*, Jan. 6, 9, Mar. 5, 1944.

38. Johnson, *Willkie*, 263–83; *Time*, Apr. 17, 1944, pp. 17–19.

39. *CSJ*, April 1944, p. 13; *HC*, May 3, 6, 1944; *NHR*, Apr. 6, June 26, 27, 1944.

40. Johnson, *Willkie*, 284–95; Divine, *Second Chance*, 209–11; *New York Times*, June 28, 1944; *NHR*, June 27, 29, July 10, 12, 1944.

41. Author's interview with Baldwin, Jan. 28, 1975; *HC*, Mar. 21, May 7, 13, 1944; *NHR*, Mar. 23, Apr. 16, 25, June 11, 1944.

42. *HC,* July 8, 15, 1944; Johnson, *Baldwin,* 147–49; author's interview with Baldwin, Jan. 28, 1975; *NHR,* July 16, 1944.

43. *NHR,* Nov. 27, 29, Dec. 13, 1942; *HC,* Dec. 10, 11, 13, 1942.

44. *NHR,* Oct. 31, Nov. 3, 1943; *Life,* Nov. 15, 1943, pp. 27–31; Ficken, "Democratic Party," 181–85; *CSJ,* April 1943, p. 6, Dec. 1943, p. 8; *HC,* May 16, 20, 1943, Jan. 2, Feb. 23, May 27, 28, 1944.

45. *CSJ,* Jan. 1944, pp. 12, 29; *NHR,* Dec. 26, 1943, Mar. 5, July 7–9, 12, 14, 16, 1944; *HC,* Mar. 19, May 14, July 2, 12–16, 1944.

46. Burns, *Soldier of Freedom,* 503–506; *HC,* July 19, 20, 1944; *NHR,* July 22, 1944.

47. *New York Times,* July 21–23, 1944; Divine, *Second Chance,* 212–13.

48. *NHR,* July 30, Aug. 3–6, 12, 1944; *Bridgeport Post,* Aug. 3, 1944; *HC,* Aug. 1–5, 1944; *New Britain Herald,* Aug. 22, 1944; *CSJ,* Aug. 1944, pp. 9, 34.

49. *HC,* Aug. 6, 9, 1944; *NHR,* Aug. 6, 1944; *New Britain Herald,* Aug. 7, 1944.

50. Polenberg, *War and Society,* 203–208; *Waterbury Republican,* Aug. 4, 8–10, 1944.

51. *New London Day,* Aug. 14, 1944; *Bridgeport Post,* Aug. 13, 1944; *HC,* Sept. 10, Oct. 1, 1944; *Waterbury Republican,* Oct. 4, 8, 1944.

52. *HC,* July 30, Aug. 27, 1944; author's interview with Baldwin, Jan. 28, 1975.

53. *Waterbury Republican,* Aug. 13, 19, 1944; *NHR,* Aug. 8, 1944; *HC,* Aug. 9, 1944; *Norwich Bulletin,* Oct. 31, 1944.

54. Polenberg, *War and Society,* 210–12; Opinion Research Corporation, "Dewey vs. Roosevelt: An Analysis of the Presidential Campaign," 12, in Baldwin Papers, Box 6.

55. Ficken, "Democratic Party," 235–37; Divine, *Elections, 1940–1948,* pp. 126ff.

56. Divine, *Second Chance,* 214–41.

57. *Hartford Times,* Sept. 30, 1944; *HC,* Sept. 9, Oct. 5, 7, 23, 24, 26, 31, Nov. 2, 1944; *Waterbury Republican,* Oct. 3, 26, 1944; *New Britain Herald,* Oct. 12, 1944.

58. Connecticut Post-War Planning Board, *Interim Report; NHR,* Aug. 17, Sept. 1, Oct. 1, 1944; *HC,* Sept. 6, 12–14, 20, 1944.

59. Baldwin to Samuel F. Meek, Aug. 24, 1944, Baldwin Papers, Box 6; *HC,* Sept. 3, 19, 28, Oct. 4, 5, 28, 1944.

60. *NHR,* Oct. 3, 1944; *New Britain Herald,* Oct. 26, 1944; Lester C. Burdick to Baldwin, Nov. 9, 1944, Baldwin Papers, Box 6; Robert P. Butler to Robert Hannegan, Oct. 14, 1944, Official File 300, FDR Library; *HC,* Nov. 2, 4, 1944.

61. *HC,* Aug. 28, Sept. 21, 22, Oct. 2, 12, 1944; *NHR,* Oct. 13, 1944; *Bridgeport Post,* Oct. 12, 13, 29, 1944; *Norwich Bulletin,* Nov. 4, 1944.

62. Clarence F. Baldwin to Raymond Baldwin, Sept. 14, 1944, Baldwin Papers, Box 6; *HC,* Oct. 6, 14, 23, Nov. 4, 7, 1944; *Waterbury Republican,* Oct. 26, 1944; *New London Day,* Oct. 26, 1944; *Bridgeport Post,* Oct. 24, 1944.

63. *HC*, Oct. 17, 1944; *Bridgeport Post*, Oct. 13, 1944; *Norwich Bulletin*, Oct. 31, 1944.

64. Opinion Research Corporation, "The 1944 Campaign: Connecticut," 5–7, in Baldwin Papers, Box 6; *HC*, Oct. 22, Nov. 7, 1944; *NHR*, Oct. 18, 1944; *Waterbury Republican*, Oct. 25, 1944; *New London Day*, Oct. 26, 1944; *Bridgeport Post*, Sept. 19, 1944.

65. *NHR*, Sept. 24, 1944.

66. Polenberg, *War and Society*, 208–209; Ficken, "Democratic Party," 275–81; *HC*, Oct. 7, 17, 24, Nov. 3 (editorial), 6, 1944; *NHR*, Nov. 3 (editorial), 1944; *Norwich Bulletin*, Aug. 8, Oct. 7 (editorial), 31, 1944; *New London Day*, Oct. 7 (editorial), Nov. 3, 1944; *Bridgeport Post*, Aug. 11 (editorial), 1944; *Waterbury Republican*, Oct. 7 (editorial), 1944.

67. *Bridgeport Post*, Oct. 29, 1944.

68. *Ibid.*, Oct. 11, 21, 30, Nov. 2, 3, 1944; *HC*, Oct. 21, 1944.

69. Irons, "Cold War Crusade," 341–43; Ficken, "Democratic Party," 275; Robert P. Butler to Robert Hannegan, Oct. 14, 1944, Official File 300, FDR Library; O'Brien, *American Catholics*, 81–96; Moscow, *Roosevelt and Willkie*, 46–48.

70. Burns, *Soldier of Freedom*, 524, 529–30; *NHR*, Oct. 6, Nov. 4, 1944; *Waterbury Republican*, Oct. 23, 27, Nov. 4, 1944; *Hartford Catholic Transcript*, Nov. 2, 1944; *Norwich Bulletin*, Nov. 3, 1944; *New London Day*, Nov. 3, 1944; *Bridgeport Post*, Oct. 26, Nov. 3, 6, 1944.

71. *Waterbury Republican*, Oct. 25, 1944; *Bridgeport Post*, Nov. 2, 1944.

72. *NHR*, Oct. 1, 15, 20, 27, 1944; *HC*, Oct. 14, 1944; *New London Day*, Nov. 2, 1944; *Bridgeport Post*, Oct. 23, 30, Nov. 5, 1944.

73. *HC*, Sept. 28, 29, 1944; *New York Times*, Oct. 4, 5, 1944; *Waterbury Republican*, Oct. 12, 15, 1944; *Bridgeport Post*, Oct. 23, 30, Nov. 1, 1944.

74. Divine, *Elections, 1940–1948*, pp. 138–43; *Waterbury Republican*, Sept. 20, Oct, 12, Nov. 6, 1944; *New Britain Herald*, Oct. 16, 1944.

75. Divine, *Elections, 1940–1948*, pp. 144–45; *HC*, Sept. 27, 1944; *Waterbury Republican*, Oct. 13, 1944; *Bridgeport Post*, Nov. 2, 1944.

76. *Il Corriere del Connecticut*, Sept. 29, 1944; *La Sentinella* (Bridgeport), Oct. 13, 20, Nov. 3, 1944; *Bridgeport Post*, Oct. 4, 9, 29, 1944; *New London Day*, Oct. 30, Nov. 6, 1944.

77. *Waterbury Republican*, Oct. 13, 28, 30, 1944; *La Sentinella* (Bridgeport), Oct. 20, 27, Nov. 3, 1944; *Il Corriere del Connecticut*, Oct. 27, 1944; *NHR*, Oct. 16, 30, Nov. 6, 1944.

78. *NHR*, Oct. 1, 22, Nov. 5, 1944.

79. *NHR*, Oct. 29, Nov. 5, 1944; *HC*, Oct. 22, Nov. 6, 7, 1944; *Newsweek*, Nov. 6, 1944, pp. 45–46; Opinion Research Corporation, "1944 Campaign: Connecticut," 1, 3.

80. Polenberg, *War and Society*, 212–14; Key, *Responsible Electorate*, 19–20; Pomper, *Elections*, 269, Table 5.5.

81. *Bridgeport Post*, Nov. 12, 1944; *New Britain Herald*, Nov. 14, 1944; Baldwin to Harold Stassen, Dec. 7, 1944, Baldwin Papers, Box 31.

82. *CSJ*, Dec. 1944, *passim*; *New Britain Herald*, Nov. 18, 1944; Burns, *Soldier of Freedom*, 525.

83. Key, *Responsible Electorate*, 19–20.

84. *Waterbury Republican*, Oct. 29, 1944; *New Britain Herald*, Nov. 25, 1944.

85. McLevy's vote in Bridgeport correlated at +.50 with percentage foreign-born and at +.35 with Roosevelt's 1940 vote.

86. Irons, "Cold War Crusade," 344–45, 350, 365; *Nation*, Sept. 16, 1944, p. 323, Nov. 25, 1944, pp. 640–41; Phillips, *Emerging Republican Majority*, 114–15.

87. Phillips, *Emerging Republican Majority*, 154–56.

88. *HC*, Nov. 8, 9, 1944.

89. See also *CSJ*, Dec. 1944, p. 28.

90. Key, *Responsible Electorate*, 35–37; *Public Opinion Quarterly*, IX (Spring 1945), 84.

91. Divine, *Second Chance*, 241; *Hartford Times*, Oct. 24, Nov. 8 (editorial), Nov. 9 (editorial), 1944; *Public Opinion Quarterly*, VIII (Winter 1944), 570.

92. Hadley Cantril, "The Issues—As Seen by the American People," *Public Opinion Quarterly*, VIII (Fall 1944), 336–42; Cantril, ed., *Public Opinion, 1935–1946*, pp. 638, 679.

93. Opinion Research Corporation, "1944 Campaign: Connecticut," 7.

94. Cantril, ed., *Public Opinion, 1935–1946*, pp. 160–61, 638–39, 642, 752.

95. Bruner, *Mandate*, 223.

CHAPTER FIVE

1. *Connecticut Industry*, Sept. 1945, p. 32, Oct. 1945, p. 38; Connecticut Labor *Bulletin*, July 1945, pp. 6, 12, Aug. 1945, pp. 11, 12; *NHR*, June 12, 1945.

2. *NHR*, Aug. 16, 25, 1945; *Connecticut Industry*, Nov. 1945, p. 30; Connecticut Labor *Bulletin*, Sept. 1945, pp. 1, 5, Oct. 1945, pp. 5, 12.

3. *NHR*, Aug. 15, 22, 25, Sept. 19, 1945; *HC*, Aug. 19, 23, 25, 26, 27 (editorial), 28, 29 (editorial), 30 (editorial), Sept. 28, 1945; *Connecticut Industry*, June 1945, pp. 8, 28, Nov. 1945, p. 30.

4. *Connecticut Industry*, May 1945, p. 8; *HC*, Oct. 3–5, 11, 1945.

5. *Connecticut Industry*, Dec. 1945 through Feb. 1947; Connecticut Labor *Bulletin*, Dec. 1945 through Dec. 1946.

6. Connecticut Labor *Bulletin*, Oct. 1946, p. 2; *Time*, July 1, 1946, pp. 19–20.

7. *NHR*, Nov. 19, 1945.

8. *Connecticut Industry*, March 1947, p. 43.

9. *HC*, editorials, Mar. 6, May 19, June 29, Sept. 4, 1946; *Hartford Times*, Sept. 13, 18, 1946.

10. Irons, "Cold War Crusade," 158–90; *Hartford Catholic Transcript*, Jan. 25, July 5, Nov. 27, 1945, Jan. 10, Mar. 14, June 6, 1946.

11. Athan Theoharis, *The Yalta Myths: An Issue in U.S. Politics, 1945–1955* (Columbia: Univ. of Missouri Press, 1970), 23–28; Irons, "Cold War Crusade," 301ff; *HC*, Mar. 26, May 4, 1945; *Hartford Catholic Transcript*, Feb. 15, 1945.

12. Theoharis, *Yalta Myths*, 28–29; *NHR*, June 25, 1945; *HC*, Mar. 5, Apr. 11, 12, July 9, Sept. 10, 14, Oct. 15, 1945, May 6, June 4–6, 1946.

13. *Il Corriere del Connecticut*, Apr. 13, 1945, Jan. 18, May 3, July 19, Aug. 30, Oct. 18, 1946; *La Sentinella* (Bridgeport), Feb. 22, Sept. 20, Oct. 4, 1946; *HC*, May 2, June 19, July 31, Aug. 11, Oct. 10, 20, 1946; *NHR*, July 18, 27, 1946; *New London Day*, Sept. 30, 1946.

14. *Waterbury Republican*, Sept. 9, 1946; *CSJ*, Oct. 1945, p. 17; *NHR*, Oct. 8, 1945, May 24, 1946; *HC*, Oct. 3–5, 17, Dec. 14, 18, 1945, Jan. 13, July 14, 15, Aug. 3, 17, 1946.

15. Connecticut Inter-racial Commission, 1945 *Report*, 28–29; *Time*, Aug. 6, 1945, p. 23; *Il Corriere del Connecticut*, Aug. 10, 1945; *La Sentinella* (Bridgeport), Aug. 31, 1945; *HC*, Feb. 6, May 27, 1946.

16. Oscar Handlin, *The American People in the Twentieth Century* (Boston: Beacon Press, 1963), 212–20; Warner, "American Town," 47–48, 54, 61; Warner, *Jonesville*, 288.

17. *Il Corriere del Connecticut*, Nov. 9, 1945; *La Sentinella* (Bridgeport), Nov. 19, 1945; Dahl, *Who Governs?*, 51, 84, 160–61; *NHR*, Oct. 4, Nov. 4, 6, 7, 1945.

18. *NHR*, Nov. 7, 1945.

19. *Connecticut Inter-racial Survey*, Nov./Dec. 1946, pp. 1–3; Connecticut Inter-racial Commission, 1945 *Report* and 1947 *Report, passim*. For similar patterns elsewhere, see Watters, *Illinois*, II, 258–86, and Cavnes, *Hoosier Community*, 108–79.

20. *CSJ*, Sept. 1946, pp. 12, 13, 27; *HC*, Mar. 20, 21, Apr. 19, Oct. 14, 1945, Jan. 7, Mar. 13, 1946; *NHR*, Mar. 21, Apr. 28, May 1, 3, 5, Sept. 25, 27, 1945, Aug. 6, 7, 1946; Connecticut Inter-racial Commission, 1945 *Report*, 15, 30–39.

21. *Waterbury Republican*, Sept. 1, 1946; Bert Cochran, *Harry Truman and the Crisis Presidency* (New York: Funk & Wagnalls, 1973), 202–11.

22. Connecticut Labor *Bulletin*, Oct. 1945, through Nov. 1946; *Connecticut Industry*, Feb. 1946, p. 5, June 1946, pp. 5, 26–27; *NHR*, May 26 (editorial), Oct. 5, 1946; *HC*, Mar. 1, 17, May 18 (editorial), 1946.

23. Connecticut State Housing Authority, 1946 *Report, passim*; *HC*, Feb. 14, 1946; *NHR*, Apr. 6, 25, 28, May 2–5, Sept. 20, 1946; correspondence in RecGovOff, Baldwin, 1943–46, Box 18.

24. Connecticut Reemployment Commission, *Reemployment*, Nov. 1946, p. 5; *CSJ*, March 1946, pp. 6, 24–25, April 1946, p. 11; *HC*, Apr. 10, 18, 1946; Connecticut State Housing Authority, 1946 *Report*, 43; *NHR*, May 12, 1946.

25. *HC*, Aug. 16, 17, Nov. 25, 1946; *NHR*, Nov. 24, 1946.

26. Cabell Phillips, *The Truman Presidency: The History of a Triumphant Succession* (Baltimore: Penguin, 1969), 104–108; *Connecticut Industry*, April 1946, pp. 5, 23; *HC*, Dec. 25, 1945, Jan. 11, Mar. 13, 1946; *NHR*, Dec. 23, 1945, Feb. 24, Apr. 13, 14, May 3, 17, 22, June 2, 1946; correspondence in RecGovOff, Baldwin, 1943–46, Box 25, "Office of Price Administration."

27. Chester Bowles, *Promises to Keep: My Years in Public Life, 1941–1969* (New York: Harper & Row, 1971), 126–56; Phillips, *Truman Presidency*,

106–10; *NHR*, Apr. 12, May 2, 4, July 1–10, 22, 26, 1946; *HC*, Apr. 25, May 5, 11, July 1–10, 23, 1946.

28. *Connecticut Industry*, Dec. 1946, p. 41, May, 1947, p. 44; *HC*, Aug. 21, 22, 1946; *NHR*, Sept. 10, 1946.

29. *CSJ*, April 1945, pp. 14, 29; *NHR*, Jan. 21, Apr. 15, June 6, 7, 13, 1945; Johnson, *Baldwin*, 157, 168–69; *HC*, June 14, 1945.

30. *HC*, Nov. 18, 1945; *CSJ*, Nov. 1945, p. 9; *Time*, Oct. 21, 1946, p. 23.

31. *NHR*, Feb. 13, Apr. 14, 1946; *HC*, Feb. 13, May 29, 1946.

32. *HC*, Mar. 31, Apr. 7, 28, May 16, July 16, Aug. 11, 17, 1946; Johnson, *Baldwin*, 180–87; author's interview with Baldwin, Jan. 28, 1975.

33. Univ. of Connecticut Oral History Project, Baldwin, IV, 1494–99; *Waterbury Republican*, Sept. 10, 11, 1946; *HC*, Sept. 5–7, 11, 1946; *NHR*, Sept. 10, 11, 1946; *Bridgeport Post*, Sept. 11, 15, 1946.

34. *HC*, Sept. 10, 11, 1946; *NHR*, Sept. 10, 1946; *New Britain Herald*, Nov. 19, 1946.

35. *HC*, Feb. 24, May 5, 12, June 2, 16, 30, July 7, 31, Aug. 7, 10, 11, Sept. 1, 8, 1946; Bowles, *Promises*, 163–65; Lieberman, *Power Broker*, 86.

36. *HC*, Jan. 28, Aug. 22, 25, 27–29, 1946; Lieberman, *Power Broker*, 74–82.

37. *NHR*, Aug. 25, Sept. 8–18, 1946; *HC*, Jan. 7, Sept. 2–5, 11–19, 1946, Apr. 1, 1958, Mar. 15, 1964, July 11, 1966; *Hartford Times*, Sept. 21, 1946; *New Britain Herald*, Sept. 3, 24, 1946; *Bridgeport Post*, Sept. 18, 22, 1946; *Waterbury Republican*, Sept. 22, 1946; Bowles, *Promises*, 164–68; Lieberman, *Power Broker*, 83–96, 101–102; Wilbert Snow, *Codline's Child: The Autobiography of Wilbert Snow* (Middletown, Conn.: Wesleyan Univ. Press, 1974), esp. 112–13.

38. *HC*, Sept. 17, 18, 1946; *NHR*, Sept. 18, 1946; *New Britain Herald*, Sept. 28, 1946; *Waterbury Republican*, Sept. 17, 18, 1946; Alonzo L. Hamby, *Beyond the New Deal: Harry S. Truman and American Liberalism* (New York: Columbia Univ. Press, 1973), 136; *Time*, Nov. 4, 1946, pp. 23–24.

39. *CSJ*, July 1946, p. 13.

40. *CSJ*, Oct. 1946, pp. 7, 14; *Bridgeport Post*, Oct. 23, 28, Nov. 4, 1946; *New London Day*, Oct. 17, 23, 1946; *HC*, Nov. 3, 4, 1946.

41. Hamby, *Beyond the New Deal*, 127–35; *New York Times*, Nov. 3, 1946; *HC*, Sept. 17, Oct. 12, Nov. 1, 2, 1946; *Hartford Times*, Oct. 17, 1946.

42. Irons, "Cold War Crusade," 346–58; *U.S. News*, Oct. 18, 1946, pp. 22–23; *New Britain Herald*, Nov. 19, 1946; *HC*, Sept. 8 (editorial), Oct. 19, 21 (editorial), 26, 27, 31, Nov. 2, 4, 5, 1946; *Bridgeport Post*, Nov. 2, 1946; *Waterbury Republican*, Oct. 25, Nov. 1, 2, 1946; *New London Day*, Oct. 11, Nov. 4, 1946; *Connecticut Circle*, Nov. 1946, p. 6; *Hartford Catholic Transcript*, Oct. 24, 31, 1946.

43. *HC*, Oct. 1, Nov. 3, 4, 1946; *Hartford Times*, Nov. 4, 1946.

44. *HC*, Oct. 8, 25, 30, 31, Nov. 1, 4, 1946; *New Britain Herald*, Oct. 5, 1946.

45. *Hartford Times*, Nov. 4, 1946; *NHR*, Nov. 1, 1946; *New London Day*, Oct. 26, 28, Nov. 2, 1946; *Bridgeport Post*, Nov. 4, 5, 1946; *HC*, Oct. 15, Nov. 1–4, 1946; *New Britain Herald*, Oct. 14, 1946; *Waterbury Republican*, Nov. 3, 1946.

46. *Waterbury Republican,* Oct. 10, 1946; *Hartford Times,* Oct. 25, 1946; *New London Day,* Sept. 23, Oct. 24, 31, Nov. 4, 1946; *Norwich Bulletin,* Oct. 19, 1946; *New Britain Herald,* Oct. 29, 1946.

47. *HC,* Oct. 6, 10, 13, 24, 1946.

48. *HC,* Oct. 3–18, 24, 30, 1946; *Hartford Times,* Oct. 5, 19, 1946; *Bridgeport Post,* Oct. 11, 12, 1946; *NHR,* Oct. 12, 15, 19, 20, 23, 27, 1946.

49. *NHR,* Oct. 20, 1946; *New London Day,* Nov. 4, 1946; *New Britain Herald,* Oct. 26, 1946; Irvin H. McGowan to Baldwin, Sept. 16, 1946, Baldwin Papers, Box 7.

50. *HC,* Oct. 10, 21, 22, 1946.

51. *Bridgeport Post,* Nov. 3, 1946.

52. *New York Times,* Nov. 3, 1946; *NHR,* Nov. 2–4, 1946; *HC,* Nov. 3–5, 1946; *CSJ,* Oct. 1946, *passim; Il Corriere del Connecticut,* Nov. 1, 1946.

53. *HC,* Nov. 6, 7, 1946; *NHR,* Nov. 6, 7, 1946; *CSJ,* Nov. 1946, *passim.* McLevy ran again for governor, but won only 32,000 votes and had negligible impact.

54. *HC,* Nov. 7, 1946; *CSJ,* Oct. 1946, p. 13, Nov. 1946, p. 9.

55. *NHR,* Nov. 6, 1946; *New Republic,* Nov. 18, 1946, p. 643.

56. At the town level statewide, Democratic losses correlated at +.52 with turnout decline, and the correlation was +.22 for the combined wards of the three biggest cities. (See Table V-1; the corresponding correlations for 1942 were +.19 at the town level and +.17 at the ward level.) Regression coefficients for the 1944–46 turnout and Democratic declines suggest that even had the correlations between the two been high, only in the First Congressional District might the Democratic margin of defeat—and even there not the entire Democratic decline—have stemmed from reduced turnout.

57. *Time,* Nov. 18, 1946, p. 21; *Newsweek,* Nov. 4, 1946, p. 20; *New York Times,* Nov. 10, 1946; *U.S. News,* Oct. 26, 1946, p. 25, Nov. 15, 1946, pp. 13–14, 26–27; Cantril, ed., *Public Opinion, 1935–1946,* pp. 161, 682–83, 939; *Hartford Times,* Nov. 9, 1946; *HC,* Nov. 6, 1946; *Waterbury Republican,* Nov. 7, 1946.

58. *New London Day,* Nov. 6, 1946.

CHAPTER SIX

1. *NHR,* Nov. 24, 1946; Allen Yarnell, *Democrats and Progressives: The 1948 Election as a Test of Postwar Liberalism* (Berkeley: Univ. of California Press, 1974), 28–45.

2. *NHR,* Nov. 9, 1947; *CSJ,* Nov. 1947, *passim,* Dec. 1947, pp. 10, 28, 30, Jan. 1948, *passim,* Feb. 1948, pp. 6, 7, 30, April 1948, pp. 16–17, 26; Bowles, *Promises,* 168–73; Lieberman, *Power Broker,* 111–17.

3. *CSJ,* June 1948, pp. 10–11, 24–25, Aug. 1948, p. 11; Lieberman, *Power Broker,* 117–23; Bowles, *Promises,* 173–78.

4. Irwin Ross, *The Loneliest Campaign: The Truman Victory of 1948* (New York: New American Library, 1968); *CSJ,* Sept. 1948, *passim,* Nov.–Dec. 1948, pp. 8–9; Bowles, *Promises,* 178–86; Lieberman, *Power Broker,* 123–26.

5. On the 1948 election returns in the nation, see Ross, *Loneliest Campaign*, esp. 245–71; Lubell, *Future of American Politics, passim;* Phillips, *Emerging Republican Majority, passim;* Bernard R. Berelson, Paul F. Lazarsfeld, and William N. McPhee, *Voting: A Study of Opinion Formation in a Presidential Campaign* (Chicago: Univ. of Chicago Press, 1954).

6. For analyses of the 1948 Connecticut vote, see *CSJ,* Nov.–Dec. 1948, *passim; HC,* Nov. 3, 4, 1948; *NHR,* Nov. 3, 1948.

7. See Tables A-1 to A-6 for statistics on the 1948 Connecticut vote.

8. See correlation coefficients and beta coefficients in Table A-5.

9. Theodore H. White, *The Making of the President, 1960* (New York: Pocket Books, 1961), 11–14, 18–19.

10. See, for example, Francis E. Merrill, *Social Problems on the Homefront* (New York: Harper & Bros., 1948), 10–13, 229, and John M. Blum, "The G.I. in the Culture of the Second World War," *Ventures* (Magazine of the Yale Graduate School), VIII, No. 1 (1968), 51–56.

11. See Menefee, *Assignment,* 3, 124; Herbert Blumer, "Morale," in *American Society,* ed. Ogburn, 223; Warner, *Jonesville,* 283–84.

12. Bingham, *Connecticut,* addendum, 38–40.

13. Angus Campbell et al., *The American Voter* (New York: Wiley, 1960), 50–51.

14. *Ibid., passim,* esp. 42–63.

BIBLIOGRAPHICAL ESSAY

This study rests principally on primary sources. Apart from the many illuminating studies of wartime economic mobilization, administration, and foreign policy, surprisingly little has been written about the American home front during World War II. There exists very little secondary material on Connecticut society and politics in the Roosevelt period, especially the war years. What follows is a guide to the most important sources I used. For the home front generally, Richard Polenberg, *War and Society* (Philadelphia, 1972) is an excellent survey with a full and useful bibliography. Among several recent popular studies, Geoffrey Perrett, *Days of Sadness, Years of Triumph* (New York, 1973) and Richard R. Lingeman, *Don't You Know There's a War On?* (New York, 1970) stand out. Francis E. Merrill, *Social Problems on the Home Front* (New York, 1948) and William F. Ogburn (ed.), *American Society in Wartime* (Chicago, 1943) are good for social history, while Jerome S. Bruner's splendid *Mandate from the People* (New York, 1944) insightfully analyzes American public opinion in the period. Several local studies, especially Robert J. Havighurst and H. Gerthon Morgan, *The Social History of a War-Boom Community* (New York, 1951), Max Parvin Cavnes, *The Hoosier Community at War* (Bloomington, Ind., 1961), Mary Watters, *Illinois in the Second World War* (2 vols; Springfield, Ill., 1951–52), and Karl D. Hartzell, *The Empire State at War* (New York, 1949), helped frame my inquiry into and provide perspectives for my findings about wartime Connecticut society. John Morton Blum's excellent *V Was for Victory: Politics and American Culture During World War II* (New York, 1976) appeared after my manuscript was completed. Eric F. Goldman, *The Crucial Decade—And After* (New York, 1960) and Joseph C. Goulden, *The Best Years, 1945–1950* (New York, 1976) are good on early postwar America.

There is a wealth of material on the politics of the Roosevelt era, but little of it goes beyond 1940. For the forging of the Roosevelt Coalition, I found especially useful Samuel Lubell's still valuable *The Future of American Politics* (3rd ed. rev., New York, 1965), John M. Allswang, *A House for All Peoples* (Lexington, Ky., 1971), J. Joseph Huthmacher, *Massachusetts People and Politics* (Cambridge, Mass., 1959), and David Burner, *The Politics of Provincialism* (New York, 1968). On the election of 1940, Paul F. Lazarsfeld et al., *The People's Choice* (3rd ed., New York, 1968) is the classic study of the campaign in Erie County, Ohio, while Herbert S. Parmet and Marie B. Hecht, *Never Again* (New York, 1968) is an informative narrative account. James MacGregor Burns, *Roosevelt: The Soldier of Freedom* (New York, 1970) and Robert Ficken, "The Democratic Party and Domestic Politics During World War II" (Ph.D. diss., Univ. of Washington, 1973) help understand wartime politics from the perspective of the President and the Democratic party, while Donald Bruce Johnson, *The Republican Party and Wendell Willkie* (Urbana, Ill., 1960) is valuable for GOP politics. Robert A. Divine, *Foreign Policy and U.S. Presidential Elections, 1940–1948* (New York, 1974) examines the impact of foreign affairs on American politics in the era of World War II. Roland Young, *Congressional Politics in the Second World War* (New York, 1956) briefly but helpfully chronicles the Congress. The politics of the early postwar period have received more attention than those of the war years, and I found especially useful Cabell Phillips, *The Truman Presidency* (New York, 1966), Alonzo L. Hamby, *Beyond the New Deal* (New York, 1973), Irwin Ross, *The Loneliest Campaign* (New York, 1968), and Bernard Berelson et al., *Voting* (Chicago, 1954). V.O. Key, Jr., *The Responsible Elec-*

torate (Cambridge, Mass., 1966) has valuable data and analysis for elections throughout the New Deal-Fair Deal era.

A number of other sources helped me follow wartime developments and attitudes. Public-opinion surveys—particularly the polls and related articles in *Public Opinion Quarterly*—were very helpful. Among contemporary accounts of World War II America, Selden Menefee, *Assignment: USA* (New York, 1943), Agnes E. Meyer, *Journey Through Chaos* (New York, 1944), and Jack Goodman (ed.), *While You Were Gone* (New York, 1946) were the most useful. I read *Time* magazine through the war years, and I read *Newsweek, U.S. News,* the *New Republic,* and the *Nation* for the late summer and autumn of each election year from 1940 through 1946. A variety of other publications, especially the *New York Times* and scholarly journals in sociology and political science, sometimes carried relevant articles.

On Connecticut history, I found Harold J. Bingham, *History of Connecticut* (New York, 1962) the most valuable survey. Rowland Mitchell, "Social Legislation in Connecticut, 1919–1939" (Ph.D. diss., Yale Univ., 1954) and Andrew Levinson, "Connecticut Politics, 1896–1936: Building a Democratic Majority" (Yale Univ. senior honors essay, 1972) both provided useful information on Connecticut politics in the 1920s and 1930s. Robert A. Dahl's superb study of New Haven politics and government, *Who Governs?* (New Haven, 1961) was helpful in many ways. Three other studies of New Haven, Robert A. Warner, *New Haven Negroes* (New Haven, 1940), Irvin L. Child, *Italian or American?* (New Haven, 1943), and John W. McConnell, *The Evolution of Social Classes* (Washington, D.C., 1942) all contain valuable information about and insights into New Haven's (and to an important degree, Connecticut's) social history. For the state's ethnic groups more generally, Samuel Koenig, *Immigrant Settlements in Connecticut* (Hartford, 1938) and Nathan L. Whetten and Henry W. Riecken, *The Foreign-Born Population of Connecticut, 1940* (Storrs, Conn., 1943) yielded much good information. The latter is part of the Storrs Agricultural Experiment Station (Connecticut) Bulletin series, a series which contains numerous excellent studies of Connecticut's population, residential, social, economic, and ethnic patterns.

Newspapers are perhaps the most important source of information for wartime Connecticut. The press carried good synopses of various state and federal reports, full and often shrewd coverage of Connecticut politics, politicians, and political parties, and informative articles on such topics as jobs, housing, living standards, wartime restrictions, social consequences of the war from the individual to the state and national levels, ethnic groups, and, increasingly as the war went on, blacks. (One must of course be careful in using and weighing newspaper accounts, and I tried to be so; but I came away from my study impressed by how much social, economic, and political history could be gleaned from them.) I examined the *Hartford Courant* and the *New Haven Register* daily for the period January 1940 through December 1946, and I culled them selectively for the years from 1928 through 1939 and for 1947 and 1948. (The *Courant*, as the principal newspaper of the state's capital city, provided the fullest accounts of events throughout the state and of the state government, while the *Register* was the leading newspaper of New Haven, the state's second largest city and the home of the largest and most important Italian population. Both newspapers, moreover, had excellent political coverage.) In addition, I also read selectively in the *Hartford Times* and the *New Haven Journal-Courier*, and I read daily the major newspapers in each congressional district (including newspapers in Bridgeport, Waterbury, New Britain, Norwich, and New London) for the late summer and autumn of each election year from 1940 through 1946.

Besides the daily newspapers, several other journals proved of great help. The weekly *Hartford Catholic Transcript*, which I read for every week in the period from 1940 through 1946 and selectively for 1928–39 and 1947–48, and two weekly Italian newspapers, examined every week for 1940 through 1946, *La Sentinella* (Bridgeport) and *Il Corriere del Connecticut* (New Haven), were invaluable. I read every issue from 1934 through 1948 of the monthly *Connecticut State Journal*, a privately published periodical with a Republican bent which focused on politics but covered as well a wide range of topics. Finally, I went through every issue from 1929 through 1948 of *Connecticut Industry*, the monthly publication of the Connecticut Manufacturers' Association, which besides providing essential data on the state's economy and businesses was a valuable barometer of business sentiment.

Reports and publications of government agencies constituted another essential source of information. State agencies provided the richest haul. Reports of the Post-War Planning Board, full of statistics and good analysis, were particularly valuable for the impact of the war on Connecticut's society and economy. The *Monthly Bulletin* of the Connecticut Department of Labor (which went under a number of slightly different titles in the period) yielded much information about the state's economy and labor force, and I used this publication for the years from 1936 through 1946. I found in *Public Welfare Statistics*, the monthly (1937) and then quarterly (1938–46) bulletin of the Office of the (Connecticut) Commissioner of Welfare, good data on relief and welfare in the state. The 1944, 1945, and 1947 *Reports* of the Connecticut Interracial Commission were helpful for the status of blacks in the war and early postwar periods. The *Connecticut State Register and Manual* (usually annual) contained a wealth of information about the state and its subdivisions, and I consulted it for the years from 1920 through 1950. In addition, I often found helpful the annual and biennial reports of various other state agencies in the 1930s and 1940s. Among municipal reports, I found the 1940–46 reports of the Hartford, New Haven, and Bridgeport Housing Authorities the most useful. Although I consulted various federal reports with data on Connecticut for the period 1929 through 1946, by far the most valuable were the decennial censuses. They were indispensable.

Several manuscript collections proved helpful. Most important and valuable by far were the voluminous Records of the Governor's Office, at the Connecticut State Library. These

300

records, examined for the years from 1939 through 1946, contain extensive reports, working papers, and correspondence, most of them otherwise unavailable, with information about conditions in Connecticut, pressures on the administrations, and the actions of the state government. The collection of Raymond Baldwin's personal papers at the Connecticut State Library contained assorted valuable items of information and correspondence, as did the collections at the Franklin D. Roosevelt Library.

Few autobiographies and biographies exist of important Connecticut personalities during the era. Curtiss S. Johnson's *Raymond E. Baldwin, Connecticut Statesman* (Chester, Conn., 1972) is a reliable if uncritical account of Baldwin's career which closely follows the material in the six-volume Baldwin interviews in the University of Connecticut Oral History Project. Besides these sources for Baldwin, and the official and private Baldwin Papers at the Connecticut State Library, I spent much of a delightful day interviewing Baldwin in January 1975 and gleaned some additional information about a few important events. From the material available for Baldwin, the most important political figure in Connecticut in the era, one can learn much about the Republican party, Connecticut politics, and the state generally. But aside from Baldwin there is little available about the key men and women in the era, though Wilbur Cross's autobiography, *Connecticut Yankee* (New Haven, 1943), Chester Bowles's autobiography, *Promises to Keep* (New York, 1971), Stephen Shadegg's biography, *Clare Boothe Luce* (New York, 1970), Wilbert Snow's autobiography, *Codline's Child* (Middletown, Conn., 1974), and especially Joseph Lieberman's good study of John Bailey, *The Power Broker* (Boston, 1966) all shed some light on Connecticut politics in the era.

The sources I relied on for my statistical analysis of voting returns are listed in the Appendix.

INDEX

AFL. *See* Connecticut Federation of Labor
Agriculture, 5, 7. *See also* Farmers
"Americanism" as Republican issue, 74, 257–58; in 1930s, 26, 27, 28, 49, 74; in 1940 election, 72, 73, 74–75, 84; after Pearl Harbor, 106; in 1942 election, 121, 124; in 1944 election, 186; in 1946 election, 227, 235
American Jewish Congress, Connecticut State Council of, 158
American Labor party, 187
Americans for Democratic Action (ADA), 245–46
Anastasio, Frank, 82, 121
Anti-Semitism, 157–58, 189, 202, 215
Arabs, 158, 159, 214
Atomic bomb, 210

Bailey, John M., 18, 19, 67, 175, 201; wins control of Hartford Democratic party, 229; and 1946 gubernatorial nomination, 229, 230, 231; becomes Democratic state chairman, 231; and 1946 election, 236, 239; and 1948 nominations, 246
Baldwin, Raymond E.: helps rebuild Conn. Republican party, 42–43; career of, 42, 47; wins 1938 gubernatorial nomination, 43–44; in 1938 campaign, 44; elected governor, 1938, 45; as governor, 1939–41, 45–46, 52–53, 61, 80, 98, 99, 190; political outlook of, 46, 57, 145–46; background of, 46; personality of, 46–47; gains national attention, 47; compared with Hurley, 55, 103; and 1940 state nominations, 56; as favorite-son candidate 1940, 58; supports Willkie, 71; expects vice-

Baldwin, Raymond E. (*cont.*)
presidential nomination, 71; in 1940 campaign, 71, 74, 75, 78–79, 91; on Willkie tour of Conn., 79; and blacks, 80, 99, 129, 152–53, 190; loses 1940 gubernatorial election, 91; for aid to British, 104, 105; and 1942 gubernatorial nomination, 107, 119, 120; opposition to, in Republican party, 119–20, 145–46, 170; supports Luce for congressional nomination, 119–20; in 1942 campaign, 122–23, 126–27, 129; elected governor, 1942, 131; as governor, 1943–46, 145–46, 149, 152–53, 158, 184, 208, 209, 222; and 1944 presidential nomination, 166, 167, 169; and 1944 national platform, 167; dispute with Bradley, 168, 169, 178–79; decision to seek reelection in 1944, 169–70; at 1944 state convention, 179–80; in 1944 campaign, 184, 185, 186, 187, 190; reelected governor, 1944, 195, 204; on postwar transition, 210; announces retirement, 224; persuaded to run for U.S. Senate, 225; and 1946 state convention, 225–27; and 1946 campaign, 236; elected to U.S. Senate in 1946, 239
Balfour Declaration, 158
Ball, Joseph, 162, 182
Barkley, Alben, 173
Battle for Leyte Gulf, 181
Battle of Midway, 118
Battle of the Bulge, 207
Battle of the Coral Sea, 118
Beefsteak Clubs, 43, 179
Belgium, 58
Beta coefficients, explained, 260–61
Biddle, Anthony J. D., 80–81

Index

Biddle, Francis, 127, 128
Bilbo, Theodore G., 215
Blacks, 10, 13; prejudice and discrimination against, 13, 61, 95, 96–97,
99–101, 109, 111, 152, 154, 155, 217;
housing problems of, 13, 100–101,
155, 217; employment of, 13, 99–100,
111, 150, 152, 216–17; in-migration
of, 13, 100, 153–54; and politics, 17,
28, 31, 80, 89, 129, 167, 173, 189–90,
195, 200, 201, 202, 237, 241, 248; impact of World War II on, 99, 100–
101, 152–53, 156, 216–18, 255–56;
protest of, 101, 111–12, 154, 155, 216,
217, 218, 255–56; and racial tensions,
153–55; and fair employment legislation, 217–18, 237, 250. *See also* Connecticut Inter-racial Commission
Boston, 7, 9, 76, 102
Bowles, Chester, 222, 227–30, 231, 243,
246, 247
Bradley, J. Kenneth: helps rebuild
Conn. Republican party, 41–43; early
career of, 41–42; as political leader,
42; becomes state chairman and national committeeman, 104; for aid to
British, 104, 105; supports Luce for
congressional nomination, 119–20; at
1942 state convention, 121; and 1944
presidential nomination, 166, 167; dispute with Baldwin and resignation as
state chairman, 168–69, 178–79; and
draft-Baldwin movement, 170; and
1946 gubernatorial nomination, 226
Bricker, John W., 187
Bridgeport, 5, 7, 59, 96, 110, 113, 157;
politics in, 48, 81, 88, 134, 171, 185,
198, 200–201, 230, 247; tables with
voting statistics for, 30, 86, 132, 133,
196, 240, 268–72
Bridgeport Housing Authority, 110
Bridgeport Socialists. *See* Socialist
party, Connecticut
Bureau of Labor Statistics, 150
Business. *See* Businessmen; Connecticut,
economic structure of; Connecticut,
economic conditions in
Businessmen: and Republican party in
1920s, 3, 15; in suburbs, 9; opposed to
New Deal, 28; and New Era Republicans, 41, 43; and Willkie, 57, 70, 79;
and economic mobilization, 94, 95,
96, 107–109; 117; 148–49; dislike OPA,

Businessmen *(cont.)*
115, 221, 222; and reconversion, 152,
208, 209; Republican appeals to, 167,
215; and fair employment legislation,
218; and postwar strikes, 219; pressure
Baldwin to run for Senate, 225
Byrnes, James F., 173, 211, 233

California, 149
Campaigns, role of, 264–66. *See also*
Elections; Democratic party; Republican party; *specific candidates*; *specific
issues*
Catholics, 12, 13, 14; and politics, 22,
34, 67, 173, 188–89, 200, 226, 234,
243, 246–47; and anti-Semitism, 157;
and anti-communism, 188, 200, 211
Celentano, William, 48, 81, 88, 102,
128, 156, 216
Churchill, Winston, 58, 191, 211
CIO. *See* CIO Political Action Commit-
tee; Connecticut CIO
CIO Political Action Committee, 177–
78, 185, 186–87, 198, 201, 234, 243
Cities. *See* Connecticut, urbanization
of; Elections, municipal; Urban vot-
ing; *specific cities*
Civil Defense. *See* Connecticut State
Defense Council; Connecticut War
Council
Civilian Conservation Corps, 144
Clark, Tom, 236
Class. *See* Economic class
Clifford, Clark, 245
Cold War, 160, 162, 188, 206
Colt's Patent Firearms, 52
Columbus Day, 64, 82, 115, 127–28,
156, 191, 216
Commonweal, 189
Communism: as political issue, 75, 124,
186–89, 193, 200, 202, 204, 211–12,
225, 227, 233–34, 236, 238, 243, 247,
256, 257–58; postwar concern about,
211–12
Congress, 58, 64, 140, 144–45, 159,
162, 194, 215, 220, 222, 248
Connecticut: industrialization of, 4–6;
economic structure of, 4–6, 52; economic conditions in, 6, 23, 24–25, 26–
27, 39, 52, 58–61, 91, 93, 94, 107–108,
149–51, 207–10; population growth of,
6–7, 147; urbanization of, 6–7; suburbanization in, 7, 9; immigration and

303

Index

Perriello, Patrick, 102

Philadelphia transit strike, 155

Poland, 80, 159–61, 191, 212–13; as political issue, 81, 159–61, 190–91, 212–13, 214, 233

Polish-American Congress, 161, 191

Polish-Americans, 9, 10, 11, 12; and politics, 21, 31, 44, 45, 69, 80–81, 88, 89, 120, 121, 177, 190–91, 200, 201, 202, 226, 232, 233, 236, 240–41, 242, 243; concern of, about Poland, 61, 80, 159–61, 212–13; and Yalta agreements, 212–13

Post Office Department, 192

Postwar economy, concern about, 95–96, 147, 149–52 *passim*, 163, 184–85, 204, 205, 207. *See also* Prosperity

Postwar planning, 147, 151–52, 207

Post-War Planning Board. *See* Connecticut Post-War Planning Board

Prestia, Charles, 177

Prices, 60, 95, 115, 150, 210, 222–23, 237

Prosperity: wartime concern about, 142, 163, 204–205, 207, 253, 257; as political issue in 1944, 167, 180, 181, 184–85, 204–205. *See also* Postwar economy

Pryor, Samuel F.: helps rebuild Conn. Republican party, 41, 42–43; becomes national committeeman, 41; seeks Willkie-Baldwin ticket, 47, 57; and 1940 party disharmony, 56; at 1940 national convention, 71; in Willkie campaign, 71–72; resigns as national committeeman, 104; supports Luce for congressional nomination, 120; and 1944 presidential nomination, 166, 167, 168; intercedes in Baldwin-Bradley dispute, 169; and ebbing political power, 179

Public opinion polls, used by politicians, 180, 181, 182, 185, 186–87, 228, 229

Pulaski Federation of Democratic Clubs, 177

Quebec, 10–11

Racial tensions, during war, 153–55. *See also* Blacks; Connecticut Interracial Commission

Rationing, 115–17, 123, 138, 142–43, 221

"Recognition" politics, 16; by Democrats in 1928 and after, 22, 34; in 1936 election, 28; by New Era Republicans in 1938, 44, 45; importance of, by late 1930s, 48, 49–50; in 1940 election, 69–70, 79, 81; in 1942 election, 120, 121, 128; in 1944 election, 177, 180, 192; in 1946 election, 226, 232, 237, 238

Reconversion, 149, 150, 184, 207–10. *See also* Postwar planning

Redick, Frances, 180

Reece, B. Carroll, 225

Regression coefficients, explained, 260–61

Relief, 27, 31, 34, 39, 59, 63, 94, 97, 108, 151, 209

Remington Arms, 52, 59

Rents, 60, 97–98, 110–11, 221, 222

Republican party, of Connecticut: in 1920s, 3, 14–16, 20, 22; and Great Depression, 23; and 1932 election, 25; and 1934 election, 26; and 1936 election, 27–35 *passim*; after 1936 election, 35, 39; reorganization of, 1937–38, 41–44; and 1938 election, 44–45; and 1939 municipal elections, 47–48; at end of 1930s, 49–50; 1940 disharmony in, 56–57; and 1940 presidential nomination, 57–58, 70–71; and 1940 state convention, 72–73; in 1940 campaign, 73–76, 78–84 *passim*; and 1940 election results, 85–91 *passim*; 1941 factionalism in, 104–105; early wartime partisanship of, 106–107; 1942 strategy of, 107, 118–19; and 1942 state convention, 119–21, 122; in 1942 campaign, 123–24, 128–29; and 1942 election results, 130–41 *passim*; and 1943 patronage grab, 146; and Palestine, 159, 215; and Poland, 161, 213; and 1944 presidential nomination, 164, 165–67; and 1944 national convention, 167–68; 1944 factionalism in, 168–70, 178–79; and 1944 state convention, 179–80; in 1944 campaign, 185–88, 189–93 *passim*; and 1944 election results, 195–204 *passim*; and 1946 state convention, 225–27; in 1946 campaign, 232–35, 237, 238; and 1946 election results, 239–44 *passim*; and 1948 election, 247–49; wartime image of, 257. *See also* "New Era" Republicans

Republican party, of United States: and 1940 presidential nomination, 70–71;

309

Index

Social Security, 78, 83, 145
Sons of Italy, 157, 213
Soviet Union, 160–61, 162, 163, 192, 210, 212, 213, 214, 233; American attitudes toward, 206, 210–15 *passim*
Spangler, Harrison, 165
Spellacy, Thomas J.: background and career of, 18–19; in 1920s, 18, 19; and Old Guard, 22; splits with Fitzgerald, 38, 54; political advice of, 42; and 1940 party factionalism, 54, 68; and Hartford race relations, 154; resigns as Hartford mayor, 154; tries for 1944 U.S. Senate nomination, 172, 173, 174–75; loses 1945 Hartford mayor election, 224; and 1946 state nominations, 229, 230; loses to Bailey in Hartford Democratic party, 229
"Stab-in-the-back" speech, 63–64, 69, 81–82, 128
Stalin, Joseph, 191
Stassen, Harold, 227
State Defense Council. *See* Connecticut State Defense Council
State Housing Authority. *See* Connecticut State Housing Authority
State, U.S. Department of, 159, 213
Strikes. *See* Labor relations
Suburbs, 7, 9, 116, 147, 255; and politics, 9, 15, 29, 88, 203

Taft, Robert A., 58, 70, 164, 165, 219
Talbot, Joseph, 106, 107, 195, 213, 226
Taxes, 95, 97, 123, 139, 234, 238
Third term for Roosevelt, as issue in 1940 election, 66, 73, 75, 77, 80
Tilson, John Q., 38
Time, 119, 166, 210
Tone, Joseph, 232, 236
"Towns," explained, 277 n.33
Treaty of Versailles, 16
Trieste, 214
Truman, Harry S.: wins 1944 vice-presidential nomination, 173; as president, 206, 208, 214, 219, 222, 233, 236–37; popularity of, 219, 223, 224–25, 227; and 1946 election, 232, 233, 235, 236–37, 242; and 1948 election, 245, 247, 249, 254; wins renomination, 1948, 246
Turnout. *See* Voter turnout
Tynan, John, 231

Unemployment. *See* Connecticut, economic conditions in
Union party, 45
United Aircraft, 52, 59, 99–100, 109
United Nations, 164, 182, 210, 215
United Polish Societies of Hartford, 161
Urban voting, in state and federal elections, 17, 21, 29–30, 85, 131–34, 195, 196, 198, 200–202, 239–42, 247–48; tables with voting statistics concerning, 30, 86, 132, 133, 196, 240, 268–72. *See also* specific cities; Elections, municipal

Vandenberg, Arthur H., 58, 70, 164, 167
Veterans: and housing, 147, 219, 220, 237; and jobs, 147, 150, 151–52, 209, 210, 219; and politics, 167, 220, 226, 227, 232, 237, 238; and talk of bonus for, 220, 227, 237
Victory Compact, 106, 108
Vioni, Pasquale, 60, 81
V-J Day, 207
Voter turnout, 21, 23, 25, 26, 28–29, 84, 135–40, 198–99, 242; tables with statistics concerning, 133, 241, 267, 268

Wages: in Depression, 60; in war era, 108, 115, 149–50, 151; in postwar era, 208, 209, 210, 223
Wagner Act, 78, 124, 145
Wagner-Ellender-Taft Bill, 220
Wallace, Henry A.: wins 1940 vice-presidential nomination, 66, 67; in 1940 campaign, 80; and internationalism, 162; fails to be renominated, 1944, 173, 205; fired from cabinet by Truman, 1946, 233, 242–43; and 1948 election, 246–47
Walsh, David I., 20
War contracts, 52, 58–59, 94, 107–108; subcontracting of, 59, 61, 94, 95, 107–108
War Council. *See* Connecticut War Council
War Industry Commission, 108
War Manpower Commission (WMC), 109, 147, 148–49
War Production Board (WPB), 108, 117, 149
War, U.S. Department of, 159

311

Waterbury, 5, 7, 11–12; politics in, 48, 82, 102, 171, 178, 200–201, 224, 239, 245
Welfare. *See* Relief
Weston, 88
Willkie, Wendell L.: and New Era Republicans, 47, 57; 1940 support in Conn., 57–58, 70; wins 1940 presidential nomination, 57–58, 70–71; in 1940 campaign, 73–76, 78–79, 84; as issue in 1940 campaign, 78–80; tours Conn., 78–79; loses 1940 election, 85; and internationalism, 104, 162, 164, 165, 166; and liberalism, 164, 165, 166; seeks 1944 presidential nomination, 164–66, 179, 205; post–1940 strength of, in Conn., 165–66; and 1944 national platform, 167; and 1944 campaign, 182
Willkie for President Association, 57
Winchester Repeating Arms, 52
Wisconsin primary of 1944, 166
Women: and politics, 21, 44, 69–70, 120, 121, 128–29, 177, 178, 180, 226,

Women (*cont.*)
232, 238; and employment, 95, 108–109, 148, 150; roles of, 129, 250
Woodhouse, Chase Going, 172, 175, 177, 178
Works Progress Administration (WPA), 55, 59, 108, 141, 144
World War II, 50, 51, 58, 93, 118, 142, 180–81, 207; and Roosevelt Coalition, 50, 85, 89–91, 93, 131, 138–39, 204–205, 244, 249–50, 254, 255, 257–58; public attitudes during, 92, 98, 116–17, 144–45, 149, 162–63, 252–54, 256–57; as "watershed," 250–54; change and continuity in era of, 250–58

Yalta Conference, 212–13
Yankees, 3, 4, 10, 12, 14, 34, 61; and politics, 15, 21, 23, 25, 29, 30, 35, 48, 50, 70, 85, 102, 131, 195, 201, 202, 203, 216, 226, 232

Zazzaro, Tony, 174–75
Zionists, 158, 214

Twentieth-Century America Series

DEWEY W. GRANTHAM, GENERAL EDITOR

Each volume in this series focuses on some aspect of the politics of social change in recent American history, utilizing new approaches to clarify the response of Americans to the dislocating forces of our own day—economic, technological, racial, demographic, and administrative.

VOLUMES PUBLISHED:

The Reaffirmation of Republicanism: Eisenhower and the Eighty-third Congress by Gary W. Reichard
The Crisis of Conservative Virginia: The Byrd Organization and the Politics of Massive Resistance by James W. Ely, Jr.
Black Tennesseans, 1900–1930 by Lester C. Lamon
Political Power in Birmingham, 1871–1921 by Carl V. Harris
The Challenge to Urban Liberalism: Federal City Relations during World War II by Philip J. Funigiello
Testing the Roosevelt Coalition: Connecticut Society and Politics in the Era of World War II by John W. Jeffries

This book has been composed on the Compugraphic phototypesetter in eleven-point Caledonia with two-point line spacing. Friz Quadrata type was selected for display. The book was designed by Jim Billingsley and set into type by Metricomp, Inc., Grundy Center, Iowa. It was printed offset by Thomson-Shore, Inc., Dexter, Michigan, and bound by John H. Dekker and Sons, Inc., Grand Rapids, Michigan. The paper on which the book is printed bears the watermark of S. D. Warren and is designed for an effective life of at least three hundred years.

THE UNIVERSITY OF TENNESSEE PRESS : KNOXVILLE